## Praise for *Baba Yaga's Book of Wi*

"A beautiful work of art and magic … Pamita brings us the wisdom of Baba …
a deep exploration of Slavic magic."

—Annwyn Avalon, author of *Water Witchcraft*

"Once you get pulled in by this book's inspired and informed secrets, you will not be
able to put it down … Pamita speaks to the deepest depths of your soul."

—Stephanie Rose Bird, author of *Sticks, Stones, Roots & Bones*

"Pamita draws you in with the beautiful telling of Ukrainian fairy tales, wisdom from
the legend herself, Baba Yaga, and tons of practical magic and daily rituals to live a
modern mystical life. This is one book I will be coming back to constantly."

—Pamela Chen, author of *Enchanted Crystal Magic*

"The organic approach taken in this book, rooted fully in its cultures of origin, is truly
marvelous."

—Ivo Dominguez Jr., author of *The Four Elements of the Wise*

"Weaving a mythic story throughout, and drawing from the author's Slavic cultural
heritage, *Baba Yaga's Book of Witchcraft* is an expedition into the very heart of magic…A
fun and informative read! Highly recommended."

—Storm Faerywolf, author of *The Witch's Name*

"Pamita brings old traditions alive, and then blends them into modern practices providing readers with new tools and perspectives to expand and enrich their magical
experiences."

—Sandra Kynes, author of *Tree Magic*

"This outstanding book will help connect you to this wise old woman and bring her
ancient and little-known spiritual path to life."

—Ainslie MacLeod, author of *The Old Soul's Guide Book*

"Pamita proves herself to be a brilliant storyteller, master instructor, and detailed histo-
rian in this fine homage to the powerful and mysterious female icon that is Baba Yaga."

—Katrina Rasbold, author of *Uncrossing*

"Pamita effortlessly mixes storytelling, history, folklore, magic, and her own personal journey in this beautifully written book."
— Gwion Raven, author of *Life Ritualized*

"This is one of the few books that as I finish, I open the front cover to reread."
— Jacki Smith, author of *Coventry Magic*

"This book has a compelling story, authentic folklore and folk magic, and the wisdom from an ancient forest witch."
— Astrea Taylor, author of *Air Magic*

"If you feel called to spend time in Baba Yaga's hut and to listen as she shares her ancient magical secrets, your intuition has led you to just the right place."
— Tess Whitehurst, author of *The Self-Love Superpower*

"This book offers a beautifully crafted and poetic journey."
— Patti Wigington, author of *Badass Ancestors*

"[A] delightful-to-read and easy-to-understand guide to Slavic traditions and magic. It's the perfect place to begin learning about the indigenous traditions common across all of Old Europe."
— Patricia Robin Woodruff, PhD, author of *Woodruff's Guide to Slavic Deities*

"This magnificent book reveals the ancient secrets of Ukrainian magic—many for the first time in English. A must-have for anyone interested in traditional Eastern European folk magic and witchcraft."
— Michelle Welch, author of *The Magic of Connection and Spirits Unveiled*

"A beautiful tome where the voice of Baba Yaga is strong and profound, and her magick is palpable."
— Phoenix LeFae, author of *Witches, Heretics, and Warrior Women*

"Pamita takes you on a deep dive into the world of Slavic folk magic. Rich with color, culture, and fairytale wisdom, this book is as beautiful as it is helpful."
— J. Allen Cross, author of *American Brujería*

# Baba Yaga's

## BOOK OF WITCHCRAFT

## About the Author

Madame Pamita is a teacher, candlemaker, spellcaster, tarot reader, and Ukrainian diaspora witch. She is the owner of an online spiritual apothecary called Madame Pamita's Parlour of Wonders. She is the host of two YouTube video series: *Candle Magic Class* and the weekly *Magic Q&A Tea Party*. Madame Pamita is also the host of the *Magic and the Law of Attraction* podcast and the author of *The Book of Candle Magic*.

## To Write to the Author

If you wish to contact the author or would like more information about this book, please write to the author in care of Llewellyn Worldwide Ltd. and we will forward your request. Both the author and the publisher appreciate hearing from you and learning of your enjoyment of this book and how it has helped you. Llewellyn Worldwide Ltd. cannot guarantee that every letter written to the author can be answered, but all will be forwarded. Please write to:

Madame Pamita
℅ Llewellyn Worldwide
2143 Wooddale Drive
Woodbury, MN 55125-2989
Please enclose a self-addressed stamped envelope for reply,
or $1.00 to cover costs. If outside the U.S.A., enclose
an international postal reply coupon.

Many of Llewellyn's authors have websites with additional information and resources. For more information, please visit our website at http://www.llewellyn.com.

# Baba Yaga's
## BOOK OF WITCHCRAFT

### SLAVIC MAGIC FROM
### THE WITCH OF THE WOODS

# Madame Pamita

LLEWELLYN PUBLICATIONS
WOODBURY, MINNESOTA

FIRST EDITION
Seventh Printing, 2024

Cover art by Sara Koncilja
Cover design by Shira Atakpu
Interior illustrations by Sara Koncilja

Llewellyn is a registered trademark of Llewellyn Worldwide Ltd.

**Library of Congress Cataloging-in-Publication Data**
Names: Madame Pamita, author.
Title: Baba Yaga's book of witchcraft : Slavic magic from the witch of the
   woods / Madame Pamita.
Description: First edition. | Woodbuy, Minnesota : Llewellyn Worldwide,
   Ltd, [2022] | Includes bibliographical references and index.
Identifiers: LCCN 2021062624 (print) | LCCN 2021062625 (ebook) | ISBN
   9780738767895 (paperback) | ISBN 9780738768175 (ebook)
Subjects: LCSH: Baba Yaga (Legendary character) | Witchcraft—Ukraine. |
   Magic—Ukraine. | Folklore—Ukraine. | Fairy tales—Ukraine.
Classification: LCC BF1584.U37 M33 2022  (print) | LCC BF1584.U37  (ebook)
   | DDC 133.4/309477—dc23/eng/20220222
LC record available at https://lccn.loc.gov/2021062624
LC ebook record available at https://lccn.loc.gov/2021062625

Llewellyn Worldwide Ltd. does not participate in, endorse, or have any authority or responsibility concerning private business transactions between our authors and the public.

All mail addressed to the author is forwarded, but the publisher cannot, unless specifically instructed by the author, give out an address or phone number.

Any internet references contained in this work are current at publication time, but the publisher cannot guarantee that a specific location will continue to be maintained. Please refer to the publisher's website for links to authors' websites and other sources.

Llewellyn Publications
A Division of Llewellyn Worldwide Ltd.
2143 Wooddale Drive
Woodbury, MN 55125-2989
www.llewellyn.com

Printed in the United States of America

# Other Books by Madame Pamita

*The Book of Candle Magic*

To Mary Kroll Moore, my matusya,
and
Kateryna Szegda Krol, my babusya.

# CONTENTS

# Acknowledgments

Writing this book was a monumental task worthy of Baba Yaga. There were many times when I sincerely felt like I was trying to separate a mountain of poppy seeds and wheat grains or spin a roomful of hemp in one day. Like Vasylyna, though, with the magical assistance of many amazing helpers, I was able to accomplish what at times felt like an impossible undertaking.

First, I would like to thank the awesome Ukrainian and Ukrainian diaspora women who gathered around, advised, translated, and guided me as I wrote: Christa Lynn, who generously shared her own Ukrainian spiritual practices with me and took me on countless spirit journeys to the lower world to get Baba Yaha's wise advice; my *vidma*-sister Katie Karpetz, who gave me *The Word and the Wax*, the book that opened all the doors for me (and who is probably the only one who geeks out as hard as I do about Ukrainian magic); Diana Tumminia, who painstakingly translated countless videos of the whispers of *baby sheptukhy;* and my beautiful Ukrainian angel, Lyudmyla (Milla) Rybak, who checked my spelling, corrected my accent, and verified and shared with me all the magic that still goes on in Ukraine today. A huge warm Ukrainian *dyakuyu!* Without you four magical women, this book would not exist.

I'd like to also thank some of the brilliant scholars and souls whom I only know through the internet but whose generous sharing of their research over the ether helped ground and guide me: Patricia Robin Woodruff, Luba Petrusha, Olga Stanton, and Andryi Dorosh. Thank you for sharing the wisdom and folklore of the old ways so generously.

I'd also like to thank my Llewellyn family, who continue to so lovingly support and give me wise advice, cheering me on and guiding me out of the woods whenever I leave the familiar path: Elysia Gallo, thank you for your help untangling numerous balls of verbal yarn; Kat Neff and Markus Ironwood, thank you for always singing the praises of the books I bring you; Anna Levine, thank you for giving me opportunities to teach and share; Sami Sherratt, thank you for gently combing and braiding my words; and Bill Krause, thank you for being the captain who sails us all through the sky to the paradise of a real-life book being birthed into this world. I am so deeply thankful for all your kindness and assistance.

Without my amazing team at the Parlour of Wonders keeping watch over the chicken-legged hut, I wouldn't have been able to spend the hundreds of hours it took to research and write this book. Thank you dear Chelsea Iovino, Romie Bo, Bridget Tuboly, Buchanan Moncure, and my own dear Manfred Hofer for keeping the magic flowing while I was on my journey through the forest.

To my sweet friends who listened and understood while I said a million times, "I can't! I'm working on my book," I give you all my best witchy magical blessings, and I'm ready to cash in those rain checks: Judy Pokonosky, Joseph James, Gwendolyn Pogrowski, James Divine, and Chris Onareo. I love you more than Baba Yaga loves a bratty kid and/or midnight snack.

I also want to say thank you to Kris Jecen and everyone from focused.space who kept me on track on those mornings when I would rather have been frolicking with the Spirits of the Lake instead of writing a book.

To my friends Queta Allred and Cloven, who helped me learn how to spin, and to Halyna Shepko, who taught me to weave, I am so grateful for you keeping these ancient crafts alive and sharing your gifts with me.

Thank you to my Instagram friend Maisy Bacon, who shared gorgeous images of the old Slavic aesthetic and also many hilarious quips, both of which inspired and kept me going.

So much love goes to Dakota St. Clare at Catland Books in Bushwick for hosting my classes on Ukrainian and Slavic magic and giving this old witch a place to share what she knows.

To the amazing Spell Squad, I love you guys more than words can say. When you come to my workshops and leave saying, "Hey! I can make magic!" there is nothing that makes my heart happier. I can't wait to share Baba Yaga's wisdom with you and see the amazing magic you make!

To my beautiful kids, Morgan and Isabelle, thank you for being just the best. I promise never to shove you in an oven.

To Manfred, the love of my life—so nice, you get thanked twice! Thank you for your love, help, and true partnership. It was on our vacation that this book began. I can't wait to fly through the skies with you again. If we can't find a mortar, an airplane will do.

# DISCLAIMER

The information in this book is not intended to replace the advice of medical professionals. Please consult your doctor or therapist before using herbal medicine.

# PREFACE

Bones survive. Whenever the blood and the flesh have disintegrated, the bones will remain.

The bones of our ancestors still carry their lives, their dreams, and their hopes. Deep in a grave in a Ukrainian cemetery in Pennsylvania, my grandmother's bones began to move. Somewhere under the patches of snow and frozen ground, the bones began to warm and almost imperceptibly vibrate.

Whenever I would come in contact with something that connected me to my Carpathian ancestors—a mournful folk tune, a Ukrainian Easter egg, an embroidered blouse—the bones would make a small rattle of life and then fall back into their deep sleep.

And then came the sound. As insubstantial and unnoticeable as the puff of a spring breeze. A sound so quiet that it would be drowned out by the silent pat of a leaf falling. It was the sound of a hum.

First, one small note. And then another, and then another. It became a tune. The humming got stronger and stronger. The bones of my grandmother, singing.

And then the words of the song came through.

*"Remember our magic. Our ways must not be forgotten."*

Her voice was joined by another voice. Her mother, who taught her that you can pour wax into water to determine the source of an illness.

And another voice. Her grandmother, who taught her how to use a *motanka* doll to heal a child hovering between life and death.

As each voice joined in, it gave power to the voice that came before. And voices upon voices joined in. Open throats, ritually wailing their mournful *holosinnya* laments, harmonizing, singing lustily and loudly in the chorus. Back and back through generations and generations. Mother upon mother upon mother. Back to the Trypillian ancients who created the clay eggs and clay dolls carved with symbols imbued with magical powers. Back and back to the most ancient one. Back to the *baba* of all the *babusy*, the grandmother of all the grandmothers, Baba Yaga. And it was she who sang loudest of all:

*"Tell my story, and you tell all the stories."*

The choir became even stronger and more beautiful. And then, one more voice joined in. My own mother's voice, familiar and clear.

*"Remember what I told you. Pick up the red thread and*
*make the first cross-stitch. In and out. In and out."*

It is no small spell for the dead to make their bones sing. It is challenge enough to cross over from the spirit world back to the world of the living and pass along messages, but to pass from the world of the ancestors and to shake a person in the material world awake and get them to create for you takes a great deal of powerful magic indeed. I am grateful forever for my mama's powerful magic, my babusya's powerful magic, and the powerful magic of all the bones of all the babusy who transported me back to the first baba, Baba Yaga.

# INTRODUCTION

*Yagishna, Egi Baba, Iagaia.* Every Slavic country has their own version of her name. *Babojędza, Jedubaba, Yaginya.* Spoken aloud, they sound like an ancient chant to conjure up the spirits. *Ega, Iagaba, Egabova.* Those hundreds of names that were told in hundreds of stories. *Indzhi Baba, Iagonishna, Iezhibaba.* Spread out over Eastern Europe like an embroidered cloth stitched over generation upon generation. *Ježibaba, Iagaia-Babitsa, Aga Gnishna.*

When the famous Russian author Alexander Afanasyev collected the stories of the Russian peasants and created his book *Russian Folk Tales* in the mid-1800s, he selected just one of the hundreds of names for the witch of the woods. The beauty and magic he wove with his stories captured the imagination of the world, and the name he gave her was solidified in the public consciousness: Baba Yaga.

Her stories were part of an oral tradition going back hundreds of years that spanned cultures and countries as diverse as Poland, Belarus, Bulgaria, Slovakia, the Czech Republic, Croatia, Moravia, Serbia, Slovenia, Galicia, Ukraine, Ruthenia, Lithuania, and dozens more. She is truly a witch without borders. From the widespread nature of these stories, cultural anthropologists and folklorists believe that Baba Yaga was originally a spirit or deity who was revered and honored as the Mistress of the Woods.[1] This once-wild nature spirit who assisted the hunters and gatherers became branded as "evil" once Christianity was introduced, and some of her stories evolved to reflect that. However, for those who are willing to look beyond her wrinkled skin, her tangled hair, and her bony leg, there is a powerful teacher for them indeed.

My own familiarity with Baba Yaga comes from my Ukrainian side of the family. To us, she was Baba Yaha, the famous old crone who ate children just like the witch in the story of Hansel and Gretel—except far more exciting, because she flew around in a giant mortar and had a sentient house that walked around on chicken legs.

---

1. Andreas Johns, *Baba Yaga: The Ambiguous Mother and Witch of the Russian Folktale* (New York: Peter Lang, 2010).

It wasn't until I began diving deeper into Ukrainian spiritual practices that I began to see the connections between Baba Yaga and the spiritual healers, wise women, and witches of Ukraine. This book centers on the spiritual practices of my own heritage; however, people who are interested in Slavic magic will discover many correspondences and similarities with their own traditions.

In some of the stories told about her, Baba Yaga appears not as one woman, but as three sisters all named Baba Yaga. So, perhaps think of what I have written in these pages as the Ukrainian Baba Yaga looking for her many other sisters scattered throughout the Slavic world. Baba Yaga has inspired stories in so many countries for hundreds, if not thousands, of years and will continue to do so for hundreds and thousands of years to come. I hope that my words will inspire people from other countries and cultures to pick up this thread and tell the stories of her many sisters.

If you've ever heard one of the fairy tales where the hero or heroine meets Baba Yaga, you know that she is quite the trickster. Tricksters are actually teachers. Like all the best teachers, she is indirect in her approach, offering the student puzzles that seem mysterious in the moment but elicit the most profound flashes of brilliance in the end.

This book is like that. As you turn the pages, you will be entering a fairy tale and walking a mystifying, twisty path that may at times seem capricious, hazy, too slow, too fast, and sometimes even frustrating. This path is open to anyone, but it is not *for* everyone. Like the characters who meet Baba Yaga, a person who picks up this book may decide to take the shortcut, put off the meeting until later, or turn back home completely. However, if you walk the roundabout path beside the heroine of our tale, you will develop a deep relationship with Baba Yaga and emerge with gifts and wisdom that you never knew you held within you.

Your journey in this book begins, as all good journeys begin, with a story. Each chapter starts with an episode of a fairy tale that will meander throughout the entire book. Like all fairy tales, it is more than it seems. You will befriend characters and enter their world to receive insights to bring back to your life. The story I spin for you here loosely follows the plot of the famous story "Vasilisa the Beautiful"; however, elements from other stories of Baba Yaga have been woven in to create something completely new. This newness includes the heroine's Ukrainian name, Vasylyna.

In the second part of each chapter, Baba Yaga herself will take the stage to share her wisdom in her own charmingly cantankerous way. She has her opinions, of course, and will also tell you about the special beliefs and traditions that show up in the tale. You may not always appreciate what she has to say (old women are notorious for not having a filter), but she will always be truthful, and what she tells you will always be useful.

In the third part of the chapter, I will offer another take on the topic, teaching you how to bring traditional Slavic magic into your own modern spiritual practice. I will take you out of just reading a fairy tale and introduce you to magic that will bring you directly into Baba Yaga's world. Like three tresses of a braid, these three strands will give you three different threads you can weave together to make deep connections that are all your own.

I can see that you are eager to start your journey. Remember, when you meet Baba Yaga, be humble, be willing, be respectful, and be gracious. Show up with your best manners, and she might even invite you to sit beside her near the woodstove. If you get a seat by the fire, she might even tell you her stories.

And if you are worthy of hearing her tales, you might even be able to figure out the secrets of her magic. And if she teaches you her magic, you will be a very, very lucky one indeed.

## Chapter 1

# Vyshyvanka: The Magical Stitches

It all started in a small village. There was a good woman and a good man: a husband and wife who were merchants. They had a successful little shop in their home. They traded their fine cloth and tools, ribbons and saddles for eggs and wheat, milk and meat. They had a fine house, warm and cozy in the winter. They ate well, they were kind and fair to all, they shared with those who were less fortunate, and so they had many friends. They had everything that they could want—except a child. How they longed to have a little baby, a girl or a boy they could raise up to be good and kind, brave and strong.

Finally, after many years, the man and the woman's wish came true, and they had a little daughter whom they named Vasylyna. She was a perfect child and beautiful, as all babies are, and everyone in the village celebrated and shared in the happiness of the couple.

Vasylyna grew, as all children do, first toddling around on chubby legs, and then running through the village, her skirts and braid trailing behind her as she laughed and scampered. Her mother was an excellent seamstress and embroidered beautiful vyshyvanky for Vasylyna by hand. She embroidered the dresses with flowers and birds, goddesses and trees in stitches of red and black, yellow and orange, green and blue, on the white linen she wove. Vasylyna helped her mother at the loom, and her mother taught her to spin and weave and sew, and she also taught her to embroider protective and magical symbols into the cloth.

Each day that she grew, she became more and more beautiful—not just with her sweet face, but in her kindness to others: the people of the village, the animals, and even the trees and flowers. She helped all those around her, especially her mother and father. They taught her how to fold cloth and polish brass. They taught her how to add and subtract and write neatly in a

5

ledger. And when her father was away getting the silks and ribbons and tools and other items for their shop, she would assist her mother with the chores.

She would help her mother sell the goods, cook the meals, fetch water from the well, and chop and haul the wood for the pich, the giant old wood-burning stove that cooked their meals and warmed them through the winter. Each morning, as the sun was just peeking over the distant mountains to the east, Vasylyna and her mother would go outside and bring in wood to feed the pich so that they could warm the house and bake the bread and cook the food they would eat that day.

One early morning before dawn, in the cold of late winter, Vasylyna's mother lay in her bed and said to Vasylyna, "Vasylyna, I think you are old enough to get the wood for the pich by yourself today."

So, Vasylyna went out to the woodpile and brought in the sticks and logs. When she brought them in, her mother was still in the bed. She put the wood in the stove, and by the firelight, she saw that her mother was pale. "Matusya, are you unwell?"

Her mother coughed and pushed herself to sit up straighter in the bed. "I just need to rest a little. Can you bake the bread today, Vasylyna?"

"I can try," said Vasylyna.

"And can you bring me my needlework please, dear Vasylyna? I will embroider while I rest and get better."

Vasylyna brought her mother her basket with the cloth scraps and needles and thread, and then she busied herself doing the chores while her mother embroidered.

Her mother stitched all through the day, and when it was time to go to bed, Vasylyna went to take the needlework from her mother's hand.

"No. Go to sleep, dear Vasylyna. I want to embroider a little more." So Vasylyna went to bed and left her mother to work by the firelight.

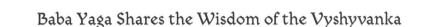

## Baba Yaga Shares the Wisdom of the Vyshyvanka

So, you're ready to begin your journey, are you? Well, I just want to give you a bit of warning that you will be venturing out of what you know into all that is unknown. I know it all seems safe and familiar now—you're sitting at home, reading a book, cozy and warm. But this is the time for you to prepare. It's no good carving a wooden pail to carry water when your house is already ablaze. We witches know that the time to do your magical work is *before* you need it.

As you go on this adventure, you are going to meet with strange spirits and encounter supernatural forces, and I don't just mean me. Listen: at the heart of it all, I am a grandmother, and like a wise grandmother, I will tell you what's what. If you are going to wander out into the world, you better not go out there unprepared. The world can be an unpredictable place, so do your magic to bring good fortune and avoid disasters before you venture out so that you don't have to clean up a mess after you are already in it.

Before you head out there like a newborn kitten with your eyes only halfway open, you need to understand how the spirit world works. There are good forces: the things you want to bring more of into your life. There are also the not-so-good ones: *vroki* and *prychyna*. Prychyna is a curse, someone actively trying to harm you. Vroki is the evil eye, when someone looks at you with a jealous or an envious feeling that causes you misfortune, even if they have no ill wishes toward you.[2] An illness, a misfortune; yes, these can just be the result of your carelessness, but they can also occur because someone looked at what you had with an envious glance, or because they were angry at you and wanted you to be harmed.

This might sound a little scary, and yes, if your fate were controlled by everyone's whims, that *would* be scary! But the good news is that you can create your own protection: *oberehy*, or charms.[3] If you stick with me, you are going to learn to create many

---

2. *Etnografichniĭ Zbirnik: Vidae Naukove Tovaristvo Imeni Shevchenka* (L'viv, Ukraine: Nakladom Naukovoho tovarystva Imeny Shevchenka, 1895).

3. Nikolay Fedorovich Sumtsov, *Lichnyye Oberegi Ot Sglaza* (Saint Petersburg, Russia: Tipografija Gubernskago Pravlenija, 1896).

oberehy on your journey, but there is one that will become as familiar to you as the clothes on your back.

Ah! It *is* the clothes on your back! Your clothing is one of your layers of magic—a physical manifestation of what you wish to wrap your body in. Just as your clothing can protect you from the scorching summer sun or the icy winds of winter, it can also protect you from a burning jealous glance or a coldhearted curse. Your clothing can attract love, encourage fertility, and bring abundance as well.

We old ones know this. Those intricate stitches you see on the vyshyvanky, the embroidered shirts and shifts that we wear, are not just pretty decorations, oh no. Open your eyes, little one, and you will see. Those designs are a detailed coded language of magical charms, oberehy, an ancient symbolic language with its roots winding back to the oldest times. To stitch powerful talismanic symbols is to program your future.

Our vyshyvanky are covered with sacred symbols. These charms are embroidered down the sleeves or over the front of the bodice, but they are also applied to the neckline, cuffs, and hem: the openings of the garment. These are the places where that vroki or prychyna could get under your clothing and get to you—the places where extra support and good fortune are needed. For men, there is heavy embroidery on the wrists, so that their hands might be empowered; around the neck, so that they may always hold their head high; and on their chest, so that they might feel love and courage. For women, there is light embroidery on the wrist and neck—sometimes on the hem of the garment as well—and large talismanic embroidery on the sleeves to strengthen the arms for hard work and protecting the loved ones they hold close.[4]

The symbols themselves are there to bring in the good and keep out the bad. You can encode prosperity, health, beauty, fertility, strength, love, and protection into your embroidery so that every time you wear it, you weave a cloak of positive magic around yourself without having to give it a second thought. When we sit down to embroider, we are sewing our wishes, hopes, and dreams into reality.

Once you learn how to make these charms, you can create magic for yourself and your loved ones. You can even use these embroidered oberehy to bless your home and

---

4. Chumarna Mariya, *Taynopys Vyshyvky* (L'viv, Ukraine: Apriori, 2018).

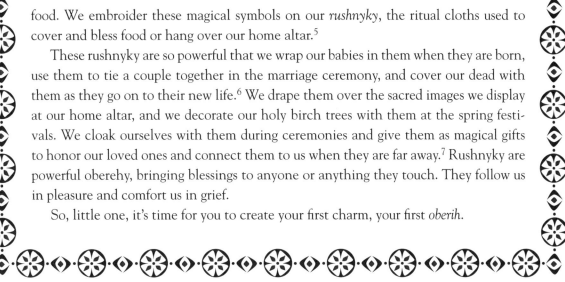

food. We embroider these magical symbols on our *rushnyky*, the ritual cloths used to cover and bless food or hang over our home altar.[5]

These rushnyky are so powerful that we wrap our babies in them when they are born, use them to tie a couple together in the marriage ceremony, and cover our dead with them as they go on to their new life.[6] We drape them over the sacred images we display at our home altar, and we decorate our holy birch trees with them at the spring festivals. We cloak ourselves with them during ceremonies and give them as magical gifts to honor our loved ones and connect them to us when they are far away.[7] Rushnyky are powerful oberehy, bringing blessings to anyone or anything they touch. They follow us in pleasure and comfort us in grief.

So, little one, it's time for you to create your first charm, your first *oberih*.

## Madame Pamita Teaches the Magic of the Vyshyvanka

When I was growing up, my mother taught me to embroider. My little hands would make clumsy crosses and French knot stitches that were more knot than stitch, but to my mother, it didn't matter. My creations, made with love and given to her for her birthday or Mother's Day, were perfect in her eyes. She had been taught to embroider by her mother, who had been taught by *her* mother, back through the generations, and to pass this gift along to her daughters was to pass along our heritage and our magic.

As I grew, I loved to dress up in vintage costumes. I remember buying a pattern for a vyshyvanka as a young teen and dreaming of embroidering it with beautiful cross-stitch patterns. At the time, I had no idea that the symbols themselves had any meaning, but I must have sensed their magic. To me, they looked like something from a fairy tale, and they made me believe that if I wore something that romantic, I could have encounters with magical beings and turn my dull teenage life into something dramatic and exciting.

---

5. Ludmyla Bulhakova-Sytnyk, Lubow Wolynetz, and Natalie O. Kononenko, *The Tree of Life, the Sun, the Goddess: Symbolic Motifs in Ukrainian Folk Art* (New York: Ukrainian Museum, 2005).

6. Mike Dixon-Kennedy, *Encyclopedia of Russian and Slavic Myth and Legend* (Oxford: ABC-Clio, 1999).

7. Natalie O. Kononenko, *Slavic Folklore: A Handbook* (Westport, CT: Greenwood Press, 2007).

## Vyshyvanky Today

Even though Ukrainian embroidery might look like something from a charming fantasy story, there has been a modern-day resurgence in making, wearing, and collecting vyshyvanky and rushnyky. For native Ukrainians, wearing a vyshyvanka has been a badge of national pride and a symbol of Ukrainian independence. For diaspora Ukrainians, it connects us to our heritage. There is such a love of this embroidery that there is even an international Vyshyvanka Day celebrated by Ukrainians and embroidery-lovers all over the world on the third Thursday of May.[8]

While people today wear vyshyvanky with the colors and patterns that appeal to them, in the past, each region, and even each village, had its own style. Embroidery was a secret language that could identify where a piece was made and, therefore, where someone who was wearing it was from. Some regions of Ukraine specialized in heavy embroidery in multiple colors, and others embroidered delicate white thread on white cloth. In still other areas, the protective patterns were not embroidered at all, but woven directly into the cloth.

While many wear embroidered shirts solely for expressing Ukrainian pride, most Ukrainians are at least conscious of the talismanic properties of these designs. Just as someone may wear a "lucky shirt" when competing in a sporting event, there are many who feel just a little more spiritually protected when wearing their charmed vyshyvanka.

## The Magic of Cross-Stitch

Throughout history, talismanic cloth was woven, and we have evidence of complex stitches being added to cloth for protective power as early as the Bronze Age.[9] Embroidery styles have evolved over the centuries, and today, the most identifiable vyshyvanky are the cross-stitched designs that became popular in the nineteenth century.

There is magic inherent in every cross-stitch. Each cross is made up of two stitches making an X, a symbol of protection. When embroidering, the first part of the cross-stitch initiates the opening of the new reality you are creating, while the second stitch

---

8. Clare Hunter, *Threads of Life: A History of the World through the Eye of a Needle* (New York: Abrams Press, 2020).

9. E. B. Shcherbyna, "Ukrayins'ka Narodna Vyshyvka i Yiyi Terminosystemy," *Visnyk Kharkivs'koyi Derzhavnoyi Akademiyi Dyzaynu i Mystetstv* 1 (2010): 79–80, http://nbuv.gov.ua/UJRN/had_2010_1_21.

fixes that new reality into place. The completed X splits, crosses out, or negates any unwelcome energies and enhances positive ones.

Our ancestors embroidered symbols of nature, abstract symbols of protection, and even hidden images of goddesses in their embroideries to protect themselves, their loved ones, and their homes against negativity and to invite blessings, spiritual connection, health, wealth, and abundance.

In all styles of embroidery, the symbols created with the stitches had magical meaning. The colors of the threads stitched onto white or natural-colored cloth also had significance, whether simple white, bold red and black, or complex multicolored designs.[10] If you would like to learn more about color magic in embroidery, refer to appendix II, where you'll see a listing of colors and their meanings.

## Make an Embroidered Charm

Your first step on your magical journey is to create a cross-stitch talisman, working from one of the traditional patterns. You can plan your stitching by creating a design on graph paper or by using the designs below. Reading a pattern is easy: one square equals one cross-stitch.

### Your Magical Supplies

Stitching on Aida fabric is the easiest for cross-stitch. It has a tight, even weave with premeasured holes to guide your stitches. Aida is measured by "count": a lower number, such as fourteen-count, will set you up for bigger stitches, which are perfect for beginners; a higher number, like twenty-eight-count, is for tighter and finer work.

Here's what you'll need to get started:

- White or light-colored cross-stitch cloth, such as Aida fabric
- Embroidery floss in black and red or other colors of your choosing
- Cross-stitch or embroidery needles
- Embroidery hoop (one that measures five inches to eight inches in diameter is about the right size)

---

10. O. V. Dobrovolska, "Filosofiya Ukrayins'koyi Vyshyvky," *Visnyk Kharkivs'koho Universytetu*, no. 57 (2017): 140–144, https://openarchive.nure.ua/handle/document/7029.

### *Create Your Cross-Stitch Talisman*

There are several ways to create a talismanic cross-stitch to protect and bless you. You can stitch a single symbol and pin the embroidered cloth to your clothing or carry it in your wallet or purse. You can create a repeating pattern and turn your embroidered cloth into a patch or a pouch. Advanced stitchers may want to embroider clothing along the cuffs, collar, and hem for protection and down the sleeves or front placket to bring in blessings.

Traditionally, new work was started during a waxing moon (the cycle when the moon appears to get larger, after the new moon and before the full moon). Just as the moon was growing, the protection and blessings were expected to grow as well. In the folk practice, stitching was done on any day of the week except on Friday and holidays.[11] Stitchers would refrain from weaving or stitching on Fridays to honor the weaving and stitching spirits *Mokosh*, *Paraskeva P'yatnytsya*, and the *Rusalky* on their special day.[12]

When you sit to stitch, take a moment before you begin to center yourself and let go of any stress or cares. When creating talismanic embroidery, it was considered essential that the stitcher's thoughts be positive and their feelings light. What you were thinking and feeling would go into your work and would be locked into the resulting magical item. If you stitched with a peaceful mind and happy thoughts, whoever wore or used the item cloaked their life in that positivity. So, if you're feeling frustrated, anxious, or unhappy, it's not the time to make your talisman. Set it aside and do something to relieve those negative feelings first. Find your best feelings and thoughts before you begin.

Meditate on each stitch itself as a cross that initiates and then locks your intention into the spell as you make it. If you are embroidering cross-stitch style, avoid making any knots in your stitching, as it is believed that knots will create unnecessary impediments to your incoming blessings.

---

11. Joanna Hubbs, *Mother Russia: The Feminine Myth in Russian Culture* (Boulder, CO: NetLibrary, 1999).

12. Cherry Gilchrist, *Russian Magic: Living Folk Traditions of an Enchanted Landscape* (Wheaton, IL: Quest Books, 2009).

## Talismanic Embroidery Designs

There are many powerful traditional symbols used in embroidery and weaving. The oldest ones, going back to prehistoric times, are the most obscure and purely symbolic: stars, sun, meanders, and the geometric shapes, for example. The representational shapes—such as plants and hearts—are more modern but still imbued with powerful magic.[13] Whether you choose an ancient or a more modern design, select the one that brings the blessings you desire or appeals to you most.

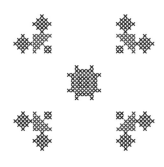

### *Kvadrat/Square*

The *kvadrat* is used in spells to enhance the material, draw abundance, or create good boundaries or protection. The kvadrat also carries an essence of orderliness and perfection—a calm and harmonious stability—and is therefore good in spells where you want peace and prosperity. The kvadrat also represents the number four and all things associated with four: the four directions, the four seasons, the four parts of the day, the four elements, and the four stages of life.

### *Rhomb/Lozenge*

The *rhomb* is an ancient diamond shape connected to fertility and the womb as well as the abundance of Mother Earth. If the lozenge is divided into four more rhombuses, it is a symbol of a fertile field and therefore invokes fertility of all kinds. If those rhombuses have a dot in the center, they represent the sown field, a pregnancy, or abundance and success. If the rhomb has hooks around the border, it is a *zhaba*, or frog, and represents life-giving water.

13. S. S. Skliar, *Starovynni Ukrayins'ki Uzory Dlya Vyshyvannya Khrestom. Mahiya Vizerunka* (Kharkiv, Ukraine: Klub Simeinoho Dozvillia, 2016).

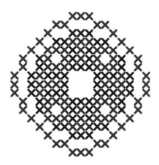

### Kolo/Circle

The *kolo* is a primary magical symbol representing the sun and the moon. It is used in spells for long life, vigor, and health. If the kolo has a dot at its center, it represents the universe and our connection to all. The kolo also refers to eternity and the never-ending cycle of life and rebirth.

### Kalyna/Guelder Rose

The *kalyna* is a berry bush that symbolizes youthful beauty, love, wealth, health, and motherhood, with the bush symbolizing the mother and the berries representing her children. Because of this meaning, it also represents the blessings of the ancestors and has an association with ancestral lands, family roots, and blood ties. The ripe red berries also represent passionate and sensual love.

### Dub/Oak

The *dub* is the oak, considered the king of the trees. The oak is a holy tree associated with strength and longevity, and there are ancient records of sacred oak groves being used for worship in pre-Christian times.[14] Often the dub is embroidered on masculine clothing to make the owner strong and courageous, and it can be combined with kalyna to symbolize the union of strength and beauty.

---

14. Mychajlo S. Hrusevs'kyj, *History of Ukraine—Rus'* (Edmonton, AB: Canadian Institute of Ukrainian Studies Press, 1997).

### Vynohrad/Grapes

*Vynohrad* signify the family and domestic happiness. Images of vynohrad strengthen family connections when embroidered on clothing but especially empower the rushnyky that are used by the entire family in the home. The vynohrad can be used to create warm familial ties, bless loved ones, and bring abundance to the bloodline.

### Mak/Poppy

*Mak* is a powerful emblem that has many magical meanings. It is often used for spiritual protection from negative entities as well as for banishing negativity, curses, and hexes. It is a symbol for remembrance of the ancestors, so it can be used as a talisman to tap into deep wisdom from one's lineage. Mak is also used in spells to encourage psychic abilities and have prophetic dreams, so it is the perfect symbol if you wish to develop these skills. It is also seen as a symbol of abundance and can be added to embroidered spells for increasing prosperity. Mak is sometimes used as a love charm for attracting a new relationship filled with happiness as well.

### Derevo Zhyttya/Tree of Life

The Tree of Life is an ancient symbol with multilayered secret meanings. First, the Tree of Life is rarely shown as a representational tree. It is usually depicted as a *vazon*, a flowerpot. This potted plant or tree motif also represents the goddess *Berehynia*, the oldest Mother spirit, who is the progenitor of life and is associated with the birch tree. The motif is often depicted with a stylized shape that resembles the upraised arms of ancient goddesses. The *Derevo Zhyttya* can be used as a charm for soul renewal, immortality, resurrection, and abundance.[15]

---

15. Bulhakova-Sytnyk, Wolynetz, and Kononenko, *The Tree of Life, the Sun, the Goddess.*

### Sertse/Heart

*Sertse* as a symbol of love is a more modern concept, but incorporating a heart into your embroidery can be a way to encode a love charm into your work. Should you want to be more discreet, you can embroider heart-shaped leaves or petals as part of a plant motif. However, as an older symbol, the heart shape stands for the dual spirits of fate, the *Rozhanytsi*.[16] Embroidering this image of the Rozhanytsi on one's clothing ensures good luck and solidifies a positive fate.

### Zori/Morning Star

*Zori* is the eight-pointed starburst symbol representing the ancient morning star or dawn, a spirit who protects one from evil, disease, and weakness. Stars scattered on a sleeve represent the orderly and harmonious structure of the universe. Incorporating zori in your oberehy will encircle you with peace, calm, love, and protection.

### Shevrony/Chevrons

These ancient symbols are an expression of the union of female and male essence and the meeting of spirit and matter. The angles pointing down are said to represent the feminine or the material, while the angles pointing up are interpreted as the masculine or the spiritual. *Shevrony* are added to oberehy for the union of the spiritual and the material to bring blessings to fruition or to invite a divine love.

16. Hubbs, *Mother Russia*.

### Khvylyasti Liniyi/Wavy Lines

*Khvylyasti liniyi* represent the element of water, life-giving rains, cleansing, the flow of time, and the evolution of the universe. Waves that run vertically represent gentle rains falling from above, while horizontal lines signify running waters flowing from springs and melting snow. This is a powerful ancient symbol to invite flowing good fortune, longevity, and the blessings of the universe.

### Khrest/Cross

*Khrest*, the equal-armed cross, is an ancient sacred symbol representing the sun and fire. When tilted to become an X, it represents the moon. As either the sun or moon, it is seen as a protective amulet against evil spirits. As the sun, it represents life force and expansive energy. As the moon, it represents a more quiet and mystical power. The two intersecting lines symbolize the meeting of the material and the spiritual, and the four arms of the cross represent the balance of the four elements: air, fire, water, and earth. The cross can be used for protection and as a symbol of harmony and peace.

### Svarga/Sun

*Svarga* is another ancient symbol for the ever-turning wheel of the sun. Solar symbols bring all to light and are incorporated to protect a person and their property from negativity, to bring enlightenment, and to bless the home and family with happiness. Use a svarga to invoke strength, energy, ancestral wisdom, and protection against misfortune.

### Povna Rozha/Mallow Flower

When the upright cross of the sun is superimposed over the X of the moon, they form a double cross, or an eight-pointed star, which symbolizes the union between these two spirits. It also represents the union of male and female, which brings in new life. The eight-pointed star is also called the full mallow flower, *povna rozha*, and is one of the most popular symbols in Ukrainian talismanic magic. It represents the bursting forth of life energy in all directions, the big bang that occurs when an egg is fertilized or when a star is born in the heavens. When you want to incorporate big dreams and expansive wishes into your oberehy, a povna rozha is the perfect addition to your design.

### Kryvi Tanets/Meander

*Kryvi tanets* literally means "the winding dance," the old ritual steps that Ukrainians performed in the spring. This symbol represents the life journey, eternity, strength, and vitality. Sometimes this design is called *bezkonechnyk*, meaning "infinite line" or "meanders." It provides powerful protection against negative forces. Any evil that attempts to attach itself will follow the meander, becoming confused and trapped in its endless circuit.

### Trykutnyk/Triangle

*Trykutnyk* symbolizes trinities of all kinds: the lower world, the middle world, and the upper world of the World Tree; the three elements of water, fire, and air; birth, life, and death; and mother, father, and child. If the triangles are touching point-to-point to become an hourglass shape, they represent the meeting of the natural world and the supernatural world and can be used as a charm to connect to the spirit realm.

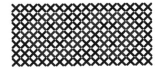

### *Klyuchi/Keys*

*Klyuchi* is another multifaceted symbol called keys, S figures, or snakes. In ancient times, they symbolized the serpent, a powerful emblem of the waters of the earth (as opposed to the waters of the heavens). Snakes are the guardians of the lower world and an avatar of Baba Yaga. Using klyuchi in your charm will protect you and connect you to Mother Earth, Baba Yaga, the lower world, and snake spirits.

## Utility, Beauty, and Magic

For Ukrainians in the past, every object they touched would be useful, beautiful, and imbued with magic. Almost everything they owned was layered with these three attributes. A wooden spoon with a simple carving on it was not just a utensil made to look pretty, but an amulet for abundance and a tool for making meals that would bless the family with health. A home loom with symbols carved into the wood had magical meaning as well as a mundane purpose. And an embroidered shirt was not just a way to protect your body; it was a beautifully decorated talisman to spiritually protect and bring in blessings.

This depth of meaning is well-known to Baba Yaga as well. Her wild hair, her hut on chicken legs, the giant mortar that she travels in, and so many other aspects of her are more than just quirky attributes. They all have secret symbolism that empowers and protects her.

You can create your own secret symbols as well through your embroidery. Once your stitching is complete and you have created your charm, reflect on its meaning. Use it, wear it, carry it with you as an obereh, or display it in your home to protect yourself and your loved ones and to bring bountiful blessings.

# CHAPTER 2

# MOTANKA: THE LIVING POPPET

*T*he next morning, when Vasylyna woke up, she saw her mother still working on her needlework, but she looked even paler than before. "Matusya! Matusya! You shouldn't be working! You should be resting and getting well!"

But her mother just laid her cold hand on Vasylyna's and said, "Vasylyna dear, can you fetch the wood for the pich today?" Vasylyna quickly got dressed, ran out to the woodpile, and brought in the wood. Then she gathered some blankets and made a little bed in the warm nook over the oven and helped her mother up there.

"Bring me my needlework please, dear Vasylyna," said her mother.

"Matusya, please rest and get well," pled Vasylyna, but her mother would not be consoled until she had her needles and thread. So Vasylyna brought the needlework basket to her mother and went outside to pick some healing herbs.

When she returned, she made her mother a nourishing and healing soup and did the daily chores of the house. Finally, nighttime came. Vasylyna's mother called for her daughter to come close to her. She took Vasylyna's hands in her own and gave her what she had been working on. It was a small doll, made of folded cloth and dressed in a tiny vyshyvanka, a skirt, and a delicate embroidered shawl that went over her head. Vasylyna took the doll into her hands. "This, dear Vasylyna, is a special motanka, a magical doll that will guide and protect you. Keep her close to you; give her a little food and a little drink, and she will watch over you." And Vasylyna's mother kissed each of Vasylyna's hands, laid her head down, and closed her eyes.

Vasylyna took the motanka with wonder. She was so small yet so beautiful. A true tiny miracle. She did as her mother told her to do and gave her doll a little bread and a sip of water, and, since it was the end of the day, she took her to bed with her. She soon drifted off to a peaceful sleep with the motanka at her side.

## Baba Yaga Shares the Wisdom of the Motanka

I don't live at the center of the most remote forest for nothing. If you're going to find me, you are going to need a guide, and a good one. I keep myself well-hidden on purpose. I don't like nosy neighbors, disrespectful kids, or arrogant young men any more than the next *vidma*. People are a nuisance, and I don't need any of them stumbling upon me just because they went for a nature hike. No; if you want to find me, you're going to have to get someone who knows what they're doing to show you the way.

You're going to need a guide, yes, but also a guardian. The forest is not always a friendly place. You'll also want a companion by your side, someone who can give you courage and strength when you feel overwhelmed and afraid. You'll definitely need more than hired help. And a friend … well, a friend is good, but do they have an investment in your success? What you need is family, an ancestor who gives a damn about you. But ancestors are not easy to call forward, and once you do, how do you know they're with you? What you're going to need is some really old, old magic. You're going to conjure up your ancestor spirits using a motanka.

A motanka is so old that your oldest ancestors created one to call in *their* ancestors. I am talking about the oldest ancestors. Yes, the ones who lived in the mammoth-bone huts on the steppes. Motanky are used to house our guardian ancestors so that they can protect us, give us strength, provide insight and inspiration, heal us, and bless us. Throughout millennia, they have been created and given from mother to daughter, weaving a golden thread of lineage connecting generation to generation.[17]

Back in the oldest days, we created our motanky out of straw, or birch bark, or sticks of holy wood. We didn't let a little thing like not knowing how to make cloth slow us down. But when your foremothers learned the magic of weaving and making cloth of hemp fibers, *that* was when we began to roll out some very special magic.

Throughout the years, there were many occasions when someone might gift a motanka to a loved one. They would be given by mothers to their grown daughters to aid them in pregnancy and childbirth. The world can be a risky place for a little one. A motanka could be placed in the cradle before the child was born. It represented that

---

17. O. Tarasova, *Lyal'ky-Motanky* (Kharkiv, Ukraine: Glagoslav Distribution, 2014).

future child being healthy and happy, but it also strengthened their connection to their ancestors and to future generations. It would guard the mother and child during this important life transition, keeping them both safe and sound during the liminal time of childbirth. After the baby was born, the motanka would become an ancestor companion to the newborn, protecting them from vroki, keeping watch over them, and, for those who listened carefully, passing on ancestral wisdom.[18]

Even as the child grew, if they became sick, a special motanka was placed in the bed to take the illness away. When the child grew to adulthood, moved into old age, and passed on, a motanka would be buried with them to accompany and welcome them to the afterlife and into the arms of the ancestors who had watched over them while they were alive. They, too, would then join the ancestors to watch over future generations.

The motanka is crafted in a very particular way. The word *motanka* comes from the Ukrainian word *motaty*, which means "to wind or roll." While we can dress one up in embroidered cloth, the doll itself is never pierced by a needle, made with seams, or tied with knots. We wind hemp or linen cloth into rolls and secure the doll by wrapping threads around the rolls.[19]

We never give a motanka a face. Either we leave the face blank or weave a khrest pattern by wrapping colorful threads in a cross over the front of the head. Why? Well, a face attaches a soul to an item. The motanka is meant to be merely a temporary home for the ancestors that they can freely use, not an object that binds a soul to it.

And another thing: we never put eyes on the doll. The eyes are the "windows of the soul," as they say. An open window is an invitation to any stray creature looking for a free handout. Eyes are an opening that a mischievous spirit could use to enter into the doll and inhabit it. Getting in there, they might even take a piece of the maker's soul. Oh, and one more thing: we never give a motanka a name, particularly the name of an ancestor, for a name binds that ancestor to the doll.[20]

Womb to tomb, whether you know it or not, your ancestors accompany you throughout your life, little one. When the body goes, the spirit still lives on, coming back to

18. A. V. Stakhurskaya, "Traditsionnaya Kukla-Motanka V Kul'turakh Vostochnoslavyanskikh Narodov," *Gumanitarnyye Nauki v XXI Veke: Nauchnyy Internet-Zhurnal* 6 (2016): 78–90, https://humanist21.kgasu.ru/files/N6-N7_Stahurskaja_AV.PDF.

19. Viktoriya Sadovnycha, *Starovynna Mahiya Ukrayintsiv* (Kyiv, Ukraine: Knyzhkovyy Klub, 2018).

20. Ol'ha Oleksandrivna Tarasova, *Taiemnychyi Svit Lialky-Motanky* (Kyiv, Ukraine: Lybid', 2015).

experience life again and again. The way that we make a motanka is a secret message about the eternal nature of the spirit. The spiral design connects the motanka symbolically to the cycles of life—birth, growth, death, and rebirth—and to the golden thread of eternity.

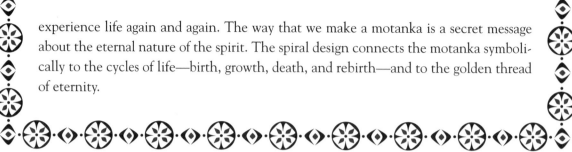

## Madame Pamita Teaches the Magic of the Motanka

When I was growing up, my mother would tell a story about when she was a little girl. When she was three or four years old, she came down with a serious illness. Whether it was a flu or measles or one of the other things that kids can pick up, she never knew. What she *did* know was that she was so sick and feverish, her own mother was afraid she was going to die. My grandmother had lost her young infant son just a few years before, and so she was probably even more anxious that she might lose her little daughter, too.

My mother would tell me that when she was lying in her sickbed, her matusya made her a special doll to help her get well. My grandmother gave her the doll and told her that she had to take care of her dolly, and so my mother talked to the doll and cuddled her as she rested and slept. After a few very worrisome days, my mother finally began to improve and was soon healthy again. And the doll? Well, my mother never mentioned keeping it or playing with it after the illness.

As my mother told me this story, I always just assumed that my babusya gave my mother the doll to keep her, a small, bedridden child, occupied, but my mother always emphasized the importance of the doll and how it was given to her to help her get better. It wasn't until years after my mother had passed away that I learned about the magic of the motanky and realized that my grandmother had crafted a magical poppet to heal my mother.

## Motanky Today

For generations, the motanka was revered as a magic talisman with its roots stretching back to the most ancient times. By the middle of the twentieth century, however, many people had dismissed the idea of magic, and motanky were demoted to being merely playthings. Nevertheless, with the revival of folk traditions in post-Soviet times, interest in the ancient protective magic of the motanky has also increased. Today, there are many talented craftspeople lovingly creating these powerful poppets. Motanky workshops are regularly held in Ukraine and other countries where Ukrainians have emigrated, and there are even museum exhibits devoted to these magical dolls.

## Creating a Motanka

Before you create your first motanka, there are a few things to keep in mind. As with crafting any magical tool in the Ukrainian way, make sure you have a light spirit when you create your motanka. Your emotional and mental states will become part of the doll, so be sure to release any negative emotions or thoughts and bring a positive outlook to imbue your talisman with happiness and joy. If you wish to be the most traditional, plan on crafting your motanka on any day of the week except for Friday, which is reserved for honoring the weaving spirits. Have all your materials ready before you start, and be prepared to assemble your motanka in one sitting, without interrupting the process. Finally, when you wind your cloth or thread, do so in a clockwise direction to bring in good luck.

### *What You Will Need to Create a Motanka*

- **Hemp or linen cloth.** Both linen and hemp are imbued with protective magic. The measurements below are just suggestions to get you started. You can change these proportions for a smaller or larger doll.
  - Square about 18 inches (45 centimeters) wide for the body
  - Smaller rectangle piece about 8 inches by 6 inches (20 centimeters by 15 centimeters) for the arms
- **Embroidery floss** for tying off the hands and neck of the motanka. If you are wrapping a khrest over the face, you will need a variety of colors of embroidery floss or threads.
- **Scraps of colorful fabric for clothing.**
  - Square piece of about 6 to 8 inches (15 to 20 centimeters) for the scarf
  - Rectangle piece of about 5 inches by 8 inches (12 centimeters by 20 centimeters) for the skirt

◆ Wide ribbon or a rectangle piece of fabric 2.5 inches by 4 inches (6 centimeters by 10 centimeters) for the apron

- **Needle** for tucking in the loose ends of the wrapped embroidery floss.
- **Extra magical bits.** You may want to wrap up some additional talismans in your motanka as you roll it.
  - ◆ Small coins for prosperity
  - ◆ Magical herbs for attracting good things
  - ◆ Grains for abundance
  - ◆ Wool for prosperity
  - ◆ Ashes collected from your hearth or woodstove to connect to the ancestors

### *Making a Basic Motanka Body*

You have some options when creating a motanka and can choose the difficulty level based on your skill and the amount of effort you'd like to put into it. The simplest option is to create a basic motanka with a blank face and unembellished clothing. For a little more challenge, you can wrap the face with a khrest, or, if you are skilled with stitchery, you can embellish your motanka's clothing using the cross-stitched symbols discussed in chapter 1.

1. Roll a square piece of heavy linen or hemp fabric into a tight roll. As you roll, you have the option of adding any of the extra magical bits mentioned above to your roll, such as herbs or coins. Place them toward the center of the cloth so they won't fall out. When you get to the end of the rolling, tuck under the unfinished edge to make the roll neat.

2. Fold the roll in half to make a body and wrap embroidery floss about 1 inch (2.5 centimeters) from the fold to create a neck. Wrap in a clockwise direction several times and then tuck the ends of the thread into your wrapping without tying a knot. You can use a needle to tuck the end of the embroidery thread behind the wrapped threads.

3. Take the smaller rectangle of fabric and roll it tightly to make the arms. Again, you can tuck the raw edges of the cloth under to create a neater roll.

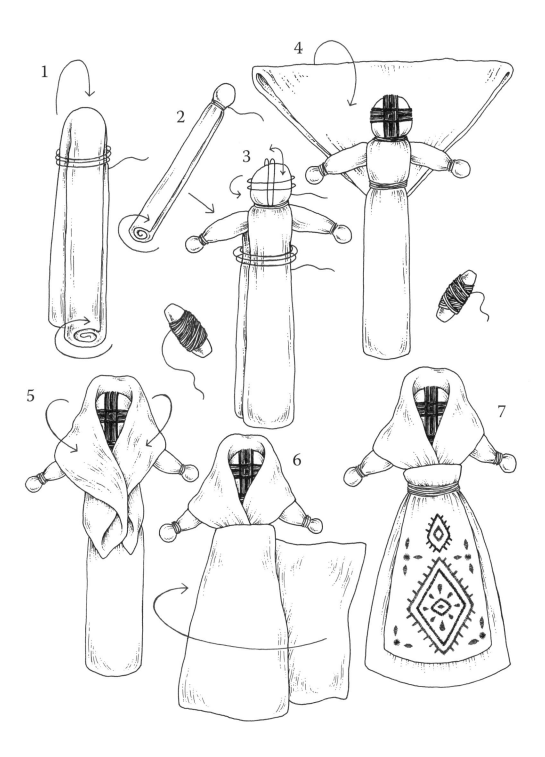

1

2

3

4

5

6

7

4. Create hands by wrapping embroidery floss in a clockwise direction around where the wrists would be.

5. Slip these arms between the flaps of the body and push them up to just below the neck.

6. Wrap and tuck another piece of floss clockwise around the torso and under the arms to hold the arms in place.

### *Wrapping the Face*

Motanky can be made either with no face or with a khrest pattern wrapped over the face with embroidery floss. If you choose to have a blank face, you can skip this section and go to Dressing a Motanka.

1. Wrap a colorful piece of embroidery floss around the neck of the motanka several times and then bring it up over the front of the face vertically and in the center. Wrap behind the head two times so that you have two vertical threads lying flat next to one another in the middle of the face. Make additional wraps around the neck to hold the threads in place.

2. Bring the thread behind the head and then wrap two times horizontally across the middle of the face, laying the threads flat next to one another and creating a cross over the middle of the face.

3. Tuck the end of the thread into the neck wrapping and start a new color of thread by wrapping it a few times around the neck.

4. Wrap the new color around the face vertically, laying the threads on either side of the original vertical threads.

5. To keep things neat, bring your thread up from the left side of the neck to wrap the right side and up from the right side of the neck to wrap the left side.

6. Wrap one thread to the left and one to the right, then another to the left and another to the right until you have two threads in the second color on either side of the original cross.

7. Repeat wrapping the horizontal threads, laying them next to the previous threads until you have two threads lying flat to either side of the original cross. Tuck the end of your thread in the wrapping at the neck.

8. Continue adding new colors, adding two threads to the right and left and two threads to the top and bottom of the horizontal arm until you build up a colorful khrest that is to your liking.

9. Tuck the end of your thread into the neck winding. Now you're ready to dress your motanka.

### Dressing a Motanka

Dressing a motanka allows you to imbue your magical doll with your creative flair. The clothing you create can be as simple as a scrap of cloth or as luxurious as an intricately embroidered vyshyvanka. Fabric with patterns in contrasting colors look the best and allow you to bring color magic to your doll. See appendix II for a list of colors and their magical meaning.

1. Take a small square of colorful fabric for the scarf and fold it in half to make a triangle with the point facing down.

2. Place the doll's head on top of the triangle with about 1 inch (2.5 centimeters) of fabric above the head.

3. Fold the top over the forehead and the right and left points across the body.

4. Take the rectangle of colorful fabric and wrap it around the waist for a skirt. Tuck the bottom points of the scarf into the skirt to secure them.

5. Put the small swatch of fabric or ribbon on the front of the skirt for an apron. Wrap thread clockwise around the waist to secure the scarf ends, the skirt, and the apron.

### Using Your Motanka for Magic

Once your motanka is completed, you will need to tend to it. It is not a decoration, nor is it strictly a toy; however, if you need comfort, you may hold it close and feel the warmth of your ancestors' love around you. When you are not attending to it, you may set it in a place of reverence in your home. Traditionally, a motanka is kept at the *pokut'*, the home altar corner where ancestors are honored.

If you want general protection for your home or loved ones, you can craft one and place it on your ancestral altar, but you can also create ones for specific magical purposes. If your loved one is ill, you can roll a special motanka and tuck it next to them in bed to draw out the illness. Once they recover, traditionally you should burn the motanka to destroy the disease. You can also use a motanka to change the weather. If you want to control the forces of nature, you can make a motanka to call in rain or hold back devastating storms.

### The Help of the Ancestors

You know the Beatles lyric "I get by with a little help from my friends"? Well, creating a motanka allows you to get a little help from friends in very high places. If you want to speak with your loved ones who have moved on to spirit form, you can talk to your motanka and ask for their support. If you want your ancestors to help you accomplish all your daily tasks efficiently, you can make a motanka with extra arms. And, of course, if you have a difficult mission to fulfill, akin to going into the woods to meet Baba Yaga, you can bring along your motanka for companionship and helpful guidance along the way.

# Chapter 3

# Domovyk: The Spirit of the House

**W**hen Vasylyna woke up the next morning, her mother neither called for her to fetch the wood nor bring her sewing, because her spirit had left for the otherworld. Vasylyna's father came home, and together they wept and grieved. When the time came, they buried Vasylyna's mother.

For a few years, Vasylyna and her father lived and worked, cried and laughed together, and over that time, she grew to be a great help to him. But a well-to-do widower will not stay single long, and after a while, her father remarried. Vasylyna's stepmother had two daughters. They all moved in, and the stepmother became the new mistress of the home.

As with any big change, there was sure to be strife. Vasylyna and her father had one way of doing things, and the stepmother and her daughters had their way. Vasylyna's father wanted peace in the home, and so he asked Vasylyna to do the bidding of her new mother. When the father was there, the stepmother and her sisters were as sweet as honey, but when the father went away for business, the three of them would order Vasylyna about and treat her like a servant girl. All day they made her life a misery, but when nighttime came, Vasylyna would take her motanka out from her pocket, give her a piece of bread and a sip of water, and hold her close while she slept and remembered her mother.

The girls all grew, as children will, and as kindhearted as Vasylyna was, her beauty radiated just as brightly. The time came for Vasylyna's elder sisters to begin to accept suitors, but each young man who came to visit took one look at Vasylyna and was no longer interested in her older stepsisters. It would not do for the youngest child to marry before her sisters, and the *stepmother and sisters became envious, and their envy turned to cruelty. Whenever the father was away, the stepmother and her daughters took away the intricately embroidered vyshyvanky that her mother had made and instead gave her patched and stained clothes that had no protective embroideries on them. They gave her even more dirty and difficult tasks around the home and mocked and abused her, but still the young men who came by would see her kind and gentle nature shining and would ignore the sisters. Finally, the stepmother concluded that nothing would do but to get rid of Vasylyna for good, and so she devised a plan.*

*When the father was away, the stepmother told Vasylyna that they had sold the home and they were moving to an isolated wooden hut, a khatynka, far away from the village at the edge of the forest. When they were ready to leave, she asked Vasylyna to bring a live coal from the old fire to set in the woodstove of the new home to bless it. Vasylyna spoke to the Domovyk, the spirit of the house who lived behind the stove, asking him to give her an ember to carry to the new home. The shy little bearded man came out from behind the pich and gave her a live coal from the fire, carefully placing the glowing ember in a strong iron pot for her to carry. Vasylyna picked up the pot and then invited the Domovyk to the new home.*

*"Didus', Didus', don't stay here, but come with our family to our new home!" But the Domovyk sadly shook his head, retreated behind the pich, and could not be enticed to leave.*

## Baba Yaga Shares the Wisdom of the Domovyk

I think you're about ready to meet my brethren, the spirits. I don't know if you know this, but you'll be encountering quite a few otherworldly creatures on this journey you're taking with me, and not all of them will be … how shall I put this … not all of them will be "housebroken." So, I think it's best if you meet one of the friendlier ones first, just to get you warmed up.

What you young ones don't realize is that the whole world is filled with spirits. There are spirits in the waters, the trees, the rocks, the weather. But not just in nature. No! There are spirits who live in more domesticated spaces, too: the fields, the yards, the barns, and even the houses. Treat these spirits with the respect and reverence they deserve, and things will go well for you. But be disrespectful, rude, unkind, and, well, after a while, they might ignore you, or worse, actively start up a rebellion.

The first spirit you are going to meet is your Domovyk. The Domovyk is a house spirit, a tiny little man with gray shaggy hair, a long beard, and bright eyes.[21]

Like many spirits, the Domovyk has mastered the art of shape-shifting. Yes, he can choose to appear before you as a little man, but he might also show up in your home as a cat, a dog, a frog, a bird, a rat, or even a snake.[22] He's a shy fellow, though, so most of the time he will make himself invisible, and when he is, you'll only be able to detect him by the sounds he makes as he rustles through your things or scampers through your house.[23]

Even though he is unseen by most people, adults who are gifted, young children, and animals can see him in his true form. The Domovyk is very fond of the small children and pets under his care in the home and will make himself visible to them so that they can play together. If you ever see your pet staring at nothing, hear your child having a conversation when no one is in the room with them, or see them playing with an invisible creature, they may be communicating with your Domovyk.[24]

If you are lucky enough or gifted enough to see him, he might look a little familiar to you. He can bear a family resemblance or appear as a tiny version of a strong and positive male ancestor of yours. He'll be dressed like a typical peasant from the old country, with loose pants, an embroidered shirt, and a woven belt wrapped around his waist, but his hairy feet will be bare. It's not just his feet that are hairy; he'll be covered with shaggy hair from head to toe. This is a good thing! His hairiness tells you about his well-being. The more hair he has, the happier he is and the more prosperous your home will be.[25]

Even if you don't see him face-to-face, you might find signs that a Domovyk is living in your home. If you see shaggy footprints in the snow around your house on a winter's night, hear someone calling your name when no one is there, or even feel the touch of a hairy hand … well, that's probably your Domovyk. And if it's a touch, pay attention!

---

21. Claude Lecouteux, *The Tradition of Household Spirits: Ancestral Lore and Practices* (Rochester, VT: Inner Traditions, 2013).

22. Yulia Buyskykh, "Domovyk u Tradytsiynykh Viruvannyakh Ukrayintsiv: Pokhodzhennya Obrazu," *Etnichna Istoriya Narodiv Yevropy* 26 (2008): 120–127.

23. Dixon-Kennedy, *Encyclopedia of Russian and Slavic Myth and Legend*.

24. Louis Herbert Gray, *Mythology of All Races Volume 3* (London: M. Jones, 1918).

25. Gilchrist, *Russian Magic*.

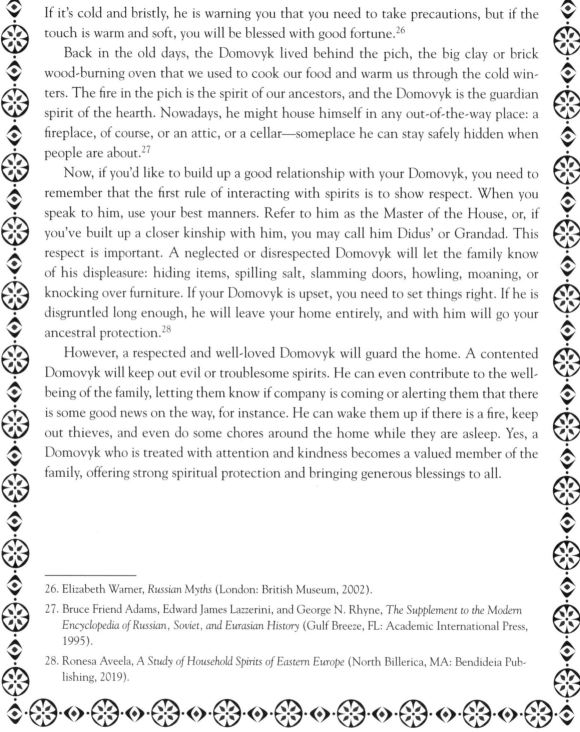

If it's cold and bristly, he is warning you that you need to take precautions, but if the touch is warm and soft, you will be blessed with good fortune.[26]

Back in the old days, the Domovyk lived behind the pich, the big clay or brick wood-burning oven that we used to cook our food and warm us through the cold winters. The fire in the pich is the spirit of our ancestors, and the Domovyk is the guardian spirit of the hearth. Nowadays, he might house himself in any out-of-the-way place: a fireplace, of course, or an attic, or a cellar—someplace he can stay safely hidden when people are about.[27]

Now, if you'd like to build up a good relationship with your Domovyk, you need to remember that the first rule of interacting with spirits is to show respect. When you speak to him, use your best manners. Refer to him as the Master of the House, or, if you've built up a closer kinship with him, you may call him Didus' or Grandad. This respect is important. A neglected or disrespected Domovyk will let the family know of his displeasure: hiding items, spilling salt, slamming doors, howling, moaning, or knocking over furniture. If your Domovyk is upset, you need to set things right. If he is disgruntled long enough, he will leave your home entirely, and with him will go your ancestral protection.[28]

However, a respected and well-loved Domovyk will guard the home. A contented Domovyk will keep out evil or troublesome spirits. He can even contribute to the well-being of the family, letting them know if company is coming or alerting them that there is some good news on the way, for instance. He can wake them up if there is a fire, keep out thieves, and even do some chores around the home while they are asleep. Yes, a Domovyk who is treated with attention and kindness becomes a valued member of the family, offering strong spiritual protection and bringing generous blessings to all.

---

26. Elizabeth Warner, *Russian Myths* (London: British Museum, 2002).

27. Bruce Friend Adams, Edward James Lazzerini, and George N. Rhyne, *The Supplement to the Modern Encyclopedia of Russian, Soviet, and Eurasian History* (Gulf Breeze, FL: Academic International Press, 1995).

28. Ronesa Aveela, *A Study of Household Spirits of Eastern Europe* (North Billerica, MA: Bendideia Publishing, 2019).

## Madame Pamita Teaches the Magic of the Domovyk

Over the years, I've had experiences out in nature where I have sensed, heard, and even seen otherworldly creatures; I've always described these experiences as faery encounters. But these experiences always happened when I was far from civilization, and I always viewed these beings as wild nature spirits. That is, until my Domovyk demanded my attention by "borrowing" my brass safe-deposit box key as I held it in my hand and walked from my bedroom to the car. After leaving offerings for a few weeks and conversing with him to find out what he needed, he eventually returned the key by placing it on the grass just outside my door—a place I had searched dozens of times before.

Since that unintended misstep with my house spirit, I have developed a happy relationship with my Domovyk, setting up a special altar to him at my fireplace and making sure he is well-fed, honored, and contented. Ancestral house spirits will let us know when they want to begin a relationship with us and if they need our attention—they'll keep hammering home the message until we get it through our thick heads. If you start to see some unexplainable phenomena in your home, it just might be a sign that your Domovyk needs your attention and is ready to get acquainted with you.

## Domovyky Today

While a house spirit might seem like something only found in movies and not a concept connected to the modern world, a surprising number of people honor their Domovyk in small ways: acknowledging his presence when they hear noises in the home, talking to him, and sitting for a few minutes with him before they leave on a trip.[29] Even these small nods to the house spirit are believed to bring positive energy to the house and family, but there are so many other ways you can build and deepen your relationship with him.

## Inviting Your Domovyk into Your Home

If you've never had a Domovyk live with you, you can invite one to bring you blessings. Before you begin, you need to remember that by inviting a Domovyk, you are inviting

29. Gilchrist, *Russian Magic*.

your ancestors into your home.[30] This is going to be a lifelong relationship—one you should not enter into without feeling a sense of commitment. Maintaining a relationship with your Domovyk doesn't require much, but like adopting a pet, you should only begin this process if you will continue it.

To begin, go outside dressed in your best clothes and call out to invite your Domovyk to come to you:

> *Grandpa Domovyk,*
> *please come into our house,*
> *and tend to your family.*

## Inviting a Domovyk Back to Your Home

If you feel you had a Domovyk at one time but he has left, you will need to do a similar ritual to get him to return. Dress up in your best clothes, go outside, and call out,

> *Grandpa Domovyk,*
> *come back to us.*
> *Make our house a home and care for us!*

## Moving a Domovyk to a New Home

When you move to a new home, it's important to invite your Domovyk to come with you. He *is* family, after all. There are two methods for transporting the Domovyk. If you have a fireplace, firepit, or woodstove, take an ember from your fire in the old home and invite your Domovyk to come with you. The proper invitation is to say,

> *Domovyk, Domovyk, don't stay here.*
> *Come along with our family.*

When you get to your new home, put the ember from your old home into the new fireplace and invite your Domovyk to settle in, saying,

> *Welcome, Grandfather, to your new home.*

---

30. Buyskykh, "Domovyk u Tradytsiynykh Viruvannyakh Ukrayintsiv: Pokhodzhennya Obrazu," 120–127.

If you don't have a fireplace, woodstove, or firepit, you can invite the Domovyk to follow you by bringing a broom from the old house to the new. Get a straw broom that you have used in your old house and ritually sweep the already-clean floor. After you do so, hold out the broom and call out an invitation to your Domovyk.

*Grandpa Domovyk!*
*Come with me!*
*A new mansion awaits us,*
*warm walls await us.*
*Come with me!*
*The food there will be hearty,*
*and the kitchen will be bright.*
*Come with me!*

Put the brushy part of the broom in a cloth bag (a pillowcase is perfect for this) and bring it to the new house. Unwrap the old broom and set it next to a new straw broom overnight so that your Domovyk can move in.[31]

## How to Rid Your Home of a Stranger Domovyk

If you arrive at a new home and the prior family has left their Domovyk behind, it may be difficult for you and your Domovyk to move in peaceably. Two Domovyky from different families will battle and create chaos.[32] Once your Domovyk has moved in, you can banish the old family's Domovyk by beating the walls of the home with a broom and asking your Domovyk to assist you, shouting,

*Stranger Domovyk, go away home!*
*Grandfather Domovyk, help me chase away this intruder.*

Another way to prepare a new home is by scattering poppy seeds or performing *obkuryuvannya*, fumigation by burning dried herbs. Burn dried thistle, wormwood, or nettles to clear out the old Domovyk before inviting yours in. An alternative to burning herbs is to make holy water by soaking these fresh herbs in water and then sprinkling that water around the home.

---

31. Aveela, *A Study of Household Spirits of Eastern Europe*.
32. Warner, *Russian Myths*.

## Dedicating Space to Your Domovyk

To make offerings to your Domovyk, you will need a small, dedicated bowl, some food, and a dedicated place where you will feed him. Once you've called your Domovyk, go inside and meet him at your dedicated spot. If you have a fireplace or woodstove in your home, this is the equivalent of the pich, and you can use this as your place of honor. If a fireplace is not an option, you can meet with him in the attic or the cellar. And if you have neither of these, find a quiet corner of the home with a small table or shelf, set a small figurine of a Domovyk on it, and set your offerings there. Little gnome statues, troll dolls, or other similar figurines will work well in place of a Domovyk statuette.

Find a small pottery bowl or saucer that you can dedicate to him. The dish can be one that you have used before, but once you dedicate it to him, it will be for him only. As you set down the dish for the first time, you may want to recite a special blessing, letting him know that this is his dish and that this is where you will be placing your offerings to him.

*This is your dish, Grandpa Domovyk,*
*and it will be set here.*
*This is food for you, my beloved ancestor,*
*you and I share this home and this table.*

While the plate should be his designated plate, when not in use, it should be stored with the plates the rest of the family uses to symbolically make the Domovyk an accepted member of the family.[33]

## Food Offerings for Your Domovyk

You don't have to necessarily prepare special food for your Domovyk every time you make an offering. In fact, sharing with him what you are preparing for yourself is a close and cozy way to feed him, just like sharing a meal with a loved one. Offering him a corner of your sandwich, a bit of bread, or a saucer of milk can be just the right thing for connecting you and your Domovyk.

A Domovyk is small, so the offerings can be small. A bite, a piece, a teaspoon—these amounts will generously feed a spirit. Your Domovyk is happy to eat whatever you

---

33. Aveela, *A Study of Household Spirits of Eastern Europe.*

offer, but you may discover that he has special preferences. If you leave out foods that he seems to favor, you can prepare those especially for him. There are foods that generally seem to be well-received by Domovyky: baked goods, such as breads, pastries, and cookies; breakfast treats, such as pancakes, porridge, yogurt, or cooked grains; sweets, such as candies or honey; and drinks, such as milk, sweetened tea, or water are all favorites of the Domovyky.[34]

Homemade foods made with quality local ingredients are preferable over mass-produced, overly processed packaged foods filled with artificial ingredients. Foods that you have prepared with your own hands and filled with love and happiness will feed the Domovyk more energy than store-bought foods or foods made when you were anxious or stressed.

When you make an offering to your Domovyk, it's important to address him and tell him that the food is for him. The Domovyk is not a thief, so if you don't let him know that it is for him, he will not touch it. When you place the offering, say something out loud to alert him, such as,

> *Grandpa Domovyk,*
> *I brought you delicious dishes,*
> *sweet dishes.*
> *Share my food with me.*

Or,

> *Grandfather Domovyk,*
> *I brought you a delicious dish,*
> *a hearty dish.*
> *Share my food with me.*

## Schedule Your Offerings

You don't need to feed your Domovyk every day. Offering food every few days or once a week is sufficient. Don't leave food out so long that it gets moldy or spoiled. You can leave an offering and remove it a day or two later without replacing it with new food immediately. Set a schedule for feeding your Domovyk. If you can feed him once a

---

34. Aveela, *A Study of Household Spirits of Eastern Europe.*

week, stick to that. If you feed him three days in a row, but then don't feed him again for a month, he may get bothered and begin hiding items from you or creating disturbances at night. And if he is consistently forgotten, he may leave the home, and you will have to entice him back.

If possible, make your offering in the morning and leave it overnight, so that your Domovyk can have his meal in peace and privacy. If you have a schedule that doesn't allow you to spend a few minutes with your Domovyk in the morning, choose a different time for your get-togethers.[35]

## Removing Food Offerings

When you make an offering to your Domovyk, what happens? Sometimes the food or beverage will appear untouched, sometimes it may appear smaller, sometimes it may disappear. Know that even if it looks untouched, the life force of the food has been taken in by the Domovyk. The Domovyk is a spirit and eats the spirit of the food.

You can leave your offering out for him as long as it's fresh. Once it has gone stale, you can remove any remaining food or drink and say a thank you to your Domovyk:

*Thank you, Grandpa Domovyk,*
*for the honor shown by eating with us.*
*We are always glad to see you.*

If there is food remaining, it is traditionally offered to the pets in the house as long as it is safe for them to eat. If you have no pets, then it is appropriate to leave it for the living things outside. Take breadcrumbs and scatter them for the birds, pour water offerings on plants, or pour milk into another dish for animals to drink. Water or food can also be left at the base of a tree as trees are able to receive and transform the remains of our spell work.

## Leaving a Domovyk Temporarily

A Domovyk likes a neat, well-kept, happy home with love and life in it. A Domovyk left behind in an abandoned house becomes angry and morose and may even burn the

---

35. Aveela, *A Study of Household Spirits of Eastern Europe.*

property to the ground. For this reason, it's important when going on a trip that you let your Domovyk know you'll be back and are not leaving him behind.[36]

Before you leave the house, sit on your suitcase for a few minutes to signal to your Domovyk that you'll return. As you sit, clear your mind to receive messages, reassurance, and any advice that your Domovyk has to offer. And if you can't find an item when you are packing your bags, it means that the Domovyk has hidden it to let you know that it doesn't need to be taken.

## Appeasing an Unhappy Domovyk

A happy Domovyk can bring good fortune to a home, and so if you have an unhappy house spirit, it's a good idea to turn things around. A neglected or disrespected Domovyk will let the family know of his displeasure by causing mischief, making loud noises, or, if very disgruntled, even causing destruction.[37] If your Domovyk is upset, you need to set things right, for if he is unhappy long enough, he will leave your home entirely and take his blessings with him.

Before you go to sleep, ask the Domovyk why he is dissatisfied, and in your dream, you should receive an answer. Sit down in your kitchen and have a conversation with your Domovyk, telling him that you will correct the situation. Keep your home tidy, make sure that there is no quarreling, and maintain harmony in the household. Once you've addressed these things, leave out an offering, and your Domovyk should settle back down into his happy rhythm.[38]

## Signs of a Contented Domovyk

The dramatic signs of an unhappy Domovyk can be fairly easy to identify, but there are subtle signs to watch for to know that your Domovyk is content. You might hear gentle knocks on the floors, walls, or ceiling, or hear floors creaking or doors opening and closing. Pets or children may stare at something that appears invisible to you or play with invisible friends. Objects may get moved or go missing and then be quickly returned. Lights might flicker, turn on and off, or flash out. You might hear a grunt or a cough

---

36. Aveela, *A Study of Household Spirits of Eastern Europe*.

37. Buyskykh, "Domovyk u Tradytsiynykh Viruvannyakh Ukrayintsiv: Pokhodzhennya Obrazu," 120–127.

38. Howard Percy Kennard, *The Russian Peasant* (New York: AMS pr, 1980).

or feel a pleasant but unusual sense that someone else is in the home.[39] None of these things will feel scary or unsettling, just unusual and interesting.

## The Gifts of the Domovyk

It is lovely to develop a relationship with your Domovyk just for the sake of connecting to the spirit world and your ancestors; however, there are beautiful gifts of service that your Domovyk can offer you.

### *Protection from Malicious People*

When a Domovyk is empowered in a household, people with bad intentions won't be able to enter. As soon as they cross the threshold, the Domovyk will send you signs. Things that the negative person picks up in the house, such as silverware or cups, will slip out of their hands. If the person is exceptionally malicious, the Domovyk will begin pushing them out of the house.

### *Babysitting*

If there are small children or pets in the house, the Domovyk will watch over them and play with them. Domovyky are very protective of these innocent ones and will prevent them from getting into dangerous situations, distracting them from playing with household items that might harm them.[40]

### *Reminders*

When you've established a strong relationship with your Domovyk, he will wake you in the mornings in time to get ready for the day and will alert you if you've forgotten anything before you leave the house.

## Your Domovyk Is Family

While the primary job of the Domovyk is to spiritually protect the house and the people and pets who live there, never forget that he is also family. Having this positive spirit in the house will protect you against troubles, quarrels in the family, or any other kind of

---

39. Linda J. Ivanits, *Russian Folk Belief* (Armonk, NY: M. E. Sharpe, 1992).

40. Ivanits, *Russian Folk Belief*.

negativity. Invite yours in, keep him happy, enjoy all the good things that he brings to you and your loved ones, but also feel the loving warmth that he brings as well. When you welcome this friendly being into your daily life, you begin to access the spirit realm and all the beautiful possibilities it holds for you.

## The Importance of the Ancestors

Throughout this book, you will discover how deeply important the ancestor spirits are in folk magic practices. They are our protectors and guides from the otherworld, the spirit realm where Baba Yaga resides. As the gatekeeper of this realm, she traverses between the world of the living and the world of the spirits and can give you access to the magic found there. Whether you have a detailed family tree going back ten generations or have no information at all about your family line, you do have ancestors going back thousands of generations. Think with wonder on all the magic that brought you here today and all the support that you have from your ancestor spirits who look upon you with love and pride.

# Chapter 4

# Rozdorizhzhya: The Crossroads

Vasylyna went out the door and joined her stepmother and stepsisters, and they began walking with the wagon full of their belongings toward the new khata. She trudged along, carrying the pot with the ember in the cold weather while the stepmother and the stepsisters bullied her along the way. Finally, they arrived at the small, dark, and dusty little hut, but just as Vasylyna was bringing the blessed ember through the door so that they could light their new fire, her sisters tripped her so that she fell into a bank of snow at the side of the path. The lid of the iron pot flew off, and the ember tumbled out into the snow and was instantly extinguished.

"You stupid girl!" the stepmother screamed. "Now we will have no light to see and no fire to keep us warm. We will all surely freeze to death because of your clumsiness."

Vasylyna offered to go back to the village to get a new ember from a neighbor, but the stepmother was crafty and said, "That's foolish to go all the way back to the village when we have a neighbor much closer. Go into the forest and find Baba Yaga. Steal some fire from her and bring it back to us."

What choice did Vasylyna have? She could stay and freeze with her stepmother and stepsisters tormenting her, or she could risk stealing some fire from Baba Yaga. So, she put on an extra shawl, packed up a basket with bread and salt to eat on the journey, felt to make sure her motanka was in her pocket, and set out on the path into the dark forest.

She walked deeper and deeper into the woods, staying to the path and never venturing off it. But then she came to a crossroads, a place where the path branched off in two directions. Vasylyna became alarmed. How would she find Baba Yaga? Which road should she take?

*As she stood at the crossroads trying to decide, she felt a chill pass through her as if there were eyes watching her, though she could see no living creatures nearby. She began to get even more anxious. The fear and worry about unseen beings and getting lost grew so much that she decided facing the wrath of her stepmother was preferable to the otherworldly dangers in the woods.*

*She turned and took a few steps to go back when she felt a tug at her pocket. She stopped, took out her doll, and held her close to her heart so that she wouldn't feel so afraid. Then she reached into her basket to give her a pinch of bread. The doll ate the bread and then spoke to an astonished Vasylyna:*

> *No need to face your family's wrath.*
> *Go to the left on the forest path.*
> *Move swiftly on your own two feet,*
> *for Baba Yaga you must meet.*

*Vasylyna was amazed to hear the doll speak, but she knew her words held great wisdom. So, she held the doll even closer and turned back around. She made haste as she passed through the crossroads, taking the road to the left and continuing on her way.*

## Baba Yaga Shares the Wisdom of the Rozdorizhzhya

Ah, the crossroads! Everyone must meet their *rozdorizhzhya*, their crossroads. It's true! No matter how many friends you have or how big your family is, you travel through life on your own, and the life experience you have depends on the choices you make. Do you turn left or turn right? Do you go back to a life that is miserable just because it's safe and known, or do you go forward into the unknown? Well, I can tell you one thing: there is no learning, no experience, no wisdom gained without going into untested territory. That is something that has always been true.

It's the same with meeting me. If you came to this book looking for all the answers to be handed to you on a silver platter, well I am sorry for you, because the path to meet me is your unique path, and it requires daring, wit, and work. For you, it might mean a turn to the left, and for someone else, it might be a turn to the right. What I will say is

that the path to meet me can only be found through the tests, through experiences. If you want to gain my gifts, you have to earn them. And your first test is the crossroads. Are you going to go forward or backward? Left, or right? Are you willing to step into the center of the crossroads, to stand in the liminal?

To know me, you must understand the liminal. Liminal is "in-between." The liminal rests outside of the familiar and resides in the strange and unknown. There are times that are liminal—a dusk that is neither day nor night, or the time between childhood and adulthood. There are spaces that are liminal—the edge of the field as it blends into forest, the threshold of a door that is neither inside nor outside, or the crossroads leading in new directions.

When you leave the known and step into the unknown, you have entered my domain. Liminal times and spaces are magical. They open you up to all possibilities and are the passageway to traverse between the worlds, but they are also risky and unpredictable. And therefore, as the one who reigns over the liminal, I, too, am considered dangerous and capricious.[41] And yes, I can be, but I can also be infinitely beautiful, helpful, powerful, and miraculous. *That* part of my story has been forgotten.

The rozdorizhzhya is a sacred and magical location, a liminal place, a portal between the material world and the otherworld, the world of the *Mavky*, the wandering spirits.[42] It is a space that can empower your spells and divinations, but it is also a tricky location where things might go awry for the unaware. The rozdorizhzhya can be used for attracting abundance, but it can also be the site for picking up a curse. It is a place where divinations and incantations are magnified, where talismans and amulets are hung or buried for empowerment. The crossroads is a place where *all* places and directions meet, where time has no meaning, and where magic crackles in the air. Take care and follow the rules of the spirit realm, little one, and all will be well—but disrespect the Mavky or carry an attitude of arrogance, and you may find yourself in trouble.

The rozdorizhzhya is a place where the unusual can happen. Listen carefully and you can hear the Mavky. This is the place where we would bury our loved ones who had a bad death, a death that was unexpected and came too soon through murder, or drunkenness,

---

41. Johns, *Baba Yaga*.

42. Kononenko, *Slavic Folklore*.

or even their own hands. These spirits need easy access to the other realms, and so we bury them at the crossroads in the hopes that they will find their way.[43]

Luck can come from using or even touching a blessed object. Likewise, curses, diseases, and traumatic events can become attached to items and to you if you pick up a cursed object. At the crossroads, people leave curses, bad luck, and prychyna behind. That means that there are items left at the crossroads like money, spell packets, and offerings, and they may be holding some questionable energy. If a person has a big curse or a terrible illness, they might have to pay a big price to the spirits. Payment for taking away the illness can be something like leaving a piece of fine jewelry or a tempting expensive gadget. So, as enticing as that delicious bauble sitting at the crossroads may be, don't pick it up; don't even touch it. You might be picking up someone else's disease or bad luck. Even if it's just someone's positive spell or intention, you don't want to mess with anyone else's work. That gift is meant for the Mavky, not for you. Let the spirits handle it.

At the crossroads, you decide your destiny and take the risk to step into the unknown. It's a place where strength and courage can be found as well, and where, in the blink of an eye, you can change your destiny. It is a place of powerful magic, indeed. We vidmy, the witches, adore the crossroads. Why? Well, where the veil between the seen and unseen is thin, we can access the spirits, perform divinations, and conjure up some potent spells. It's the place where we can leave our magical items, both blessed and cursed. The crossroads is indeed a holy place of power—if you know the intricacies of working with its energies.[44]

## Madame Pamita Teaches the Magic of the Rozdorizhzhya

When I was a little girl, I sensed the magic of the crossroads as if it emerged from some deep ancestral knowing. My friends and I weren't afraid of the crossroads, but when the grown-ups would drive us through the streets of the city, we'd perform little rituals as

43. W. F. Ryan, *The Bathhouse at Midnight: An Historical Survey of Magic and Divination in Russia* (Stroud, PA: Sutton, 1999).

44. Hubbs, *Mother Russia*.

we crossed over intersections to make the journey more exciting: lifting our feet off the car floorboards or closing our eyes and holding our breath.

It wasn't until I began studying magic in my teens that I first learned of the power of the crossroads: the place where the Greek goddess Hekate ruled or where one could make a deal with a demon in exchange for talent. As my magical studies expanded, I discovered that this belief in the power of the crossroads is part of the folk magic of many cultures and is deeply ingrained in Slavic magical practices.

## The Rozdorizhzhya Today

So much of the old magic of the rozdorizhzhya came from our agrarian ancestors who had a rural way of life. However, that doesn't mean that the beliefs about the power of the crossroads were left behind when people stopped traveling over dirt roads and moved to the cities. While most people might not perform the old rituals at busy city intersections, there are many people today who had a Ukrainian baba admonishing them not to eat when walking across the street or never to pick up anything lying in a crossroads. The idea of picking up money found near a city intersection is unthinkable to most Ukrainians, who have a real sense that if they did, they would be picking up someone else's bad luck. The power of the crossroads has never truly been forgotten.

## Types of Rozdorizhzhya

One unique aspect of working with the rozdorizhzhya is that each type has a different energy. Today, with most of us living in cities with paved streets, crossroads magic requires us to step outside, get back in touch with nature, and go into less domesticated areas, the realms of the wild Baba Yaga. While you don't have to go deep into virgin forest to do this magic, you will find so much power in going out of the city and into more natural surroundings. Before beginning this work, you may want to do some exploration to find some suitable dirt paths with secluded crossroads where you can do your spells in private. Of course, rural areas may have many magical paths, but even big-city vidmy can find paths in quiet gardens, on hiking trails, or in parks where they might do their magic.

### Unpaved Paths

Rural Ukrainians believed that different crossroads had different energies and that the most powerful crossroads were unpaved footpaths. Dirt roads have an open, wild energy, connect closely with Mother Earth, and can lend the best results to your magic.

### X- or +-Shaped Crossroads

The standard crossroads where four roads meet is suitable for any kind of crossroads work or ceremony.

### T-Shaped Crossroads

A crossroads that is shaped like the letter *T* has a dead end, blocked energy, and so it blocks any magic you may attempt there. If you attempt to do spells there, you may find that they fall flat. It is not recommended as a place to do magical work and doesn't count as a crossroads when you are counting crossroads for journey magic.

### Y-Shaped Crossroads

A forked road is different than a T-intersection. It is quite magical and especially good for spirit encounters. This is a favorite of witches and is especially good for crossroads divination and fortune-telling.

### Star-Shaped Crossroads

A crossroads with five or more roads meeting is quite powerful. The more roads that meet, the more concentrated the energy. These unusual crossroads add power to any work that is done here. In particular, a crossroads of seven roads is helpful for changing your fate, and a crossroads of eight roads is so powerful that a stone picked up from here is a power object that can be used in sacred rites and protection magic.

## General Rules for Working at the Crossroads

When choosing a crossroads at which to do spiritual work, there are some recommendations on how to find the perfect spot. Choose a special crossroads to work at on a consistent basis. Select one that is easy to access, day or night. The most magically powerful crossroads are found on unpaved trails and footpaths, and older roads are more potent than newer ones.

## Do Crossroads Work Alone

Crossroads magic is usually done as a solitary practice. For crossroads spell work to be effective, you must walk to the crossroads and back home in reverent silence. Don't bring friends or do your spell work on a busy pathway with other people around. Only bring with you what you need for the spell. Don't bring anything you will consume, and avoid bringing anything there and back. Leave everything for the spell.

### Avoid Eating or Drinking

Never eat at the crossroads. The crossroads is a place where spirit activity of all kinds is high, and so some tricky energy might be roaming around. When we eat, we not only absorb the nutrients of the food, but also the life force of the food. There might be some stray energy that attaches to your snack, and, well, you don't want to give a hitchhiker a free ride. Save your snacks for after your ritual and eat them away from the crossroads. If you need to bring water or food for the hike, leave it beside the road before you get to the crossroads and retrieve it on your way back.

### Keep Your Money in Your Pocket

The crossroads are a portal, and the spirits there are attracted to energetic things. Displaying money attracts the spirits, and not leaving it for them is considered rude. The spirits may take retribution for your insult by drawing your prosperity away from you. If you are at a crossroads, keep your money in your purse or wallet and only pull out money you are going to leave as an offering.

### Cover Your Yawns

Make sure you don't yawn with an open mouth when standing in the crossroads. If you do so, you are creating an entry point for a wandering entity, who can settle in your body and sap your vital energy. If this happens, you may find that bad luck follows you. This problem can be easily prevented by covering your mouth when you yawn or making sure to suppress the yawn until you're out of the intersection.

### *Avoid Spitting*

Don't disrespect the spirits at the crossroads by spitting there. There is an old saying that if you spit at the crossroads, you are spitting out your own life. When you leave your spit there, you leave a direct connection to your spirit and body. Spitting also implies a curse, and this double action of offending the Mavky and leaving them a connection to you is just too tempting for trickster spirits that may be lingering around. With that connection to you, they are given an opportunity to make you pay for your insulting behavior.

### *Go to the Crossroads with a Purpose*

Avoid loitering at the crossroads without a purpose. If you just hang around the crossroads for no reason, you are opening yourself up to picking up problems that others have left there.

### *Don't Look Back*

After working at the crossroads, resist the temptation to look back over your shoulder at your work. If you are making a payment to the spirits, throw a coin or coins over your left shoulder after you turn back home and don't look back. To do so would be taking a forbidden look into the world of spirits, which will offend them.

Likewise, don't go back to the crossroads just to check on your work or keep doing the same spell at the same crossroads day after day, unless otherwise specified. Doing one crossroads working per month is usually sufficient. Doing more than one working in a moon cycle may dilute your intention.

## Rozdorizhzhya Journey Magic

Take a journey on a path, and you may encounter more than one rozdorizhzhya. Count the crossroads as you leave your home or other starting point, and you will find that each one is used for a different type of spell. Ideally, you will want to do this work on natural dirt walking paths, not on paved roads. If you live in a rural area, finding these paths should be easy. If you live in the city, look for a footpath out in a natural setting and begin walking it to discover your places of magic.

### Counting the Crossroads

Begin walking and counting the crossroads that you pass through. You can select the crossroads at which to work based on whether it's the first, second, third, and so on. You can use a path that you have walked many times and take the route you normally take, or, if you don't know the area well and want to make sure you don't get lost, you can plan your route with a map.

If you know the area well and feel safe, you can also choose your path intuitively. When you come to the first crossroads, choose the direction based on your intuition or by spinning clockwise in the center of the crossroads with your eyes closed. When you have spun enough to disorient yourself, stop, open your eyes, and take the path in front of you. If the path leads you back the way you came, the spirits are telling you that today is not the day to do your spells.

Only work at one of the crossroads on the journey and only go as far as the cross-roads where you wish to do your working. For example, if you are doing a money spell at the third crossroads, go only to the third crossroads, do your working, and then go back home.

These are sacred personal rituals. While you are waiting for your good outcome, don't speak too much about the work that you have done. In fact, it's preferable that you tell no one of your spell. Any work at the crossroads, apart from divination, should be done alone so you can focus and commune with the spirit world without distraction.

### Focusing Your Rozdorizhzhya Work

Keep your rozdorizhzhya work focused. Don't try to do more than one crossroads spell at a time. If you have more than one issue you would like to work on at the crossroads, do one each lunation (one month or one cycle of the moon). Only do crossroads work if your intent is serious and you have a real need. For example, if you are wealthy and you do money magic, the spirits may judge you as greedy. At the very least, they may not grant your wish, and if they feel that you are really out of line, they may take your prosperity away from you.

Choose just one of these workings to do at a time. Visit the crossroads where you will be working ahead of time so that you can plan your work thoughtfully. Follow the recommendations but amend them if the spirits tell you that they want something different. Whatever you do, don't leave litter at any crossroads. Trash, particularly noncompostable plastic, left at a crossroads will disturb the spirits. Either leave something of value, something natural that can be safely consumed by wildlife, or something that will harmlessly disintegrate and feed the earth.

### First Crossroads

The first crossroads you encounter on your journey can be used for spells for your family and home. You can bring domestic peace, health, protection, and prosperity to your household by leaving offerings of paper money or banknotes there during the daylight hours. Speak your wish out loud and leave the money in the center of the crossroads.

The bigger the problems that you must overcome, the larger denomination you should leave. For example, if you have just a small problem, you may leave a one-dollar bill, but if your family life is filled with strife, arguments, and separations, you may want to leave a twenty, a fifty, or even a one-hundred-dollar bill, depending on the degree of the unhappiness. If you are unsure, start with a smaller denomination, and if there is no resolution, wait one month between workings and make subsequent offerings of increasingly higher denominations. The belief is that whoever picks up the money will bring the strife home with them, and your family will be free.

### Second Crossroads

The next crossroads you encounter can be used for love spells. You can draw a new love into your life, bring back an old lover, or improve your love relationship. Bring a piece of red wool yarn spun by your hand and whisper your wish into it (you'll learn more about spinning in chapter 12). Find a nearby tree or bush and ask the spirits and the spirit of the tree to bring your love to you. Speak your wish three times and tie a knot with each wish. Do this spell any time between sunset and sunrise.

### Third Crossroads

The third crossroads you come to is a place for money magic. Speak your wish and take out the number of coins corresponding to the number of roads and add one. For example, a typical X crossroads has four roads, so you would take out four coins plus one for a total of five coins. Leave one coin at the beginning of each road and one at the center of the crossroads. Speak your wish as you leave each coin. Do this spell work between dawn and noon.

### Fourth Crossroads

The fourth crossroads is a place to do spells to compel people who owe you money to pay you. When you come to the crossroads, pick up a nearby stick or stone and write the name of the person in the dirt. This work should be performed after midnight and before dawn.

### Fifth Crossroads

The fifth crossroads is for justice work. If someone has wronged you and you wish for them to receive their just deserts, you can do this spell so that the perpetrator will receive the appropriate punishment, spiritual or legal.

At any time of day, take a piece of raw meat, a coin, and a trowel to the crossroads. Dig a hole as close as you can to the center of the crossroads and bury the piece of meat in the ground. As you do, say this incantation three times: "May [person's name] receive their just reward." Once you've buried the meat, pick up your trowel and turn back the way you came without looking back at your work. Throw the coin over your left shoulder and say, "Everything is paid for!"

### Sixth Crossroads

The sixth crossroads is used to attract luck or bring back good fortune that has gone dry. This crossroads must be X-shaped. Go there at dusk, stand in the center, and say the following incantation:

> Good luck, I miss you.
> I will bow to the four directions and smile at each of you.
> Come back to me, good luck; go away, misfortune.

Bow to each of the four roads and then return home. Repeat this ritual for three days in a row to bring back good luck.

## Some Other Special Workings at the Rozdorizhzhya

As a liminal space, the rozdorizhzhya can be a tricky place, but big risks lead to big rewards. Yes, you can meet the spirits there at midnight, but there are many other ways to access the power of the crossroads for wishes, spells, and other less risky workings.

### *Relief from Sadness and Grief*

If you are inconsolably sad and can't seem to let go of your grief, you can leave your heartache at the crossroads. Take a handkerchief to wipe your tears. When it becomes completely damp, collect dust from the corners of each room in your house and put it in the handkerchief. Add a pinch of ashes from your fireplace. If you don't have a fireplace, burn incense or dried herbs in your home and use a pinch of these ashes. Tie the handkerchief in a knot and leave it at the crossroads at midnight during a waning moon to relieve yourself of your grief.

### *Spiritual Healing*

When the rivers and lakes begin to thaw, there is a belief that crows carry their children from the nest to bathe in the river before sunrise. There is a saying that those who bathe earlier than the crow's children on Holy Thursday will be healthy all year. Anyone who sees a crow bathing and gets at least a drop of water from that crow will be healthy all their life, because the crow is one of the caretakers of the Waters of Life and Death.

To wash away illness and protect good health, use water from a living source at the first thaw. You might plunge yourself into the icy water in the predawn hours, but a better method is to bring a bucketful into the home and add it to a bath in the early hours before dawn. After bathing and before the sun comes up, take some of this bathwater, carry it to the crossroads, and pour it out just as dawn is breaking so that any illness leaves the body and is taken away by the hungry spirits. Knowing that people may be leaving this water at the crossroads, cautious people avoid walking through crossroads on Holy Thursday morning so that they don't step in this water and inadvertently pick up someone else's discarded illness.[45]

### *Love Divination at the Rozdorizhzhya*

While most crossroads work requires solitude, fortune-telling is empowered when performed in a group. Gather some friends and go to the crossroads with a white tablecloth at midnight. Begin the ritual by picking up a stick and tracing a circle on the earth in the center of the crossroads, making sure that it is large enough to contain everyone. Sit as a group inside the circle and put the tablecloth over your heads like a tent. Each

---

45. Oleksa I. Voropaj, *Zvychayi Nashoho Narodu: Etnohrafichnyy Narys* (Kyiv, Ukraine: Vydavnycho-Polihrafichne Tovarystvo Oberih, 1993).

person should take turns, calling out their own name one by one. Then, everyone listens for a sound coming from an animal, such as a dog or an owl, to foretell that person's love fortune.

- If you hear a loud sound, it means that you will win the love of someone.
- If you hear a hoarse sound, an older person will fall in love with you.
- If you hear a distant sound, your love will be from far away.
- If the sound is close by, then your true love lives close by.

Every member of the group must call their name, and when all have heard their fortune, you can take the tablecloth off and erase the circle. If anyone should get frightened and leave the circle before all have heard their fortunes, it is believed that the predictions will not come true.[46]

### *Protecting a Community from Illness*

If there is widespread disease and you wish to protect your community, it's possible to do a cleansing and protection ritual for all by burning juniper at the crossroads. Go to the crossroads at noon near the area you wish to protect and burn dried juniper bundles. Take extra precautions if your crossroads is in a dry area prone to fires.

### *Removing Your Own Illness*

One of the most traditional things that can be done at the crossroads is to perform a ritual to rid yourself of an illness. On the day of the new moon, the sick person must go to the center of the crossroads and shout the name of the illness. Each day, the person must make their way there and repeat the ritual for a complete twenty-eight-day lunar cycle. It is said that the spirits will take the disease away and the person will get well.

Both the full moon and new moon increase the power of the crossroads, and so working this magic through two new moons and a full moon will strengthen the spell work. Like all healing magic, it might bring you direct healing from the spirit realm, but it is more likely to bring you synchronicities—the healers, the treatments, or the information that you need to heal your body, mind, or spirit.

---

46. Olga Kruchkova, *Slavic Seasonal Rituals and Divinations* (Teaneck, NJ: Babelcube, 2019).

If there is no time to wait for a full moon cycle, bring a small glass jar, a trowel, and a small piece of paper with the name of your illness written on it. Dig up some earth from the crossroads and put it in the jar along with the slip of paper and bury the jar in the hole. Leave without turning around, and do not tell anyone about your ritual. When this is done, it is said that the illness will go away after the first rain that falls on that crossroads.

### Removing the Illness of a Loved One

If a loved one is ill and cannot leave the house to go to the crossroads, you can remove any spiritual cause for the illness by doing crossroads work on their behalf. Take a coin or a banknote and, with the sick person sitting on a chair or lying in a bed, walk around them three times. Immediately take the coin or bill to the crossroads, speaking to no one as you go there and back.

When you arrive at the crossroads, turn back toward home and throw the money over your left shoulder, saying, "It is paid!" Let the amount of money reflect the seriousness of the problem. If someone sees the money and picks it up, they will take on the disease and relieve the one for whom the spell was cast.

### Cleansing Troubles from a Home

Make an attractive besom from branches or straw and sweep the dust from all the rooms of your house. Collect the sweepings and take them and the broom to the crossroads and leave them there. When someone picks up the broom and takes it home, they will take your troubles with them.

### Removing a Curse

If you have had a curse placed on you and are willing to pass it along to someone else rather than suffer anymore, you can leave it at the crossroads. Take a valuable item that will attract the attention of someone walking the road. A piece of jewelry is ideal, though any item of value that someone might pick up will work. At home, place this item between two candles and repeat the following incantation six times during a waning moon:

*Dryness, misery, bad luck, troubles, misfortune, and curses,*
*step away from [name].*
*I take you off me and transfer you to [name of the object].*
*Whoever takes the [name of the object] will take you with them.*

Snuff the candles, take the object and six coins, and walk in silence to a crossroads. Place the object of value in the center of the crossroads. Turn back toward home and throw the six coins over your shoulder, saying, "Paid!"

Leave the crossroads without looking back and without speaking until you reach home. Whoever picks up the object will take on the curse.[47]

### Banishing Poverty

Take a coin and a button made of wood, shell, or other natural material from some old, worn-out clothing to the crossroads at midnight when the moon is waning. Walk toward the crossroads in silence. When you arrive, turn your back to the crossroads and your face toward your home and say the following incantation:

*Poverty has overcome me.*
*I don't live a day without fear.*
*Come down from my roof, poverty,*
*and stay at the crossroads where you will not bother anyone.*

Throw the button and the coin over your left shoulder and head home. Don't say a word until you get home and don't look back over your shoulder.

### Simple Wishing Spell

When you are on a journey and come to a crossroads, you can make a simple wish. When you come to the next crossroads on your way, make the same wish again. And when you reach a third crossroads, make the wish one more time. This wish repeated at three consecutive crossroads in a single journey is potently empowered to come true.

---

47. Oleksandr Bosyy, "Svyashchenne Remeslo Mokoshi," in *Tradytsiyni Symvoly Ta Mahichni Rytualy Ukrayintsiv (Typolohiya. Semantyka. Mifostruktury)* (Vinnytsya, Ukraine: Vydavnytstvo-drukarnya «Dilo» FOP Rohal's'ka IO, 2011), 39–40.

### Wishing at the Rozdorizhzhya

Start this working just as the first rays of dawn are breaking. Gather a handful of coins, a small loaf of homemade bread, a small beeswax candle, and matches. Walk to the crossroads wearing your clothes inside out. Light your candle just before the dawn breaks and say the following incantation:

> The sister sun rises, the joy of the people shines, and I stand at a crossroads.
> I call to the spirits, I turn to the spirits, I demand their help.
> Go, spirits, to the fire.
> Come to me and stand behind me.
> Sharpen your ears, listen to my desire: [state your desire].
> As the new day comes, so you, spirits, leave your chambers,
> go around the world, find what you are looking for,
> bring it to me, fulfill my wish.
> And now feast and celebrate, meet the coming day,
> remember me with a kind word, do not forget my request,
> receive your payment, and do not demand anything more.

Place the bread at the crossroads, turn back toward home, and throw the coins over your left shoulder. Snuff out the candle with moistened fingers and walk back toward your house without looking back and without reacting if you hear any rustling behind you. Save the candle, and when your wish comes true, return to the same crossroads and silently burn the rest of the candle there to complete the spell and seal your good fortune.

### Leaving Negativity at the Rozdorizhzhya

Go to the crossroads at noon and whisper everything you wish to get rid of. Stand in the center of the intersection and turn clockwise, facing each of the roads, and say the following incantation to each road:

> I will turn in all directions; I will pray in all directions.
> My words will be heard, my prayers will be fulfilled.
> Evil leaves me, blows out with the wind, and burns up with the sun.

Walk home and light a beeswax candle on your home altar to seal your spell.

***Fulfilling Your Desire***

On a clear night when the moon is visible, go to the rozdorizhzhya in complete silence. Bring offerings of wine and coins for the spirits of the south and the west. Make sure that no one sees you walking. If you meet another person, go back home and try again the next clear night.

When you arrive at the crossroads, stand in the middle and place the coins on the road closest to the west. Pour the wine on the road closest to the south. Face the moon and say,

> *I stand neither in the field nor in the forest,*
> *but where my dreams come true.*
> *The power of the four roads is woven into a knot.*
> *This place is endowed with power.*
> *I do not steal that power, I do not borrow it, but*
> *by right I buy it with blessed coins*
> *[bow toward the coins in the west]*
> *and sweet wine*
> *[bow toward the wine poured in the south].*
> *I want my desire to be fulfilled.*
> *Exchange these gifts for [state your desire].*

After speaking your petition, leave without turning around, even if you hear that you are being called by name. If the spirits receive your gift, in three days you will receive what you want. If not, reformulate your wish and do the ritual again.

***Gaining Wisdom and Psychic Knowing***

If you are an experienced magic practitioner, you may be able to contact the spirit of the wind and receive insight. Go to the crossroads on a windy day and say the following invocation:

> *I ask the winds of the fields and forests,*
> *winds of the mountains, winds from the ice, and winds from the crossroads.*
> *Windstorms and gentle breezes,*
> *gather together and tell me [ask the winds your questions].*

Listen to the wind afterward and see if you can make out words or get impressions about your request. If you have some difficulty the first time you do this, persist and try again until you hear or sense the answer.

### *Meeting a Spirit at the Rozdorizhzhya*

The riskiest yet most rewarding spiritual work to do at the rozdorizhzhya is to meet the spirits there at midnight. Go alone, bring your protective charms with you (your oberehy and your motanka), and plan to arrive a little before midnight. Find a comfortable place to sit and wait. You might meet an ancestor, a teacher, or perhaps a Mavka. The spirit who shows up may be in any form, including shape-shifting into an animal. Be prepared, for at the crossroads, you will meet the spirit you are destined to meet.

When you meet this spirit, you may ask them three questions, and they will be obliged to give you truthful answers. Prepare your questions ahead of time so you don't get tongue-tied at the critical moment.

Once you've asked your questions, you are obligated to the spirit. If you want to avoid this obligation, which is recommended, you must leave an offering at the crossroads. Leaving money or valuable jewelry is traditional as an offering for the crossroads Mavky. Leave it out in the open. If someone else picks it up, they assume the obligation, and you are free and clear of any contract to the spirit you contacted.

## Baba Yaga and the Rozdorizhzhya

In many ways, the energy of the rozdorizhzhya reflects so much of Baba Yaga and her magic. The crossroads possess a wild power that can bring amazing blessings, but if treated carelessly, they might bring unintentional consequences. Some scholars see a direct connection between Baba Yaga and Hekate, the Greek goddess associated with liminal spaces, the world of the dead, and the crossroads.[48] It is said that if you go to a Y-shaped crossroads at midnight, you will meet Hekate, but the same can be said for Baba Yaga.

---

48. M. K. Matossian, "In the Beginning, God Was a Woman," *Journal of Social History* 6, no. 3 (January 1973): 325–343, https://doi.org/10.1353/jsh/6.3.325.

If you would like to encounter Baba Yaga, go to the rozdorizhzhya at midnight with your questions prepared. Come with respect and an offering and see if she appears. She may show up as an old woman, or she may shape-shift into the form of an animal. No matter how she appears, if you come with the proper respect, you will gain great wisdom from your encounter.

# CHAPTER 5

# LISOVYK: THE LORD OF THE FOREST

*After Vasylyna had gone a bit farther down the road, she sat under an oak tree. She pulled out her doll, fed her a little bread and gave her a sip of dew from a leaf, and then held her close.*

*"Dolly of mine, what do I do? I don't know where to find Baba Yaga, and being alone in the forest is dangerous."*

*And again, the wise doll spoke to her:*

*Even if it's hard to do,*
*you must see your journey through.*
*To find Baba Yaga will be good,*
*but first attend the Lord of the Wood.*

*And the doll told her to leave some bread and salt for the Lisovyk, the spirit of the forest, and then wait. So, Vasylyna pulled one of the loaves from her basket, sprinkled some salt on top, and wrapped it in the beautiful rushnyk that her mother had embroidered so many years before. She nestled it all in the roots of the tree and sat and watched and waited.*

*Night began to fall, and the light in the forest began to dim, and the moon rose. In the light of the silvery moon, Vasylyna's eyes began to play tricks on her. The wind began to blow in gusts, and the trees began to move and sway, seeming to come alive.*

*She focused her eyes on the trees and reminded herself that it was only her imagination. Or was it? One of the trees really did seem to be moving slowly closer and closer to her. As it inched toward her, she could see it wasn't a tree at all, but a giant man, his skin as weathered and brown as the rough bark of an old oak, his long beard and hair as green as long-hanging* moss. Vasylyna was astonished and afraid of this giant man, but as he got closer, his sparkling green eyes radiated kindness, and his shy and gentle movements calmed her fears.

"Good evening, good sir. My name is Vasylyna. Are you the Lord of the Wood?" she said as she dipped her head in a respectful way. The Lisoviy Cholovik, the Forest Man, spoke with a voice that sounded like the creak of old wood.

"That I am, and my name is Chuhaister. What is a little girl like you doing in the woods by yourself so late in the evening?"

Vasylyna picked up the bread wrapped in the rushnyk, offered it to Chuhaister, and explained her predicament as he nibbled at the bread.

"I know where Baba Yaga lives. I can walk with you part of the way," he said kindly. So Chuhaister and Vasylyna walked side by side through the forest. Chuhaister sang beautifully mournful songs about falcons and doves, roses and oak trees, and his singing voice sounded like the song of birds and the rustle of wind through the leaves. Vasylyna learned the songs and sang along with him as they walked through the night. Finally, they found a cave where Chuhaister built a fire and made a bed of moss for Vasylyna, and she snuggled down and fell fast asleep.

## Baba Yaga Shares the Wisdom of the Lisovyk

You might find the Lisovyk in the woods, but my own story begins there as well. The forest is where I come from. Born at the same time as the Sun, the Moon, and the seventy-seven Sister Stars. Born as one of three sisters. Like all multiple births, we had our individual identities, but we also were identified as a unit. We all became known as the Baba Yaga.

And the humans, oh, they were so different back then. You know when an old woman says, "Back in my day, people had much better manners?" Well, it's true. They were not these curiosity seekers or the ones who feared me or the show-offs trying to destroy me. As if they could!

No. Back then, humans loved and respected me. I was their grandmother, the wise and powerful one. I was the one they sang to, asking for help with the hunt and for protection in the woods. They knew what I was: the *Hospodynya Lisu*, the Mistress of

the Forest.[49] Before people left me to become planters, farmers, and herders, I was the source of their food, their water, and their shelter. Honor me, and I could bless you. Disrespect me? Curse me? Ah, do that, and I could destroy you.

All power emanated from me and still does. I am the Mother of the Animals, daughter of the *Maty Zemlya*, Mother Earth. The old ones loved and respected my forest, building their altars under my trees and burying their dead in my groves.[50] To begin to know me, you need to know my sacred domain.

First, you must become acquainted with the forest. If you live in the wilds, you already have this knowing. The darkness of the night on the new moon, the breathing of the trees, the noises of the hidden ones. If you live in civilization, this knowing can still come to you. Go outside and observe the plants and the animals. Touch a tree with a loving hand. Go for a solitary hike. Camp in the wilderness. Get out of the safety of indoors and connect in any way you can to the wild out there. The forest is a place of initiation, the entrance to the land of the spirits, and when you enter my home, you truly do begin your spiritual initiation. So, you want to be a vidma, the one who knows? Then let the initiation begin.

If you connect to the wild in authentic ways, you will learn the lesson of the wild, which is that you can only impose your will so far. It's always a compromise. Try too hard to keep the wild out, and you will suffer. Meeting with nature is always a marriage. You have to dance with nature. Like a *khorovod*, a circle dance, you cannot go your own way. You follow the one to your left and lead the one to your right.

In the old days, the ancient ones relied on nature for everything, but they also needed protection from the dangers of nature, too: foul weather, hungry beasts, and dangerous spirits. So, they called on me, the Mistress of the Forest, to help them, to protect them. They made me offerings and sang me songs. Oh, how they would praise and flatter me. Their *molfars* and *molfarkas*, their shamanic magicians, would commune with me, sing their first song in the tongue of the birds and the cry of the animals and translate my messages for my children. Yes, they were *all* my children—the beasts, the birds, the fish, and even the humans. My work was to make sure that my children got along, that all were fed, that all were protected, and that all thrived and prospered.

When the hero or heroine of the story needed the help of the animals, they came to me. When the hunters needed food, I was the one they called on. They made offerings

49. Johns, *Baba Yaga*.

50. *Ethnologia Slavica*, vol. 1 (Bratislava, Slovakia: Slovenske pedagogicke nakl., 1969).

to me of bread and salt, the symbol of good wishes—a humble offering of a blessing to those who receive it.

In times past, all our rituals took place in nature, in the sacred groves or near the holy ponds that were worshiped. The people knew very well back then that trees were sentient beings with souls.[51] No one dared to cut down a tree, hunt an animal, or even pluck a flower without first asking my permission.

Now, in more recent times, I am the Forest Woman, the *Lisova Baba*, the sister of the Lisovyky, the Forest Lords, and the one whom mothers plead to when their child is crying through the night.[52] The Lisovyky are my guardians of the forest. Even someone as magical as me can't be everywhere all the time, and alas, though my aim is peace in the forest, sometimes my children, the humans and the beasts, need protection or direction, and so my Forest Men are there to protect the ones who need protecting and guide the ones who need guiding, and, if need be, they step up if there is someone getting out of line.

If you enter the forest, how will you recognize my guardians? In their true form, they appear naked or with just a simple white garment on. They are giants with skin as rough as the bark of a tree, flashing emerald eyes, and beards as green as grass. They might carry large wooden cudgels—the better to protect their forest home. Some have hairy bodies like their more domestic cousins the Domovyky, and others have curling horns like a ram. If you do see these horned ones, pay attention, for the one with golden horns is the leader of the Lisovyky and should be paid extra respect.[53]

However, Lisovyky are not always easy to spot. They are powerful shape-shifters and can grow to the height of the tallest trees or shrink to be small enough to hide behind a blade of grass. They can appear and disappear at will and can transform into any forest animal: a hare, wolf, bear, raven, or boar, for example.[54] The horned owl is a particular favorite of theirs, and they may appear as one or have one upon their shoulder. If you are sharp enough to spot a horned owl in a tree, that is the Lisovyk guarding his forest, and such a tree should never be cut down.

---

51. Stanisław Rosik and Anna Tyszkiewicz, *The Slavic Religion in the Light of 11th- and 12th-Century German Chronicles (Thietmar of Merseburg, Adam of Bremen, Helmold of Bosau): Studies on the Christian Interpretation of Pre-Christian Cults and Beliefs in the Middle Ages* (Leiden, Netherlands: Brill, 2020).

52. Johns, *Baba Yaga.*

53. Dixon-Kennedy, *Encyclopedia of Russian and Slavic Myth and Legend.*

54. Kennard, *The Russian Peasant.*

Master shape-shifter that he is, the Lisovyk is not limited to just turning into an animal. He can turn into a flaming fir tree or even a mushroom, particularly the *mukhomor*, the red-and-white-spotted mushroom that you call fly agaric, the one used for dream journeys.

The trickiest form that the Lisovyk can take is the form of a human—a poor peasant, perhaps. The only way you can be sure he is a Lisovyk and not a new neighbor is that he will have a small detail out of place: shoes on the wrong feet, clothing inside out or backward, missing buttons on his clothes, or not wearing his sash. Or there might be more obvious signs on his body: a missing eyebrow or ear, or a wart that moves from place to place on his face. There are also other more mystical signs, like his footprints being swept away by the wind the moment he lifts his foot, or standing in the sunlight and not casting a shadow.[55]

Lisovyky are generally solitary spirits. They are territorial and roam the woods alone. Some say that should two Lisovyky have a dispute over territory, they will play a game of cards. The losing Lisovyk must send his squirrels and hares over to the winner's forest.[56]

The Lisovyk, like nature, is ambiguous. To people who respect the forest, he is benevolent, protecting them from danger and guarding their cattle or sheep. But to those who disrespect our home, he has a subtle way of reprimanding them. He can mimic the voice of your loved ones calling out your name, leading you off the path and deeper and deeper into the forest. He can shift road markers and obscure paths to keep you wandering in circles. At best, this may mean you are delayed and frustrated, but very disrespectful interlopers may be led deeper and deeper into the woods until the forest takes them into itself.[57]

Should you get tricked by a Lisovyk in this way, sit down on a nearby stump or fallen log, take off your clothes, and put them back on inside out or back to front; also, put your shoes on the wrong feet. Chant "sheep's muzzle, sheep's wool" as you walk, and he will no longer be able to trick you into walking in circles.

To meet me, you will have to come to my home in the woods, and so you will have to move through the realm of the Lisovyk. You may just want to pass through the woods

55. Warner, *Russian Myths.*

56. Ryan, *The Bathhouse at Midnight.*

57. Gilchrist, *Russian Magic.*

unmolested, and for that, all you have to do is respect the forest and leave him an offer-ing. However, you may want to meet a Lisovyk and befriend him. Hunters and shep-herds who traverse through the woods regularly have been known to gain great boons from befriending Lisovyky: successful hunts, having the Lisovyk tend their flocks, or even learning the secrets of magic. So, respect the Lord of the Wood, and you may not only be safe as you travel, but you may gain powerful wisdom as well.

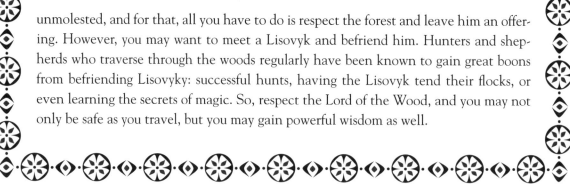

## Madame Pamita Teaches the Magic of the Lisovyk

My own stories of encountering woodland spirits have happened halfway around the world from the beautiful spruce forests of the Carpathian Mountains; my ancestral know-ing of forest ways has translated to seeing the spirits in a redwood forest on the Califor-nian coast just as easily as my Ukrainian grandparents could see them in the pines.

Even as a child, I sensed the otherworldly life in the woods. Through my own intui-tive exploration, I learned that if you find a quiet place in the forest among the trees and you sit down to listen, you will start to sense the life force of the forest, feel the personality of each individual tree, and receive profound downloads of wisdom.

When I opened up to this deep knowing, I began to see the spirits of the forest: tiny plant guardians, large treelike giants, and human-sized beings who would appear, say something to me in a language I couldn't understand, and then retreat back into the woods. The spirits of the forest are there for you if you are willing to meet and honor them.

## The Lisovyk Today

Most modern people who live in cities are sadly far removed from having the ability to see the spirits of the forest. Some may think the Lord of the Forest is just a fairy tale character; however, they haven't lost their inner knowing that the trees have some-thing special to offer humanity. Going back to ancient times, Slavic people worshiped in groves and had deep spiritual connections to the forest. This loving relationship to the trees hasn't been entirely forgotten. In many Slavic countries including Ukraine, *dendroterapiya* (dendrotherapy) is a popular alternative method of healing that descends from the ancient practices of tree worship.[58]

In dendrotherapy, contact with trees offers energetic healing benefits. Whether you are interested in meeting the Lisovyk in his physical form or just want to benefit from connecting to trees, dendrotherapy is an excellent place to begin your journey.

## Dendrotherapy Techniques

In dendrotherapy, it is believed that each species of tree offers a different type of energy. Some trees are seen as donors that offer energy when we are feeling depleted, while others are seen as receiving trees, the so-called vampire trees that take away negative or unwanted energy. Any kind of tree can be partnered with for healing purposes, but there are some traditional trees that are known to be donors or receivers.[59] For a list of common dendrotherapeutic trees, see appendix I.

When you are searching for a tree for therapeutic purposes, first find a tree that is healthy and at least eighteen feet (six meters) from other species of trees so that you connect with clear energy from your tree. From a few feet away, hold your palms outward toward the tree. If this is the appropriate tree for your healing, your hands will feel a gentle energetic pull toward the tree. It may feel like warmth or a tingling in your palms, and it indicates that the tree has a large reserve of energy to share and is willing to work with you.

When you are ready to spend time with the tree for healing, meet with it one to two hours after sunrise or one to two hours before sunset and wear clothing made of natural fibers to facilitate the transmission of energy. Go alone with a peaceful and positive intention to meet with your tree and receive healing.

### Working with Donor Trees

Work with a donor tree when you feel tired, depleted, depressed, or sick (except from inflammation) or need more energy. To begin working with a donor tree, stand a foot or two away (forty to fifty centimeters) from the south side of the tree, close your eyes,

---

58. I. M. Mineyev, *Entsiklopediya Traditsionnoy Narodnoy Meditsiny: Napravleniya* (Moscow, Russia: Metody. Praktiki. AST, 2002).

59. P. N. Yudina, "Derev'ya–Tseliteli," *Dialog Kul'tur* (2016): 169–171.

and mentally make your request for healing. After asking for assistance, step closer and touch your forehead or cheek to the trunk and breathe in and out slowly and deeply for two to twenty minutes, imagining each breath drawing silver, blue, or violet light into your body. You may hug or hold the tree for extra support, to receive more energy, or just to show it love.

### Working with Vampire Trees

Work with a receiver or vampire tree when you are anxious or overexcited, having trouble sleeping, suffering from inflammation, or feeling excessively emotional. Stand a foot or two away (forty to fifty centimeters) from the north side of the tree and make your mental request. Step up to the tree, turn around, and lean your back against it, touching your palms to the trunk on either side behind you. Envision the tree drawing out and transmuting the unwanted energy. Stay with the tree in this way for two to fifteen minutes.

After contact with a vampire tree, you may want to spend time with a donor tree to replenish yourself with healthy, balanced energy. If this is not possible, step away from the vampire tree into an open area, stand with your feet apart, raise your hands up to the sun, and breathe deeply for a minute or two.[60]

### Effects of Dendrotherapy

When doing dendrotherapy, pay attention to the sensations you experience. You may feel energy flowing through your body, a slight pleasant lightheadedness, or sensations of slight coolness or warmth. Your body may feel lighter, you may feel relaxed and slightly drowsy, or, conversely, you may feel energized, uplifted, and joyful. Even if you don't notice any special feelings, the energy exchange is still occurring and benefitting you. Having this intimate connection with the tree kingdom will also open you up to encountering the Lisovyk.

## Honoring the Forest

Lisovyky are beautiful forest spirits. To encounter them, you will naturally have to spend some time among the trees. Find a natural tree-filled area, the wilder the better,

---

60. Mineyev, *Entsiklopediya Traditsionnoy Narodnoy Meditsiny*.

and plan to spend some time there. If you can spend a few days camping, staying day and night in the forest, you are more likely to enhance your senses and spot the Lisovyk, and he is more likely to trust you enough to be seen.

Before meeting the Lisovyk, you would do well to show your respect for his home. When you are in the forest, behave as if you are a polite guest. Don't swear, make excessive noise, leave trash, disturb the animals, or willfully damage anything.

Before cutting down a tree or even breaking off a branch, leave an offering for the Lisovyk or ask him for permission, and never harm an old spruce, as this is said to be where the spirit of the Lisovyk resides.

Feed the trees to establish good relations with them and the Lisovyky. Leave scrambled eggs at the base of a tree, break a raw egg against a tree trunk, or pour *kompot* (juice made from boiled dried fruit) or beer at the roots of a tree as an offering.

## Offerings for the Lisovyk

Once you've shown respect for his home and made an offering to a tree, you are ready to make a direct offering to him. Leave a gift of food at a forest crossroads, on a tree stump, on a fallen log, or high up in the branches of a tree. Appropriate offerings are homemade bread with salt, *kasha* (porridge), *nalysnyky* (crepes), *salo* (pork belly), or *krashanky* (the red eggs you will learn about in chapter 13). Leave the food and then come back a day or two later. If your offering is gone, it means that the Lisovyk has received it, that you have established a positive relationship with him, and that you are safe to do your work or travel through the woods. If your offering is untouched, wait a few more days and check again. If it's still left there on your third visit, make a different offering at a new place in the forest and try again.

## Meeting the Lisovyk

If you'd like to encounter the Lisovyk and learn from him, you need to meet him and gain his trust. Like most friendships, it may take time before he feels he can share his secrets with you, but follow these guidelines and you can open the door to that magical knowledge.

The Lisovyk can sometimes be shy, so you might get other signs before you see him. Magpies are considered his special messengers, warning him anytime there are strangers in the forest. If a magpie gives its harsh, rattling call, it is letting him know that you are nearby. If so, you can prepare to see him or call to him to come out.

Bend over, look between your legs, and call out, "I walked, I found, I lost." This phrase is irresistible to a Lisovyk. If one is nearby, he will appear from behind a tree momentarily and say, "You figured it out!" and then disappear. This first encounter, though brief, will let the Lisovyk see you. Leave an offering for him nearby, and he will know that you are respectful and trustworthy.

On your next visit, go to the same place where you saw the Lisovyk and once again bend over and look between your legs, but this time say,

*Lisovyk, Lord of the Forest,*
*come to me now.*
*Not as a gray wolf,*
*not as a black raven,*
*not as a flaming fir tree,*
*but as a man.*

If the Lisovyk is nearby, he will emerge. See if you can get him to laugh, and he may perhaps stay and speak to you. Offer him some of your food or some tobacco and use your best manners. Unless a Lisovyk introduces himself to you and shares his name, call him by his honorific. You can refer to him as the Lord of the Forest, the Master of the Woods, or the Kind One.

The Lisovyk may then play his flute for you, imitating the sounds of the birds and their beautiful music. He may ask you to dance, and if he does, don't refuse him. His spirited dancing allows him to transform himself into a whirlwind. Those who refuse to cavort with him may get knocked over by the twister, but those who dance along with him, and dance with him well, will often receive gifts and blessings for their efforts.

When he is ready to share his wisdom with you, he may teach you the secret languages of the animals so that you can speak to and understand them. These secret calls will also allow you to go on spirit journeys where you can communicate with ancestors and animal spirits. He may share with you the secrets of the mukhomor, the fly agaric mushroom, and how to use it in rites and rituals. Regardless of what arcane knowledge he shares with you, it will be immensely valuable and will elevate your magical practice.

**Connecting to the Trees**

Spending time with the tree kingdom and the Lisovyk will bring you into the forest world so familiar to Baba Yaga. Get in touch with the Lisovyky and get to know their home. Be a loving, respectful guest. Take some time to notice the trees around you, spend time outside in nature, and touch the trees with loving kindness. Baba Yaga knows the tree spirits intimately. She knows that each tree has a unique consciousness and personality. If you make a habit of communicating and connecting with these powerful sentient beings, you open the doors to deeply magical worlds.

# CHAPTER 6

# RUSALKY: THE SPIRITS OF THE LAKE

When Vasylyna woke up, the sun was beginning to rise, the fire had burned down to embers, and Chuhaister was nowhere to be found. She peeped out of the cave and saw a vast carpet of forest trees and a glittering blue lake that had fresh clean water. She made her way down to the edge of the lake, pulled her motanka out of her pocket, and gave her a bit of bread and a sip of the cool, clean water.

She began to feel panic rising within her as she realized that she was lost very deep in the woods and still had not seen a trace of Baba Yaga or her house. She jumped up and began to walk quickly in one direction around the lake and then backtracked and went in the other direction, not sure which way she should go. She was about to turn back again when she felt a movement in her pocket. She brought out the motanka and spoke to her. "Dolly of mine, what do I do? I don't know where to find Baba Yaga, I have to bring home the fire, and now I really don't know how to find her."

And the motanka answered her:

> Take a rest, get off your feet,
> for Baba Yaga you will meet.
> And her fire you will take,
> but first you'll greet the Spirits of the Lake.

And the doll told her to hang her beautifully embroidered cloth, her rushnyk, in the branches of a birch tree next to the water. Vasylyna did so, and then she sat on the shore and watched and waited.

77

*As she rested patiently, the sun rose higher and higher in the sky, and it became warmer and warmer, and Vasylyna became sleepy in the heat of the sun. As she dozed, she thought she heard the echoes of people laughing in the distance and the sounds of splashing water. The gentle, happy noises woke her from her nap. As she looked far across the lake, she could see a group of beautiful long-haired women wearing verdant wreaths of flowers and sedge on their heads swimming and frolicking in the lake. They playfully swam toward Vasylyna, and, as they got closer, they called to her, "Hello, little girl! Why don't you come and play with us? The water is so cool and refreshing."*

*Vasylyna answered, "Are you the Spirits of the Lake?"*

*"Yes," they replied. "We're the Rusalky. Come! Join us for a swim."*

*"I've brought you a gift," said Vasylyna, and she touched the rushnyk hanging from the branch. On seeing the beautiful embroidery, the Rusalky came out of the water, naked and wet, and pulled the cloth down from the tree and cooed in admiration over the fine embroidery. One of the water spirits turned to Vasylyna, "Thank you for this beautiful gift. What are you doing here by yourself in the middle of the woods?"*

*"I am looking for the house of Baba Yaga," said Vasylyna.*

*"Ah, we know where she lives. Just in the forest on the other side of the lake. Come swim with us and we will take you over there and show you the way."*

*So Vasylyna stripped down to her shift and put her clothes and her motanka in the basket that held the bread. The water spirits carried her basket for her, and together they swam to the other side of the lake. When they reached the other bank, the Rusalky showed Vasylyna the path to take to get to Baba Yaga's house, and then they swam away with the rushnyk, playing and laughing as they went.*

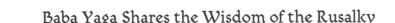

## Baba Yaga Shares the Wisdom of the Rusalky

You've met my guardians of the forest, now it's time to meet their watery counterparts, the Rusalky. They're slippery ones, these spirits of the water. So, you think you know so much? That they're just mermaids? You've got a lot to learn, little one.

First off, the Rusalky are ancient, perhaps even the oldest spirits we know. Their mother, Berehynia, the one represented in embroidery by the Tree of Life, was the first divine spirit, the mother of all, and her daughters, well, they don't follow too long after. The Rusalky live and play in our sacred waters—the rivers, ponds, and lakes—and they have legs instead of fish tails. They resemble human women in every way except for their otherworldly pale skin and the green tint to their damp hair.[61]

These beautiful creatures always gather in groups, seductively swimming or playfully romping in the water, scantily clad in gauzy shifts or wearing nothing at all. You expect them to swim fully clothed? Well, they're never completely naked—they wear wreaths of flowers in their hair.

They are usually found in the water, but they also step onto dry land once in a while to do the traditional dances, sing, or just giggle and gossip as they wash their clothes on the riverbank or spin fibers to make magical garments for themselves. They'll sit in the branches of trees by the water or on swings made from low-hanging boughs and ask passersby to give them clothing.

Rusalky are often found admiring their reflections in still waters or stroking their long, unbound hair with magical combs. Like all witches and spirits, a Rusalka lets her hair flow freely; she does not tie it up in a braid or cover it in a scarf. If a Rusalka's hair becomes dry, she dies, so they generally congregate in or near watery places. If they travel over land, they bring their combs with them. A Rusalka can produce a torrent of water by passing her comb through her hair, watering the land and keeping herself alive. If one finds a comb on the bank of a river, it is certainly a comb lost by a Rusalka. Should you find this treasure, you are a lucky one indeed, for it will give you the gift of clairvoyance and the power of healing.

---

61. Gilchrist, *Russian Magic*.

Back in the old days, people knew these spirits were the guardians of the waters and honored them. Rusalky lived in the rivers and lakes through the fall and winter and emerged in the spring and summer to bring their life-giving moisture and fertility to the fields. More recently, though, the propaganda has been that these tricksters were the unquiet spirits of women who had drowned or the vengeful ghosts of girls who died before they were baptized.[62] Yes, they can be capricious, but to call them vengeful? Well, that's just evil gossip.

Like a beautiful flowing river or the deceptively still waters of a lake, their alluring looks and charming ways may lead to danger for people who don't treat them with honor. If you decide to bathe in a river on one of the Rusalky holy days without paying them proper respect, you might find one inviting you to take a swim only to drown you, or she might clamber up onto the shore and playfully tickle you to death.[63] Don't say I didn't warn you about having manners.

The Rusalky are simply nature spirits, and if you honor them as you should, you can see them, even interact with them, and receive their blessings. They emerge in the spring and stay active until the fall, particularly during the time of the full moon. They wander onto land to bless the fields of flowering rye with beautiful singing and joyful clapping, and, if they're pleased with the offerings given to them, they create an abundant crop. The waving of the stalks in the field indicates where they are dancing and is seen as a positive sign of their visit. However, if they are disrespected or displeased for some reason, they may send bad weather or some other blight to the crops.[64]

The spirits of the water and water itself are viewed with reverence. All water comes from a miraculous source, offering both healing and nourishment. Magical waters, such as the legendary "Waters of Life and Death," heal mortal wounds or bring a corpse back to life. Sacrifices and offerings are made to the spirits of sacred wells and waters. Cloths and ribbons are tied to trees near wells. Food, money, and even jewelry are thrown into waters as gifts for the water spirits. In return, the spirits and the waters provide healing and blessings. You, too, would do well to honor my watery sisters, the Rusalky, for they bring life and abundance, playfulness and joy, to those who respect them.

---

62. Hubbs, *Mother Russia*.

63. Kononenko, *Slavic Folklore*.

64. Johns, *Baba Yaga*.

## Madame Pamita Teaches the Magic of the Rusalky

Born under the water sign Cancer, I seem to gravitate toward bodies of water for healing. I am fortunate to live within walking distance of the Pacific Ocean, that gorgeous, almost inconceivably vast expanse of water. Even though it's practically outside my door, I never lose my wonder for what I call my Mama Ocean: so vast, so mysterious, and so powerful.

Growing up spending summers playing in the ocean, it's very easy to know the power of the water. Even on normal days there are all kinds of potential threats in the water: riptides that might pull you out farther than you want to go, jellyfish that might sting you, and, of course, the big waves that push you down under and tumble you around like an old T-shirt in a washing machine. Anyone who's sailed over the sea, gone whitewater rafting, put water skis on their feet, or gone kayaking on an inland water trail will remind you that the waters of nature can be unbelievably glorious, but they demand your respect. That is the message of the Rusalky: play with us, enjoy our beauty, but don't forget that we are the ones who hold the power.

### Rusalky Today

As with most spirits, making an offering to the Rusalky is a powerful way to develop a relationship with them. Traditionally, the summer months—when the lakes, ponds, and rivers are flowing—are the best time for this work. The special holidays of *Rusal'nyy Tyzhden'* (Mermaid Week) and *Kupala* are when you are most likely to encounter them.

In modern times, belief in the Rusalky might not always be literal, but these traditionally Pagan holidays are celebrated in Ukraine to honor these spirits. And, while you might not be afraid of being drowned by spirits, heaven forbid you should disobey a baba who tells you not to swim in a lake on these special holy days.

Wearing beautiful flower crowns is a time-honored way to celebrate the Rusalky. In recent years, these wreaths, called *vinoky*, have become a powerful symbol of cultural identity. Making, wearing, and using these wreaths have become popular pastimes, and wreaths have even been adopted as high fashion.

### *Celebrating Rusal'nyy Tyzhden'*

The early summer festival of Rusal'nyy Tyzhden' honors the Rusalky. During this time, the rye is blooming, and the harvest is celebrated with feasts of fertility. There are some who believe that there is a connection between this festival and the Roman festival of the roses called *Rosalia*, and that Rosalia was adapted into a weeklong celebration to honor the Rusalky called *Rusalia*. However, there is much evidence that belief in the Rusalky and their fertility celebrations predate the time of the Romans. After Christianity was introduced, the syncretized holiday became a moveable feast coordinated with Pentecost, which takes place on the Sunday forty days after Easter. The following Monday through the next Monday is called Mermaid Week—the time when the Rusalky walk the earth, blessing the fertile fields.[65]

This festival overlaps and intertwines with *Zeleni Svyata* (Green Feast), another fertility festival when houses are traditionally decorated with the green branches of early summer. Linden, birch, and maple branches are hung around the house, and floors are covered with fragrant grasses such as wormwood and calamus to bring health, protection, and prosperity to the home.[66]

These holidays were meant for celebration, and in times past, it was forbidden to perform any work, particularly weaving, sewing, washing linen, or even making woven willow fences, during this time. To work at any textile crafts was considered offensive to the Rusalky, who are known for being master weavers. It was believed that the Rusalky would take away the abundance of those who disregarded these proscriptions.

During Mermaid Week, young people would circle the fields carrying torches and decorating the land with green boughs as offerings to the Rusalky to prevent weather damage and ensure fertile crops. Wreaths were hung in barns, green branches were used to decorate the horns of cattle, and obkuryuvannya, the smoke from burning herbs, was used to fumigate livestock to protect them from malevolent forces.

At this magical time, young single men and women would meet in the fields or forests or near streams to celebrate. They would bring food and carry doll effigies made from young trees as offerings to the Rusalky. The women would dress up as Rusalky, songs and dances honoring the water spirits were performed, and the young people

---

65. S. V. Bezuhla, "Narodni Uyavlennya pro Rusalok u Konteksti Svyatkuvannya Triytsi u Skhidnykh Slov'yan," *Visnyk Student·S'koho Naukovoho Tovarystva DonNU Imeni Vasylya* 1, no. 7 (2015): 43–48.

66. *Ukraine: A Concise Encyclopedia* (Toronto, ON: University of Toronto, 1963).

would indulge in flirtatious games. Young women offered garlands to the Rusalky, asking for loving husbands, and made flower wreaths to hang in the woods to divine the future.[67]

During these revels, it was believed that the Rusalky would leave the water to dance, sing, and bless the fields and forests as well. They would traverse between water and land until the end of June, and during these weeks, many people would hear their voices in the rustling of the breeze or their dancing footsteps in the splash of running water.[68]

### Celebrating Kupala

The Rusalky might be seen again during the midsummer holiday of Kupala. This ancient festival is celebrated today on July 6 and 7 but was believed to have originally been celebrated at the summer solstice. During this time, the Rusalky dance in fields by the light of the moon and invite shepherds to play with them. Evidence of these nighttime revels was said to be found in circles of darker, more luxuriant grass in the fields.

On the celebration of Kupala, wise women awake before dawn to pick herbs and flowers, for it is believed to be the time when their healing powers are at their zenith. As the day progresses, women also weave floral wreaths that include these healing plants, and revelers wear these flower crowns to bless themselves throughout the year. Later in the evening, young women float their wreaths on the water as a love divination. During the day, people swim in the waters, and a holy bonfire is lit with a living fire created by rubbing sticks together. All through the night, the people dance and sing around this bonfire and jump through the flames as an ancient purification ritual. Couples jump through the flame hand-in-hand as a rite to cement their relationship.[69]

During these days of midsummer, Rusalky roam back and forth between the land and water until the first frosts of winter, when they return to their watery home before it freezes over.

---

67. Y. E. Smolyns'ka, "Perezhytky Prymityvnoyi Obryadovosty v Ukrayins'komu Pobuti.(Peredmova d-r. Ist. Nauk. Prof. Valentyny Borysenko).," *Etnichna Istoriya Narodiv Yevropy* 15 (2003): 77–93.

68. Gray, *Mythology of All Races Volume 3*.

69. L. F. Artyukh, "Vohon' i Voda v Systemi Zvychayevykh Zaboron," *Narodna Tvorchist' Ta Etnolohiya* 3 (2012): 31–41.

## Meeting the Rusalky

Like most spirits, the Rusalky are shy creatures, but you might have an opportunity to encounter one during the summer months. Carry wormwood if you want to avoid meeting a Rusalka or parsley if you would like to have an encounter with one. When you meet one, she may ask you, "Wormwood or parsley?" If you show the wormwood, she will disappear. If you show the parsley, she will say, "You are my darling!" and may further try to entice you.

Mint is also attractive to Rusalky. Throwing a sprig into the river and saying, "You have mint on you!" can entice them to surface, and they will say, "You're our [mother/father]!" Mint and parsley grown in your garden can attract them and at the same time appease the more mischievous of them.

## Honoring the Rusalky

One way to show the Rusalky your good intentions is to bake rye bread with blessed water (see chapter 19 for more information about sacred waters). Bake bread and leave it on your windowsill when it's still hot from the oven. The delicious scent of the warm loaf will entice them to come to your home, and as spirits, they will feed off the aroma. Traditionally, you would bring bread to a field at sunrise as an offering to the Rusalky, but alternatively you can bring it to a river, stream, lake, or pond, or offer it in a garden to feed the Rusalky and invite them to bless the land.

Since the Rusalky are weavers and fond of cloth, you might gift them with a hand-kerchief, skeins of handspun yarn, or a piece of fine hemp or linen cloth that they can sew into a shirt. Hang your offering on the branches of trees where you suspect they might dwell. One good spot may be branches that overhang rivers, lakes, or springs.[70] If you choose a holy spring, you can splash its water on your eyelids to ritually cleanse yourself of negativity and leave a coin in the water or tie ribbons in the branches of the nearby trees as payment for the water's blessing.[71]

During Mermaid Week, you might honor them by bringing fresh cuttings into your home in the traditional style. Fragrant lovage and calamus leaves can be scattered over

---

70. Matossian, "In the Beginning, God Was a Woman," 325–343.

71. Gilchrist, *Russian Magic*.

the floor, mint can be hung over your door or your home altar, and the outside of your home can be decorated with linden, birch, and maple boughs.

To develop a relationship with these water spirits, you might clean up a riverbank or lakeshore, go swimming in natural waters, or leave nature-respecting offerings, such as coins, bread, or eggshells dyed yellow with turmeric, in a body of water that is sacred to you.

Of course, one of the most beautiful and ancient ways you can commune with these spirits is to weave a vinok, a wreath of flowers or sedge, and wear it; give it as an offering in the forests, fields, rivers, or lakes; or use it as a divination tool.

## Vinok Magic

Vinoky are old magic. There are records of magical wreaths going back three thousand years, but it is believed that the use of wreaths in magic goes back even further to before written history. Wreaths were worn not just to adorn, but to bless and protect the wearer.[72]

Traditionally, the vinok is woven from twelve magical flowers and foliage on special festivals and holidays. These twelve special plants vary from village to village, but a list of generally accepted variations can be found in appendix I. For centuries, the tradition has been that as soon as it dawns on the morning of Kupala, women go out, wash their faces with dew collected from yarrow flowers, and go into the forests and fields to collect flowers for wreaths and herbs for healing.[73]

Magical wreaths can be created at any time, however. The herbs and flowers used in a vinok have a language and express your wishes and intentions. You can use the flowers, plants, and herbs listed in appendix I as a guideline, but if you cannot find these in your local area or if they are out of season, substitute with other magical plants of your choosing.[74]

There is a traditional method of collecting plants for magical purposes. When you pick the herbs and flowers for your vinok, you should take extra care to honor the plant

---

72. Halyna Hryhorivna Stel'mascuk, *Ukrainian Folk Headwear* (L'viv, Ukraine: Apriori, 2013).

73. Victoria Williams, *Celebrating Life Customs around the World: From Baby Showers to Funerals* (Santa Barbara, CA: ABC-CLIO, 2017).

74. O. Pen'kova and S. Boyko, "Tradytsiya Kupal's'koho Vinkopletennya v Ukrayini: Istoriya Ta Transformatsiya v Druhiy Polovyni KHKH St," *Novi Storinky Istoriyi Donbasu* 22 (2013): 255–268.

and Maty Zemlya, Mother Earth.[75] Start by kneeling on the ground next to the plant. Then, create a protective circle by placing a gold or silver necklace around the base of the plant. Alternatively, place four silver coins on the ground on four sides of the base. Once you've done this, set your hands on the earth on either side of the plant and ask the plant and Mother Earth to share their magic and power with you. Cut only a few branches from each plant, never cutting back a plant completely unless you are retrieving a root. Touch your plant pieces to the silver coins or the chain, then put your hands back on the earth and thank Mother Earth and the plant. Once these steps have been done, you can retrieve your coins or chain and move to the next plant.

Vinoky do not have to necessarily be worn. You can make a special vinok to hang on your door or window to protect the home and family from all negativity, disease, or misfortune.

## How to Craft a Vinok

1. Cut long stems and do not remove leaves so that your vinok looks lush and full.

2. Start with a small bunch of your strongest, longest, and fullest stems.

3. Tie off one end and begin to braid them into a long plait. You can use grasses, flexible bark, thread, string, or ribbons to tie them in the most authentic way, or rubber bands or twist ties for ease.

4. Add extra stems as you go along, weaving them into the braid until it is long enough to wrap around the top of your head.

5. Tie off the other end and then tie the two ends together.

6. Add additional flowers and leaves, weaving the stems into your original crown.

7. Add long, flowing ribbons to the place where the two ends are joined.

## Adding Ribbons to Your Vinok

Traditionally, ribbons were added only to wedding vinoky, but in more recent times, people add them to any wreath that they'd like to make even more beautiful. The colors of the ribbons are also magically meaningful, and so you may choose colors to express the intentions of your magic. See appendix II for a list of vinok ribbon colors and their

---

75. Alla Dmytrenko, "Zbyrannya Trav i Arkhayichni Elementy Svitohlyadu Polishchukiv," *Etnichna Istoriya Narodiv Yevropy* 11 (2001): 14–18.

meanings. Traditionally, you might choose up to twelve different colors of ribbons and, if you have long hair, braid your hair in a single braid down your back and cut the ribbons slightly longer than the length of your hair so that your braid can coyly peek out.[76]

## Care in the Creation of Your Vinok

The vinok is a magical item, and so there are some special considerations that must be noted. Whoever weaves your vinok puts their energy into it. Ideally, you should weave your own, but loving older siblings or parents can weave a vinok for a child. If you have the opportunity to have a wreath woven by a pregnant woman, it will be endowed with magical powers of fertility and abundance. Many times when people are planning to do a wreath divination, they weave two wreaths: one to wear on their head, and another for the divination.

## Aftercare of Your Vinok

Vinoky should never be carelessly thrown away. A wreath should always be disposed of ritually in some way: burned in a bonfire, thrown into water or into a well, hung from a tree, or taken to a cemetery, for example. Vinoky can also be taken home and hung on trees in the garden to increase fertility, hung inside near the door or stuffed into the eaves to protect the home, or thrown over your head onto the roof as a protective talisman for the family.

Wreaths can also be stored and dried. If edible herbs were used, they can be brewed into a decoction or tea. This potion can be consumed, added to a magical bath, used as a hair rinse to promote beauty, or poured onto a field or garden to protect it from bad weather or pests. Dried herbs can also be burned for obkuryuvannya, the censing of people, animals, or the home.

## Vinok Love Divination

To perform a vinok divination, pick your fresh herbs and flowers at dawn on Kupala. Create your wreath and wear it throughout the day, and then at sunset, gently float it on the surface of a river. If you wish, you may place a floating candle in the center of

---

76. Stel'mascuk, *Ukrainian Folk Headwear*.

the wreath, and they will float on the river together.[77] As you lay your wreath on the water, say one of these traditional incantations or similar words of your own invention.

*Flow, flow, flower crown.*
*Beautifully woven with periwinkle.*
*Go to my love, go to my love.*

Or,

*Oh, on Kupala, I float my wreath on the water.*
*I, a beautiful young woman, pulled out roots.*
*Float, wreath, on the blue waves.*
*I collected flowers and wove wreaths.*
*Float, wreath, to where my true love lives.*

Once laid on the surface of the water, how your wreath floats will give you a relationship prognostication for the next twelve months.[78]

- If you float your wreaths with others and the wreaths stay together, then the year ahead will be about close friendships.
- If the wreath spins in place, then there will be no change in your love situation.
- If the wreath floats away downstream, love will come from far away.
- If the wreath sinks to the bottom of the river soon after launching, you will fall out of love this year.
- If your wreath floats in the center of the river and stays there, your love situation will stay the same this year.
- If your wreath comes back to the shore where you launched it, you will go back to an old love.
- If the wreath stays afloat for a long time, it will be an exceptionally happy year.
- If floating your wreath with friends, the person whose wreath stays afloat the longest will be the happiest this year.

---

77. Pen'kova and Boyko, "Tradytsiya Kupal's'koho Vinkopletennya v Ukrayini: Istoriya Ta Transformatsiya v Druhiy Polovyni KHKH St," 255–268.

78. Pen'kova and Boyko, "Tradytsiya Kupal's'koho Vinkopletennya v Ukrayini: Istoriya Ta Transformatsiya v Druhiy Polovyni KHKH St," 255–268.

◆ If the wreath floats across the river or lake to the opposite shore, you will have a serious love commitment this year.

## Vinok Family Divination

During Mermaid Week or on the night of Kupala, create wreaths for each of your family members and hang them in the forest overnight for the Rusalky. On the following morning, go back to inspect them. How each wreath fares will indicate the type of year the person will have. If the stems are not broken and the greenery is still fresh, it is a good omen. If the wreath has withered, the year may have challenges great or small, depending on how faded it has become. If that is the case, untie the wreath to "untie" the person's fate and break the tips of the branches to break ties with that outcome.[79]

## Friendship Ritual with a Vinok

Wreaths can be used in rituals to cement a friendship. With a group of friends, weave wreaths of herbs and flowers and tie them off with handkerchiefs. Find a cherry, apple, or other fruit tree in a garden or orchard and hang a wreath from a branch. Two friends who wish to be *kumy* (adopted family or best friends) should look at each other through the wreath and kiss each other's cheeks. After the kiss, they can pass precious items through the wreath to lend to each other—for example, scarves, rings, necklaces, or ribbons. From this point forward, they can refer to each other as *kum* or *kuma*—in other words, best friends.[80]

## Connecting with Water

The Rusalka is the complement to Baba Yaga. While on the surface they may appear to be polar opposites—young and playful versus old and cantankerous—they have more in common than meets the eye. Both are liminal and potentially dangerous spirits of nature: Baba Yaga of the earth and woods, the Rusalka of the water and bodies of water.

---

79. Pen'kova and Boyko, "Tradytsiya Kupal's'koho Vinkopletennya v Ukrayini: Istoriya Ta Transfor-matsiya v Druhiy Polovyni KHKH St," 255–268.

80. S. V. Bezuhla, "Narodni Uyavlennya pro Rusalok u Konteksti Svyatkuvannya Triytsi u Skhidnykh Slov"yan," *Isnyk Student·S'koho Naukovoho Tovarystva DonNU Imeni Vasylya Stusa* 1, no. 7 (2015): 43–48.

They are both master spinners and weavers, and they both wear their hair loose and break the norms of society.

It's no wonder that Baba Yaga refers to them as her sisters. They are the sunnier version of her shady persona. Perhaps, shape-shifter that she is, she takes on the form of these beautiful watery mermaids whenever the weather gets warm and she'd like to go for a swim.

CHAPTER 7

# ZAKLYNANNYA: THE MAGIC WORDS

On the other side of the lake, Vasylyna lay in the sun to dry off, and when she took out her loaf of bread, she saw that she only had one small crust left. So, she took her motanka out again, and she gave her a bit of bread and water.

"Dolly of mine, we have nothing more to eat except one last crust of bread. If we don't find Baba Yaga soon, we will go hungry."

And the motanka replied,

> Take heart, dear girl, and never fear.
> The witch of the wood is very near.
> Get dressed and eat and don't delay,
> together, we will find the way.

So Vasylyna did as the doll commanded. She got dressed, ate the last of her bread, and together they entered the forest.

Vasylyna and the doll made their way through the woods, following the path that the Rusalky had shown them. Whenever they came to a crossroads, the doll directed her and told her which way to turn. The sun began to go down, and the forest was getting darker and darker and the track harder to find. Vasylyna was getting cold, hungry, and very tired, but the doll urged her on.

Finally, in the distance, she could see a light on the side of the mountain among the spruce trees, and the doll told her that this was the home of Baba Yaga. The winds began to whip up around them, and they could hear the mournful call of the crows and the howling of distant wolves, and the two of them made haste to get to the house before nightfall.

Just as the sun dipped down behind the mountains, they reached a clearing, and there they beheld a sight that caused Vasylyna to stop right where she stood. There was a dark little hut with a yard and a fence around it. But this was no ordinary home. The fence was made entirely of gleaming white bones. Atop each of these bony fence posts was a skull, some human and some animal, and from the empty eye sockets of each skull glowed an unearthly light. The gate of the fence had a latch made from the tiny bones of a human hand. Vasylyna hesitated, but the doll urged Vasylyna to touch the latch. At her touch, the hand bones let go of the fence post, and the gate slowly creaked open as if moved by an invisible spirit. Vasylyna found her courage, and she walked through the gate and into the yard.

Once inside, Vasylyna could clearly see the khata, the little hut of Baba Yaga, by the glow of the eerie lanterns. A tiny little hut it was—no more than a one-room cabin. However, it stood high on two enormous chicken legs that stepped and scratched at the dirt below. It stood with its back to Vasylyna, and neither a door nor a window could be seen. Vasylyna gathered all her nerve and walked around to the other side of the house to find the door, but no matter which way she walked, the hut would turn away and face its windowless back to her. Vasylyna felt the doll tugging on her skirt, and the motanka whispered to her the words of a charm and bade Vasylyna to speak them. So, in a clear and confident voice, Vasylyna spoke to the hut:

"Khatynka, khatynka, turn your back to the forest and your front toward me."

At those words, the hut turned toward her, its shaggy thatched roof, its door, and its windows looking like a surprised face. It crouched down low enough to let Vasylyna touch the handle on the door. Vasylyna tucked the motanka back into her pocket, reached for the door, and opened it.

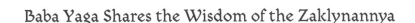

## Baba Yaga Shares the Wisdom of the Zaklynannya

And now you get to meet my lifelong companion, my khata, my khatynka, my little forest hut surrounded by its fence posts of bones topped with skull lanterns. Your feelings of dread or even curiosity may turn to terror once you notice that there is a gap waiting for just one more skull. Whoever lives here may be looking for that last human skull to collect the whole set. We all love to complete a collection, don't we?

Those bones around my khatynka are a sign that I have some good connections in the spirit world. Some people even say that my house is the gateway to the otherworld, that when you cross the threshold into my khata, you are stepping from the land of the living into the land of the spirits.

My little home is more than a shelter or a gateway, it is my companion and my guardian. It keeps out the intruders … well, at least the ones who don't know the correct whisper, the incantation, the *zaklynannya*. I don't mean to brag, but even you will have to admit that to create a living hut is masterful magic, and, well, to control that magic without even lifting a finger—to command all that power with a mere phrase—that alone should tell you how powerful words can be.

Words can become one of your most potent tools. Words are always at the ready— you don't need to grow them or craft them or buy them. They can heal a person or curse them with disease, save someone from danger or destroy them. Incantations can be cast on water or herbs, objects or substances, people or spirits. The right zaklynannya can turn a human into an animal, a tree, or a stone. The ones who know the power of the word can also be transformed by the word, can fly in the air, not drown in water, not burn in fire. With the right words, you can safely call forth spirits like the Rusalky or the Lisovyky or protect yourself from the tricky Mavky. Yes, the one who knows the secrets of the zaklynannya can control the universe.

I have a little secret to share about words. *All* of them are powerful. We have a saying, "A word is not a sparrow. Once you let it fly, you will never catch it again." Think about the words you use before they leave your mouth, little one. Even the most off-handed comment can create profound realities.

And there are even deeper secrets behind that. *Your* words have this ability. You do not have to repeat someone else's incantation like a parrot. Learn at the feet of the old ones, and then trust yourself to create your own words of power. You will create incantations

that will have the ability to heal or harm, protect or invite, bind or cut, create or destroy, control or free.

Once you understand the power of the zaklynannya, you can empower your tools, your potions, your herbs. You can add them to the elements that you use in your magic: air, fire, water, or earth. You can even invoke the help and assistance of the wind, the clouds, the sun, the moon, and the stars. You can command the spirits, and you can even bypass the powerful barriers placed by my guardian khatynka.

What? You don't know what words to use? Don't worry, little one; your ancestor spirits will guide you and whisper the words you need to speak into your ear. Say them with courage and say them with respect. If you do, my hut, and really all of life, will do as you command.

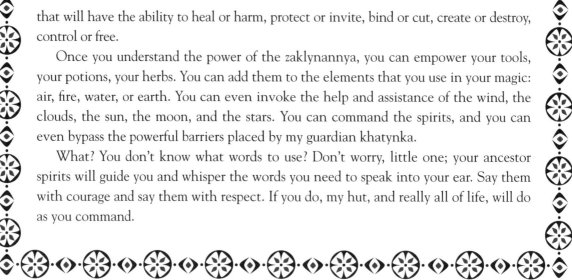

## Madame Pamita Teaches the Magic of the Zaklynannya

When I was young, my mother often told me stories of my babusya and how she would perform an unusual ritual for healing. What my mother described was a memory from her childhood so many decades before. It was just a hazy fragment that she couldn't reference, but she would tell me that my grandmother would hold a bowl of water over someone's head, pour melted beeswax into the water, and divine the source of the person's problems by reading the wax.

This mystery made a nest in the corner of my mind. What was my grandmother doing? Was it fortune-telling? Candle divination? Back when the internet was new, I tried a little amateur sleuthing, and all I could find were references to a divination game played on the eve of Saint Andrew's Day, when young girls would drip candle wax through the hole of a skeleton key into a bowl of water and read the shapes in the wax to divine whom they were going to marry. But this didn't add up. My mother never spoke about a key or prognostications of marital prospects.

Many years later, I learned that my grandmother was doing the wax pouring ritual, *vylyvaty visk*. This Ukrainian form of healing magic is a spiritual treatment performed by an elder wise woman of the community known as a *baba sheptukha*, or grandmother whisperer. These spiritual healers perform a rite where they whisper incantations into water and wax to drive out the fear that is seen as the source of someone's physical or emotional troubles.[81]

A key feature of the ritual is the zaklynannya, the words spoken over the water. Calling on the sun, the moon, the stars, and Mother Earth—as well as God the Father, Mary, Jesus, and the Saints—the baba sheptukha uses carefully crafted incantations to draw out her client's fears into the water. The Christian elements in some incantations seem to be tacked onto the original invocations to the elements of nature, a latter-day addition done to appease the church fathers.

After speaking the words, the healer cuts the water with a knife, effectively cutting and disabling the fear. Pouring the wax into the water assists with the healing process and allows the healer to divine the source of the problem. Finally, she uses zaklynannya to cast out the fear. She uses her words to gently entice it to go far away or firmly command it to leave.[82] While the water, the wax, and the knife are necessary tools, the words direct the energy of the healing and tell it where to flow.[83]

Discovering this practice was like uncovering a cavern full of precious jewels. Finally, I was able to understand what my grandmother had been doing all those years ago, and it profoundly deepened and enriched my belief in the importance of the word in magic.

## Zaklynannya Today

At one time, there were healers in every village in Ukraine, and the baby sheptukhy were respected for their contributions to the community. It was traditional for these healers to verbally pass down their special zaklynannya from grandmother to adult daughter or granddaughter to preserve the continuity of the practice. In agrarian communities, few people learned to read and write, and so these powerful incantations were memorized and passed on in an oral tradition stretching back generations.[84]

---

81. Rena Jeanne Hanchuk, *The Word and Wax: A Medical Folk Ritual among Ukrainians in Alberta* (Edmonton, AB: Huculak Chair of Ukrainian Culture and Ethnography, 1999).

82. Deatra Cohen and Adam Siegel, *Ashkenazi Herbalism: Rediscovering the Herbal Traditions of Eastern European Jews* (Berkeley, CA: North Atlantic Books, 2021).

83. Sarah D. Phillips, "Waxing Like the Moon: Women Folk Healers in Rural Western Ukraine," *Folklorica* 9, no. 1 (2004), https://doi.org/10.17161/folklorica.v9i1.3744.

84. Ryan, *The Bathhouse at Midnight*.

In the twentieth century, a combination of forces threatened to erase this once-thriving practice. Modernization, Soviet suppression of native Ukrainians, and assimilation for diaspora Ukrainians trying to fit in all conspired to eradicate these ancient rituals. Fortunately, there were individuals who kept these practices from disappearing: native Ukrainians who continued to offer the healings in secret, and diaspora Ukrainians who held on to the traditions of their homeland.

Today, interest in the ways of the baby sheptukhy is increasing with people not only healing with vylyvaty visk, but also any number of the myriad rituals that incorporate zaklynannya for healing, blessing, and removing vroki and casting out prychyna, the evil eye and curses. Modern-day healers speak these ancient words of power to enchant objects or people, to avert the undesirable, or to induce the desired.[85]

## The Power of Vocalization

The method of how you say your incantations is important. When calling to spirits, elements, forces of nature, or heavenly bodies, it may feel more natural to speak out loud and authoritatively. For example, when inviting your Domovyk to come home, you will want to use the natural voice you would use when calling someone to come to you.

However, when you are performing spells, enchanting an object, blessing food or drink, or healing a person, whispering may be the more powerful way to use your voice. Whispering implies an intimacy, gives privacy to your magic, and feels as if you are giving more concentrated and focused energy toward your objective.[86] I recommend that before you do your magic, you give each a run-through: try speaking your incantation out loud and then whispering your words. See how each method feels and sense the subtle difference in the power of each.

## Form and Flow of the Zaklynannya

A simple zaklynannya might be a single phrase such as "as this flax is drawn out [in spinning], so may all people come out to me and woo me!"[87] Or, "As ardently and hot as

---

85. I. Kolodyuk, "Suchasnyy Stan Polis'koho Znakharstva (Za Espedytsiynymy Materialamy Na Polissi)," *Volyn'-Zhytomyrshchyna* 13 (2005): 134–142.

86. Ryan, *The Bathhouse at Midnight.*

87. V. V. Zajvoronok, *Oznaky Ukrayins'koyi Etnokul'tury: Slovnykovyy Dovidnyk* (Kyiv, Ukraine: Dovira, 2006).

the copper red-hot stoves burn, may God's servant [woman's name] bake and burn at all times, at all hours, early in the morning, late in the evening … so that she might not be able to live without God's servant [man's name]."[88] There are many short incantations where an object is manipulated in sympathetic magic, symbolically representing the outcome you wish to have. For example, "As this wax melts, so let the disease melt."[89] However, for a more complex incantation, there is a traditional formula that gives extra focus to your magic.[90] These complex zaklynannya consist of several segments using the following formula:

1. The Greeting
2. The Compliment
3. The Spirit Journey
4. The Order, Request, or Proposal
5. The Vow

### The Greeting

There are many different beings you can greet depending on whose assistance you require. For example, you might call on elements, heavenly bodies, weather phenomena, trees, animals, insects, spirits, deities, saints, or ancestors to help you in your objective.

You can greet more than one and from any of the categories. All greetings should begin with "good morning/afternoon/evening" as appropriate. When greeting ancestors or spirits, do not address them by name, but instead by their respectful titles. Addressing them by name will open up a way for them to attach themselves to you, which may or may not be desirable. Here are some examples:

*"Good morning, holy water."*
*"Good afternoon to you, beautiful sun."*
*"Good evening, oak and birch."*

---

88. Johns, *Baba Yaga.*

89. T. Parkhomenko, "Vykorystannya Vosku v Narodnomu Znakharstvi," *Etnokul'turna Spadshchyna Rivnens'koho Polissya* 1 (2001): 27–38.

90. Edina Bozóky, "Mythic Mediation in Healing Incantations," *Health, Disease and Healing in Medieval Culture* (1992): 84–92, https://doi.org/10.1007/978-1-349-21882-0_5.

*"Good day, Master of the House."*
*"Good morning, Lord of the Wood."*
*"Good evening, blessed ancestors."*

## The Compliment

After the greeting, it is customary to praise or compliment the spirit you are addressing by describing their gifts with a tone of appreciation. Here are some compliments:

*Shining sun, you are holy.*
*You are clearly beautiful.*
*You are pure, majestic, and worthy of respect.*
*You illuminate mountains and valleys, land and sea.*

Or,

*Beautiful water, you run fast.*
*You moisten the meadows,*
*splash the shores, and water every root.*

Or,

*Sister Stars, evening dust.*
*You walk the world; you walk the frontiers.*
*You see good people and evildoers.*

## The Spirit Journey

In the incantation, you poetically describe a journey, taking action, or going long distances into spiritual dimensions. Through the words, you can take these actions to either retrieve something or someone or dispel something or someone. They will sound almost fairy tale–like in their description of going long distances, entering fantastical worlds, and symbolically doing the spiritual work. In reality, they are a spirit journey to these otherworlds to do your magic. Here are some examples of spirit journeys:

*I will go to a clear field and face the east.*
*There is a river in that field.*
*I will wash with that water.*

I will swim with the white dawn.
I will touch a star.
I will wrap myself with the beautiful moon.
I will be adorned with the light of the sun.
I will go into the open field, to a celebration.

Or,

I bless myself.
I go out of the hut through the doors,
through the door to the gate,
through the gate into a wide courtyard,
through the courtyard and into an open field.
In the open field I will pray.
In the open field there are twelve winds,
twelve whirlwinds, strong, violent, and dry,
that crush the field in spring.
In the middle of summer,
they will crush the field, mow the grass, dry the earth.

### The Order, Request, or Proposal

Once the journey has been made, the beings in the spirit world can be addressed. The address can be done as an order, if you are casting out something evil; a gentler request, if you are asking for a blessing or boon; or a proposal, if there is to be some exchange.

I will say, Mother Earth, give me your salt,
take away everything bad from me,
let me stand, give me vigor, give me courage.
My face will be light, my hair will be thick, my body will be well.

Or,

Disease, you are not given a home here, not given a peaceful harbor.
Go into the swamps, the deep lakes, the fast rivers, and the dark forests.
There are beds for you there, feather beds with feather pillows.
There are sugar dishes and honey drinks for you there.

*There you will have a dwelling.*
*There you will have peace.*

Or,

*Oak, oak! You are black.*
*You, oak, have a white birch.*
*You have sticks for your sons, and the birch has sticks for her daughters.*
*To you, oak and birch,*
*let your children make noise so that my child will sleep and grow.*

## The Vow

To empower the incantation, a vow is made at the end, emphasizing that your words have power and that your will is strong. This is the phrase that binds the incantation into reality. Whether whispered or spoken aloud, these words should be said with courage and confidence.

*Whatever I do, everything will be fine.*
*Whatever I think of, everything will come true.*
*Whatever I want, it will come true!*

Or,

*May my words be sticky and tough,*
*firmer than stone,*
*stickier than glue or resin,*
*saltier than salt,*
*sharper than a self-cutting sword,*
*tougher than steel.*
*What is intended, shall be fulfilled.*

Or,

*I will fasten thrice nine locks.*
*From the thrice nine locks I remove the thrice nine keys.*
*I fling those keys into the clear ocean-sea,*
*and from that sea a golden-finned, copper-scaled pike will emerge,*

*and it will swallow my seven-and-twenty keys,*
*and it will sink into the depth of the sea.*
*And no one shall catch that pike,*
*or find out the seven-and-twenty keys,*
*or open the locks,*
*or do harm to me.*

## Create Your Own Zaklynannya

Zaklynannya are such an important part of Slavic magic that no matter what you will be making or doing, there are probably words that go along with it. You will find many zaklynannya throughout this book, but understanding the form and flow of them will allow you to create your own for any situation you may want to address magically. I recommend writing out your zaklynannya on paper beforehand and polishing it before you speak the words in your ritual.

1. **The Greeting:** Decide what beings will best aid you in your magic: an element, an animal, a spirit, a part of nature, or a deity. Choose the one that is most aligned with your intention and address them in a respectful way.

2. **The Compliment:** Outline the attributes of your helping spirit. Praise them with honest compliments and imbue your appreciation for them with genuine love.

3. **The Spirit Journey:** Imagine a far-off land, a magical fairy tale place: a distant paradise island, a beautiful green field, a mountain so high that no one can reach it, a sky cradling the moon and the stars. See yourself journeying to this place and performing an action that will symbolically represent your intention of blessing, control, or protection, whether that is leaving something or bringing something. Ukrainian fairy tales have beautiful dreamlike landscapes, so if you feel stuck and need a boost of imagination, read some fairy tales for inspiration.

4. **The Order, Request, or Proposal:** Make a direct proposal, order, or request to the beings you are addressing.

5. **The Vow:** Make a vow to empower your words. In modern magic, people often close their spell with phrases: "It is so!" "So mote it be!" "It is done!" You can incorporate these confident phrases into your practice, or you can craft something more poetic, using metaphor or imagery to symbolize that your intention is now a reality waiting to happen.

Once you have carefully crafted your zaklynannya, you may use it in your spell work. Whisper it over objects to enchant them; say the words with gusto as you address the sun, moon, or stars; softly speak them over your candles, water, or other magical tools to bless them; murmur them as part of a morning or evening ritual for connection to the spirits.

## The Power of Words

Baba Yaga intimately knows the power of words. In many of her stories, she speaks an incantation over objects or people to transform them. She knows that words have power and that the only way to truly *know* the power of words is to start creating and using incantations in your magic.

When you use the words, feel their power and see the incredible changes they bring to your life. Once you do so, you will truly understand and be able to harness the power of the witch of the woods.

# CHAPTER 8

# KHATYNKA I POKUT': THE HUT AND THE ALTAR

*asylyna pushed the door gently but stood outside and peered in. She knew better than to stand on the threshold, but she didn't want to step into the hut without knowing who or what was inside. The room was dimly lit by the fire in the pich, and she could barely discern anything inside the hut.*

*When her eyes adjusted a bit, she could see that the khatynka was very small indeed—just a single cramped room with whitewashed walls and protective talismans carved into the wooden beams. Like all peasant huts, the pich, the massive earthen woodstove, sat in the corner to the left, crouching and dominating the space like a sulky cat stuffed into a box that was too small for him. The pich, too, was whitewashed, but it was painted with colorful symbols unlike any that Vasylyna had seen before. By the light of the oven fire, she could barely make out the mystic designs, herbal motifs, and cryptic images painted across the stove. They seemed like the symbols of a forgotten language. Near the pich, bundles of herbs and mushrooms were strung up to dry, like leftover decorations from a party.*

*In another corner was a large loom and a wooden chest. There was a half-finished blanket on the loom with intricate and colorful designs woven into an indecipherable magical code. The chest next to the loom was made of a heavy dark wood and painted with fat red poppies and fiery birds with flowing feathers.*

*In yet another corner was a bed: a small straw mattress on a shelf, cozy and covered in colorfully woven wool blankets. After her long travels, the bed looked very inviting, and though it wasn't her home, she longed to get cozy under its covers and have a deep sleep.*

*In the last corner, diagonal from the stove, was a small wooden table draped in an embroidered tablecloth and flanked by benches in the corner against the walls. Above the table and in*

*the corner was a pokut', the altar of the home. An image of an ancient goddess sat on the corner shelf, and an intricately woven rushnyk was draped above it. And in the shadows on the bench below the pokut' was an old woman, a very old woman, sitting as still as a statue. The only thing about her that moved was the curl of smoke from the pipe she clenched in her mouth as she looked at Vasylyna through squinted eyes.*

## Baba Yaga Shares the Wisdom of the Khatynka and Pokut'

So, you finally get a peek inside my little hut, my khatynka, my ally, my guardian on its chicken legs. My hut, like all houses, is a living thing with its own spirit. Yes, little one, even "inanimate" objects like a home can be imbued with life.

When we made our homes in the olden times, we placed offerings—eggs, bread, wheat, salt, coins, wool, incense—in the foundation beneath the corners of the house so that it might be willing to protect the family within. In even older days, an offering of a sacrificed chicken head—or the skull of a sheep, bull, or horse—might have been made along with beeswax, honey, bread, and grains. Without these offerings, the living "bones" of the house would not come together as a whole; the house would not be alive and could not work to protect the people who lived within, like my little khata on its chicken legs does.[91]

I know what you're thinking: What's up with those legs? Well, going back to the oldest times, we had special huts far out in the woods that we created for initiation rituals. Some of these would be constructed to appear as a giant animal, built high up on tree trunks that looked like legs and fashioned with a doorway shaped like a big animal mouth. Any young person being initiated would enter through the door and be "swallowed up" by the creature or monster, their old life symbolically put to death so that they would emerge as a full-fledged member of the community.[92]

Spirituality, mystery, and magic were incorporated into all the elements of the initiation. Ritual entry into the land of the dead was required to gain skills, secrets, or

---

91. Lecouteux, *The Tradition of Household Spirits.*

92. Johns, *Baba Yaga.*

otherworldly objects. While inside the hut with the community elders, the initiate would be taught spiritual secrets and magical practices and given tests to see if they were truly ready to be a member of the group. So, if you dare to step into my hut, you are entering into the mysteries.[93]

Don't stand there at the threshold like a ninny! The threshold is a liminal space, neither inside nor outside, and if you're not careful, it opens you up to who-knows-what. Back in my younger days, it was where we buried our dead, so standing on a threshold is like standing on top of a grave; it's gravely disrespectful. Hah! And you thought I didn't know how to tell a joke.

Anyway, that liminal space is why we paint our protective symbols over the door; hang sheaves of fresh stinging nettles; stick a knife blade, pins, or needles into the doorpost; tuck mugwort into the eaves; or hammer an iron horseshoe into the lintel—to protect our ancestors and the house from wandering tricksters, malicious spirits, and the odd thief or two.

Some people take extra precautions when crossing thresholds by crossing themself, and no person in their right mind would ever shake hands or conduct business over one. If you know how to work with this liminal space, however, it can come in handy. For example, if you need to rid a loved one of an illness or they have been crossed up with prychyna and you can't take them to the crossroads, the threshold will work in a pinch. All you have to do is set them over the threshold and wash them with a wet cloth and let the water run out the door. With the help of the ancestors, the curse or illness will leave them and the home. But unless you're experienced at moving through these liminal spaces like me, the three worlds forbid that you should ever sit down on a threshold.[94]

Speaking of the three worlds, you do know about those, right? The world is divided into three parts: the lower world, the middle world, and the upper world. This is not your concept of heaven and hell—this is the land of nature spirits, the land of the material world, and the land of the ethereal spirits. We see these three worlds symbolized by the World Tree with its roots, trunks, and branches. We also see these three worlds

---

93. Hubbs, *Mother Russia*.

94. Ryan, *The Bathhouse at Midnight*.

reflected in our khaty: the floors are the lower world, the walls are the middle world, and the ceiling is the upper world.[95]

Those designs you see carved into the wooden beams and painted on the walls? Well, a house is not considered habitable until these charms of flowers, leaves, and protective symbols are painted on the whitewashed walls to confuse and keep out the forces of evil, disease, and unhappiness. And the red stripe painted on all the walls just above the floor? It becomes a magic circle that keeps the mischief at bay.

So, don't stand out there. You can't see anything. Come in, come in, and take a really good look at my home. My little khatynka is not so different from anyone else's back in the olden times. You had one room, yes, and everything went on in there. You cooked, you worked, you wove, you sewed, you ate, and you slept. But it was never a confused jumble. It was very organized. Every peasant khata had the same necessary things placed in a certain order. In this one room, each corner had a purpose: a corner for spinning and weaving in the north, a corner for sleeping in the south, a corner for the pich used for cooking and heating in the west, and a pokut', or home altar, in the east.

The directions were critical to the placements of these corners. Place the wrong items in the wrong corner or direction, and you open up your home to all sorts of spiritual mischief. Everyday folk followed strict conventions for the placement of the corners of their house when it was built and traditional rules for which things belonged in which directions. So, you can see why my house spinning around and around on its chicken legs breaks the rules and upturns the order of things. A khatynka where nothing is stable, yes, but also one where anything is possible.

While all the corners have their power and magic, the pokut' is the most spiritual corner in the khata.[96] In many homes, it is in this sacred corner where the *ikona*, the icon, is placed on a shelf on the wall and draped with a rusknyk. These powerfully magical images of saints and deities are said to protect and bless the home in miraculous ways. But the pokut' goes back even before the days when they brought their new gods and saints to the people. The ancient Trypillians, an advanced Neolithic culture centered in what is now Ukraine, Moldova, and Romania, had home altars in the east

---

95. Gilchrist, *Russian Magic*.

96. Johns, *Baba Yaga*.

that housed their deity figurines.[97] The east is where dawn breaks and so is sacred in our spiritual connection to the sun. And in the oldest times, the east corner of the house was the place of honor for the ancestor altar.

Even today, the *didukh*, the sacred sheaf of wheat that you will explore more in chapter 20, is placed at the home altar. The name *didukh* itself translates to "grandfather spirit," and this blessed sheaf houses the spirits of our ancestors over winter holidays. During different seasonal celebrations, the wheat porridge *kutya*, the soft crepes *mlynets'*, and the fruit drink *uzvar* are left for our ancestor spirits at this altar as well. The family meal takes place at the table under this altar, inviting the spirits of our loved ones to dine with us on a daily basis and share in our special occasions.

In olden times when people were more in touch with the power of the khata, when someone would enter a home, they would cross themselves while going over the threshold, that liminal place of chaotic magic, and then they would bow to the pich and the pokut' before socializing with the people who lived there. This bow was a way to honor the real presence of the saints and ancestors in this corner, just like taking off your hat and nodding to your elders to show them respect.[98]

So, step into my khata and pay your respects to the ancestors at the pich and pokut'. Once you've come inside, you begin your initiation into the mysteries of the vidmy, the witches, and Baba Yaga.

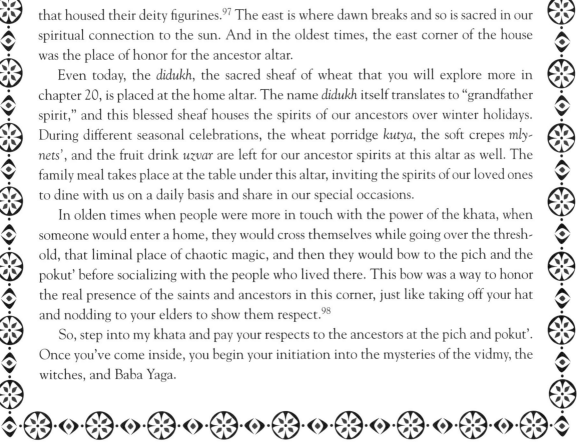

## Madame Pamita Teaches the Magic of the Khatynka i Pokut'

I can't remember a time in my life when I didn't know of a home altar. As a girl growing up, I remember visiting my great-aunt and seeing her pictures of saints draped with lacy rushnyky in the corner of her living room. In our own house, my mother created a little altar to Mary in a cupboard in our hallway.

---

97. P. V. Pysarenko and O. I. Harmash, "Etnohrafichni Osoblyvosti Ukrayins'koho Narodu Ta Yikh Rol' u Stvorenni Ekoposelen' Na Terytoriyi Ukrayiny," *Isnyk Poltavs'koyi Derzhavnoyi Ahrarnoyi Akademiyi* 4 (2016): 83–88.

98. Gilchrist, *Russian Magic*.

Whether it's a product of my upbringing or just a natural part of being a witch, everywhere I go, I seem to set up altars. Outside in nature, I might place some bread as an offering to the spirits on a tree stump, but I'll collect some daisies and acorns to place around it to make it pretty. In my office at work, I have a community altar for my clients' petitions festooned with magical talismans for prosperity, love, and health. And it seems like every room in my house has an altar or two for spell work or to honor the ancestors. I even have a small pokut' in the eastern corner of my kitchen to honor my favorite spirits and loved ones who have passed on. Making altars is in my blood. Incorporating these spots of high spiritual energy into where I work and live brings these spaces to life.

Decorating your rooms, imbuing them with magic, and creating sacred spaces will bring your home to life. You might not be able to bury coins and wheat in the foundation of your house as it's being built, but you can make these offerings after the fact by burying them in the ground next to your building. Find an eastern corner and set up a small altar to your ancestors, your spirits, or your deities. Bring magic into your home, and you will bring protection, abundance, and all sorts of blessings into your life.

## The Khatynka i Pokut' Today

Though most Ukrainians live in modern homes and apartments in cities, there are still old-timers who live in small traditional khaty warmed by woodstoves. There is a great affection and nostalgia for the old khaty. In fact, just outside of Kyiv is the ancient village Pyrohiv, which has been converted into the three-hundred-fifty-acre Museum of Folk Architecture and Folkways of Ukraine. This popular "living history" destination is dedicated to the display and preservation of all the unique styles of traditional architecture and decorative arts of the different regions of Ukraine.

The nostalgia for the charm of the past does show up in smaller ways in the home: flowers painted on the walls in the *Petrykivka* folk art style, decorated eggs, embroideries, and, of course, the pokut'. Diaspora Ukrainians, like my grandparents, brought the practice of the home altar with them when they left the old country. Up until the early twentieth century, most homes in Ukraine would have had a holy corner with an ikona, but as the Soviet Union began aggressively promoting atheism and punishing those who practiced, many people became hesitant to display religious artifacts. However, the pokut' never went away. People either replaced the ikona on their altar with state-mandated political figures or put up an image of something noncontroversial, such as a painting of flowers, perhaps unconsciously harkening back to the Tree of Life and the symbolic goddess Berehynia with her arms upraised. Today, Ukrainian people are free to worship as they wish, and both for those who follow traditional Christianity or the older Pagan path, the pokut' is still an important spiritual center in the home.

## The Power of the Pokut'

Belief in the power of the pokut' is so ingrained that there is an oath that can never be broken, and that is to say, "I swear to you before the holy corner." To say this meant that you were making a vow before one's deities and ancestors. In the olden times, every activity that was essential to the lineage was done at the home altar. Newborn babies were bathed for the first time, brides adorned themselves before their wedding, and the wakes for those who had passed to the spirit realm were all done under the pokut'.

## Creating a Pokut'

To create a sacred space in your home to honor your spirits, deities, or ancestors in the traditional way, you may want to create a pokut'. While you might not live in a traditional Slavic home and be able to accomplish all the specific requirements of the pokut', you may incorporate as many elements as you are able to. Feel free to make adaptations if necessary.

### Images

Though icons of saints are often seen at the pokut', the home altar dates back long before the advent of Christianity. Placing images of ancestors, deities, or honored spirits in this corner is an even older way of working with the pokut'.

Consecrated images, such as icons, have several rules in how they should be treated. First, a blessed image should never be sold. If the owner of the image dies, for example, the image should be given away, buried along with the person, or left as an offering at sacred waters. The images should never be hung directly on the wall but instead placed on a shelf. These images are given life in their role as guardians and protectors, and so they are never taken out of the home unless the family is moving or the house is burning. By keeping them with the family and in their place in the home, they gain their power.

### Shelf

Traditionally, the pokut' would be created in a corner, on the east or southeast side of the home, diagonally across the room from the woodstove, and above the dining table. In this corner, above the table, would be a shelf mounted to the wall. This shelf was where the holy images were placed. In creating your own pokut', you can install a single corner shelf or a more elaborate shelf with two or three levels. In older times, these shelves were carved with magical symbols: geometric notched motifs, six-petalled rosettes, oblique crosses, or solar symbols to bring protection, abundance, and health.

To be completely authentic, the shelf should be mounted high on the wall, up toward the ceiling and never below the eyeline. Ideally, it should have an upper and lower shelf. Holy images, candles, and an incense burner can be placed on the top shelf, and other important spiritual artifacts on the lower shelf.

### Table

The table is a symbol of the unity of the household. It is the place where we gather to share a meal, have meetings, and resolve problems. Having a table near the pokut' means that you are inviting your ancestors to join in the household community, to offer their wisdom, guidance, and protection. Ideally, you can situate your pokut' near your kitchen or dining table, but if this is not possible, then placing a small table near the pokut' where you can sit and eat a ritual meal and leave offerings will work, too.

There are some specific ways in which we treat this pokut' table. The table is seen as a holy place, so nothing except food or offerings should be placed on it. The table should not be used as a catchall. In particular, you should never lay your keys on the table, because it is believed that to do so would elicit quarrels. Nor should you lay a hat on the table, as that would invite sickness.

The table should be covered with a special tablecloth. Never sit with your back leaning against the table, and it goes without saying that you should never sit on the table itself. Sitting at the table, even to eat, is considered a sacred act that unites us with our ancestors, so it is to be treated as such. When you sit at this table to dine with your loved ones, living and dead, you must pay attention in particular to speaking with kindness and never swearing or getting angry. Any significant family decisions or agreements can be sealed by all parties sitting at this table, and any vow made at the pokut' is considered sacred and inviolable.

## Bench

In the past, guests of honor who came into the home would be invited to sit at the pokut' and offered bread and salt, the symbol of hospitality. Traditionally, long, backless benches were placed against either wall, meeting at the corner. This spot in the corner, directly underneath the rushnyk and the images, was considered the most revered and honored place in the home. It was reserved for people who were going through a life transition: a newly born baby, a married couple, or the deceased as they make their transition into the afterlife.

## Rushnyk

While rushnyky woven or embroidered with sacred symbols can be displayed on the walls of the home, the best and the longest rushnyk is reserved for the pokut'. This ritual cloth is draped over the image so that the spirits are dressed in their finest and treated with respect and luxury. Traditionally, this rushnyk is hung above the main icon or image like a little tent or curtain and drapes down as far as the bench.

## Water

Bottles of sacred water are collected and stored behind the images for when the need for blessing or healing arises. If someone is sick, they are given sacred water to drink, and their sickbed is wiped with holy water to wash away the disease. Sacred water is used in myriad magical ways that are discussed in detail in chapter 19.

## Greenery

During the spring, pussy willows and cherry blossoms are put in vases at the pokut'. In summer, especially during the week honoring the Rusalky, sheaves of flowers and greenery such as cornflowers, mint, periwinkle, and lovage are draped around the pokut'. At other times of the year, paper flowers can be used to decorate and add some color, or dried poppyheads can be added to strengthen the connection to the spirit realm. And during the winter months, the sheaf of dried wheat called a didukh is set up in this corner. The didukh represents the ancestors and gives a temporary dwelling to the ones who come to visit at the winter solstice.

### Eggs

Eggs are always seen as an appropriate offering at the home shrine. Red eggs called krashanky, decorated eggs called *pysanky*, wooden eggs, or porcelain eggs are all beautiful amulets to add to your altar to bring blessings and protection.

### Candle

A blessed beeswax candle can be kept and used at the pokut'. There is a special candle made during the holiday *Stritennya* (meeting) or *Hromnytsya* (thunderstorm). This holiday corresponds to Candlemas and takes place on February 2 in the Gregorian calendar used by most of the world, or February 15 in the older Julian calendar used by the Orthodox Church. It is the day when winter and spring meet. Beeswax candles called *hromnytsi* (thunderbolts) are made on this holy day. The same candle can be blessed year after year, gaining strength each year that it is blessed on this special meeting day.

These candles are created by slightly softening beeswax and rolling it around a homemade linen wick and then wrapping the finished candle with flax fibers and homespun red linen thread. When not in use, the hromnytsi are stored behind the holy images and taken out to be lit in special rituals. For example, if there is weather that would endanger the home, the candle can be lit and placed in the pokut' to protect the house from floods, fires, tornados, or getting struck by lightning. If a loved one is afraid of the thunder, the hromnytsi can be lit and circled around the head to relieve them of this fear. Hromnytsi are also used to support spiritual healing and relief from fever, insomnia, and inflammation.

These candles can also be lit to assist during liminal times—if there is a difficult childbirth, for example, or to hold vigil for the spirit of someone who has recently died. When a person dies, a hromnytsi is placed in their hands and lit to illuminate their path to the afterlife so that they can find their way to the spirit world. Without this light, it is believed that their spirit will wander in the dark and will not be able to find their loved ones on the other side.[99]

---

99. Y. M. Rudenko, "Oberehove Pryznachennya Stritens'koyi Svichky Yak Osnovnoyi Rytual'noyi Zakhysnytsi," *Termyny Rynochnoy Ékonomyky: Sovremennyy Slovar'-Spravochnyk Delovohocheloveka* (2020): 180–183.

### Food

Bread, salt, kutya (wheat and poppy seed porridge), and uzvar (boiled juice made from honey and dried fruit) are all left at the pokut' as offerings for the spirits.[100] Traditionally, children are the ones who offer food to the ancestors. Twice a year, at winter solstice/Christmas Eve and spring equinox/*Provody*, a bowl of kutya and each family member's spoon were left on the table overnight to feed the ancestors, to allow the spirits to join in the dinner and feel honored and welcomed. A divination would be part of this ritual. The following morning, if someone's spoon was turned upside down, it was a sign that that person would join the spirits within a year. Kutya was also offered at the pokut' to loved ones forty days after their passing as a meal to celebrate their initiation into the world of spirits.[101]

### Amulets and Magical Tools

Amulets can also be kept in the home shrine for use in spiritual work. Charms such as woven straw ornaments and springtime larks fashioned from bread dough called *zhayvoronky* were often placed in the pokut' for blessings and abundance. Paper cutting art, *vytynanky*, can also be added for protection and blessings for the family.[102]

Protective spells can be done at the pokut'. Placing water and a beeswax candle in a copper jug at the pokut' at night was done to prevent the house from catching fire. Some people suspend a hanging olive oil lamp from the lowest shelf to keep a vigil. And many people keep their most valuable treasures tucked away around the pokut', knowing that that space is inviolable.

## Rituals of the Pokut'

There are many small rituals that surround the pokut'. In the old days, anyone who entered the home would take off their hat and bow to the shrine. You can also nod to this corner to greet your ancestors when you come into the room.

---

100. Kononenko, *Slavic Folklore*.

101. Volodymyr Halaychuk, "Narodnyy Kalendar Zarichnenshchyny v Obryadakh, Zvychayakh Ta Fol'klori.," *Naukovi Zoshyty Istorychnoho Fakul'tetu L'vivs'koho Universytetu* 13–14 (2013): 43–83.

102. Mykhaylo Stankevych, "Vytynanky i Shtuchni Kvity: Porivnyal'nyy Aspekt," *Vytynanky i Shtuchni Kvity: Porivnyal'nyy Aspekt* (2008), http://dspace.nbuv.gov.ua/handle/123456789/16748.

When a child was born, their first ceremony integrating them into the family was performed at the pokut'. A ceremonial bowl of kutya was offered to the ancestors, and the newborn was carried around the table under the shrine three times to initiate them into the family. Bringing new members of the family to the pokut' can be a beautiful way of inviting the blessings of the spirits and including them as part of the family line.

In a happy and blessed home, the family wouldn't sweep out the door, for doing so would sweep out your good fortune. They would sweep from the threshold toward the pokut' so that all of their blessings would stay with them. When life is going well for you, sweep toward the pokut' and then pick up the dust from there, but don't leave your broom under the pokut', as that would be considered an insult to the spirits.

When a family member passes away, it was believed that their spirit would stay anywhere from three to forty days at the pokut'. Leave special offerings such as kutya or uzvar for your loved ones at the pokut' during this sensitive time to honor them and help their spirit to the afterlife.

## The Magic of the Khatynka i Pokut'

As Baba Yaga does, you can view your house as a sentient guardian with a life and spirit all its own. Creating a pokut', home altar, and other personal magical spots in your home where you can honor your spirits or deities is a graceful way to bring life to your house, deepen your connection to your spirits, and make magic a part of your daily life. Making an offering to your home can awaken its protective power and help you build a relationship with it. Whatever magic you do in your home, whether with spirits or the home itself, you'll be creating connections with powerful magical allies who can support you on your spiritual journey.

# CHAPTER 9

# VIDMA: THE WITCH

he light of the fire wasn't too bright, and so it took a moment before Vasylyna could make out the features of the wizened old woman sitting under the pokut'. When she did, she could see her with her long beaklike nose and tangled greasy hair, smoking her pipe and sizing up Vasylyna through the penetrating gaze of her squinting eyes. Apart from puffing on the pipe like a dragon breathing smoke, she didn't make a move. There were several moments of awkward silence with Vasylyna too intimidated and flustered to say anything. But, as it was clear that the old woman wouldn't speak first, Vasylyna finally gathered the courage to bow her head politely to the pich, and then to the pokut', and then to Baba Yaga herself.

"Good evening, grandmother."

The old woman continued to gaze at her through the rings of smoke slowly curling around her, and she reached up and began slowly rubbing one of the animal teeth she wore around her neck on a simple string. Vasylyna cleared her throat and tentatively stepped inside the door.

"My name is Vasylyna," she said.

The old woman stared at her for a moment more, and then slowly stood up. Vasylyna could see that she was very thin and dressed in a vyshyvanka that was so dirty it was practically a rag. She came out from behind the table and silently moved over to where Vasylyna was standing. As she got up, Vasylyna noticed that one of her legs looked so thin and shriveled that she could see the shape of the bones beneath.

Nevertheless, she ably walked around Vasylyna, looking her up and down as she smoked her pipe, appraising her like a tasty morsel that divine providence had brought to her door. Vasylyna continued speaking to fill up the awkward silence.

*"I'm looking for Baba Yaga."*

*At those words, the old woman stopped in her tracks in front of Vasylyna. She squinted her eyes even more sharply and brought her face right up to Vasylyna's. Vasylyna could see hairs growing from the soft wrinkles of her chin, smell the mix of garlic and tobacco on her breath, and hear the old woman clamping her teeth on her pipe.*

*"Do you come of your own free will or are you coming on someone else's errand?"*

*Vasylyna didn't know how to answer this question. She was wise enough to know that it was a test of some kind and that getting the answer correct was imperative. She looked down into her pocket at the motanka and saw the doll nodding her head encouragingly.*

*"I come on an errand, but I desire to know Baba Yaga of my own free will."*

*The old woman squinted harder at Vasylyna and then burst into laughter.*

*"Oh ho ho!" she said. "You want to know Baba Yaga. To know her? Oh ho ho! Oh ho ho!"*
*She laughed as if Vasylyna had told the funniest joke she had ever heard.*

## Baba Yaga Shares the Wisdom of the Vidma

That little girl. Wanting to know me. Did she have any idea of what she was getting herself into? When you step into the spirit world and ask not just to *meet* a spirit but to *know* a spirit, well, that takes some moxie. You might not come back from a request like that. Well, at the very least, you won't come back the same as you were when you walked in. When you walk into the house of a magic maker, you'd better be prepared for some kind of transformation to happen. We like to show off what we do best.

Well, you've probably figured out by now that when you step into my khata, you are stepping into the initiation hut. That's why the first question I ask you is what you've come for. If you've just come to get a look at a witch, fine, feast your eyes before I give you a shove into the oven. If you've come to get a healing, remove a curse, borrow some fire, that's also fine; but if I give something to you, you're going to have to give me something in return. But if you've come to learn, ah, then I *know* you mean business. You are ready to be initiated.

If you want to be a witness to the mysteries, I will give you a few tests to see if you are worthy of the knowledge you are asking to receive. To truly *know* my magic, you can't just read about it, you must experience it. Finding me is just the beginning. An initiation is meant to *test* you. Are you serious about wanting to become a vidma or a molfarka? Good, then you'll do the work to get there. Not everyone will be able to complete the tasks I give. Many will give up. Others will put off their learning for another day. Others may find fault with the tasks I give and walk out completely. And still others may get impatient, wondering why I go so slow or why they can't be initiated right now. And they, too, may leave.

An initiation is never easy. If it were, everyone would be a member of the club, right? The tasks may seem difficult, or even impossible. Yet, what you may not realize is although they may *seem* impossible, they are not. An impossibility is not a riddle but a block. And while I may give puzzles, I never give an impossibility. Nor are my tasks punishments. The child within you might get moody and feel that I am simply giving you these chores to amuse myself, like a cat plays with a mouse before she eats it. No, they are not that, either.

The very best initiations are designed not only to teach you through experience, but to challenge you, to make you know that you can do more than you think you are capable of. When I give you a task, you may feel lost or out of your depth. You may have to seek outside helpers or search to find the needed information. You may have to come up with creative solutions or make adaptations. This is part of our work. And if you are like the lazy girls who come to me looking for a free handout, well, you may find an encounter with me to be a bit of a disappointment. It is intended to be that way, my way of turning you away at the door.

But for those who push through, who complete the tasks I set out for them, who are open to see what boon comes from the work, there is an enormous reward. Not just the gifts I give them in the end, but the magic they learn along the way. One of the first gifts I offer is the ability to see your own blocks. If you look at a task with disdain, discouragement, or resistance, that doesn't say anything about the task, but it speaks volumes about your desire and dedication. Becoming a vidma is not about going through the motions and getting a certificate of participation in the end. It requires commitment that can carry you when you are faced with a task that feels insurmountable. It requires a lifetime of overcoming challenges. Even *lifetimes*, plural. The good news is there is no final exam. The not-so-good news? You will be constantly challenged, constantly tested—but you'll also be constantly learning, growing, mastering, and perfecting.

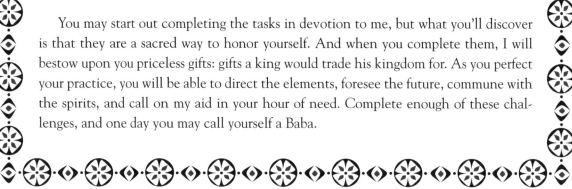

You may start out completing the tasks in devotion to me, but what you'll discover is that they are a sacred way to honor yourself. And when you complete them, I will bestow upon you priceless gifts: gifts a king would trade his kingdom for. As you perfect your practice, you will be able to direct the elements, foresee the future, commune with the spirits, and call on my aid in your hour of need. Complete enough of these challenges, and one day you may call yourself a Baba.

## Madame Pamita Teaches the Magic of the Vidma

When I was a little girl, I loved the magic my mother shared with me. There were so many tiny things that she taught me as matter-of-fact parts of life. Light a candle in a church and make a wish and it will come true. Take a piece of food that you dropped on the floor, kiss it up to God, and it will be safe to eat. Sleep with a piece of wedding cake under your pillow, and you'll dream of your future husband. Pour out some holy water, and it will cure your ills. Carry a charm of Mother Mary in your car, and you won't get in an accident.

My mother never called herself a witch, though I can see that so much of what I took for granted as typical Catholic practices were actually folk magic. When she told me stories about my babusya curing people of their illnesses by pouring wax or crafting dolls, I didn't know at the time that it meant my grandmother was a *znakharka*. Magic was just a part of our devotions, and as long as we included Jesus, Mary, the saints, and the angels in our spells, we were fine.

## The Vidma Today

This blend of traditional Christianity and older folk magic practices is a hallmark of Ukrainain faith. For eleven hundred years, there has been the push and pull between the Church and old Pagan folk magic practices—some church leaders decry them as demonic, while others accept some practices as a harmless part of spiritual life as long as the holy Trinity are brought into the mix.

Like a ribbon through a braid, magic is woven very intrinsically into Ukrainian folklore. Legends abound about the beautiful and enchanting witches of Kyiv flying up to *Lysa Hora*, Bald Mountain, to celebrate their sabbats. Nikolai Gogol's story "The Night Before Christmas" features an attractive witch named Solokha who has many admirers in the village. And, of course, there are dozens of stories featuring Baba Yaga, the witch who is evil, helpful, or ambiguous toward the people who cross her path.

Unlike in Western Europe where the witchcraft trials had a chilling effect on wise women and people who held on to Pagan practices, Ukrainians accepted magic practitioners as part of the village culture. Even today, folk magic practices are seen as truly healing or, at the very least, harmless superstitions, and almost every Ukrainian knows of a fortune-teller or a spiritual healer whom they can recommend.

## Different Kinds of Magic Practitioners

There are as many different types of magical practitioners as there are different flavors of magic. The vidma, the znakharka, the *vorozhka*, the *chaklunka*, the baba sheptukha, and the molfarka all have different specialties and talents. There are any number of ways that cunning folk might gain these magical skills. Some of these gifts are inherited, handed down from parent or grandparent to child. Others are gifted by the spirits, and still others are taught by an unrelated elder and passed through an initiation.

### Vidma

A vidma, a witch, means someone who "knows"; in other words, a wise woman. So, vidmy are not only makers of magic, they are knowers of all knowledge. Vidmy can be helpful or harmful. In the days when most Ukrainians lived on farms, vidmy were thought to have the ability to steal the milk from someone's cow, destroy a harvest, or curse with an illness. However, it was also believed that they could protect people from disease, cast love charms, bring on good weather, or counteract the spells of malicious vidmy.

### Znakharka

A znakharka is a cunning woman, healer, herbalist, and midwife who engages in folk medicine using herbs, fumigation, or whispering to heal and protect. She can interpret dreams, use magic prayers, and cast beneficial spells. She can also detect poisons, sense the witchcraft of others, hear over long distances, and counteract the evil eye and other baneful spells. Like the word *vidma*, the root of the word *znakharka* means "to know."

### Vorozhka

A vorozhka is a soothsayer, a fortune-teller who can look into the future and decipher omens and auguries. Vorozhky can use any number of devices to do their prognostications: dice, cards, palmistry, tea leaves, coals, salt, or water, for example. They might also have the gift of psychic knowing and be able to foretell the future without using tools. Besides fortune-telling, a vorozhka might also be called upon to locate lost or stolen objects.

### Chaklunka or Chaklun

The chaklunka is a sorceress of legendary power often focusing on negative magic. The chaklunka, or her male counterpart the chaklun, casts curses, controls weather, or creates malefic potions to harm or control others. They can also use spells to empower and enrich themselves.

### Baba Sheptukha

The baba sheptukha, the whispering grandmother, is an older woman who uses her whispered words to heal. Her favored method of casting a spell is to whisper zaklynannya over a mundane medium, such as water, butter, bread, salt, beeswax, or tea, turning it into powerful magical medicine, or by murmuring incantations over water, fire, and earth.

### Molfarka or Molfar

A molfarka is someone who traverses between the lower world, the middle world, and the upper world, the world of the living and the world of spirit. A molfarka, or molfar if they're male, has a role similar to the Siberian shaman: they serve the community, spiritually ministering to individuals as well as to the village as a whole. Each molfarka has particular gifts. Some can shape-shift into animal form and communicate with animals, while others create charms that can cure disease or calm troubled minds. Still others control the elements, bringing gentle rains or destroying crops with a curse bringing droughts or storms.

## Sacred Objects of the Molfarka

Every magical practitioner has their spiritual tools: their mortar and pestle, their wand, their talismans—but the molfarka or molfar has a unique set of sacred objects they use in their practice, called *molfa*, that are filled with life energy. A molfa can be an everyday object that has been imbued with magic, such as a piece of cloth, a ribbon, a ring, a medallion, or a necklace, or it can be something found in nature, such as a stone, a splinter of wood, or the bones, feathers, or teeth of an animal.[103]

What turns one of these mundane objects into a powerful molfa are incantations: the ritual, spell, or prayer performed by the molfarka. With the words of the magical practitioner, a simple object becomes a molfa with protection, healing, blessing, or attacking power. The molfarka chooses which direction to take the spell—love, death, strength, wealth, beauty, or health—and utters the words with reverence from the bottom of their heart. The molfa serves the molfarka for their lifetime and can even be passed from generation to generation. Surprisingly, if a molfa is lost, it returns to its owner in a miraculous way.[104]

### *Hromovytsi/Thunderbolts*

*Hromovytsi* are pieces of wood with natural holes that have fallen off a tree struck by lightning. People who have been struck by lightning and live often receive gifts of clairvoyance and psychic abilities. An object struck by lightning possesses this jolt of power coming from Nature herself. Hromovytsi are used to heal, protect, and remove the evil eye by lighting them and fumigating an individual with the smoke, by putting a small splinter into a bath, or simply by carrying them.

A hole in a piece of thunderstruck wood can also be used for giving the molfar or molfarka special abilities to see beyond the material. By peeping through the hole with one eye, it is said that they can spot magical practitioners who have malicious intent.

---

103. V. Bloshchyns'ka, "Kul't Karpat·S'koyi Mahiyi Yak Fenomen Hutsul's'koyi Kul'tury," *Karpaty: Lyudyna, Etnos, Tsyvilizatsiya* 5 (2014): 277–293.

104. Hromovytsia Berdnyk, *Znaky Karpat·S'koyi Mahiyi* (L'viv, Ukraine: Zelenyi pes, 2006).

### Hromova Palytsya/Storm Stick

"To disperse a cloud, one has to have a stick with which a person has hit a snake that was about to eat a frog."[105] A *hromova palytsya* is a stick or staff empowered with the special ability to control the weather. The most legendary hromova palytsya was charged by separating a snake and frog, but sticks that have had other special supernatural encounters can also become powerful hromova palytsya. A stick so blessed becomes a rod that can be used for banishing clouds and controlling weather phenomena.[106]

### Hradovyy Nizh/Hail Knife

The hail knife is a mystical tool to protect the molfar and is considered their faithful guardian and friend. It is believed that milk will start pouring from a tree stabbed with a consecrated *hradovyy nizh* or that a hail knife can transform a stone into cheese. It can also be used to heal a snakebite. Often you see the protective symbol of a six- or eight-pointed flower on the handles of these special knives.

### Zgarda/Sun Medallion

The *zgarda* is a brass charm of an equal-armed cross. This ancient sun symbol is a talisman of protection and is worn on the neck during the initiation of the molfar or molfarka. When a second initiation takes place, a second zgarda is threaded onto the chain, and so on, adding a new talisman for each initiation. These necklaces with their cross symbols have a very strong protective function.

### Mosyazhni/Brass Rings

*Mosyazhni* are massive brass rings carved with magical solar symbols or images of forest spirits. They are amulets symbolizing the immortality of the soul, the unity of Earth and heaven, and the circle of the infinite. Wearing a charmed brass ring is believed to allow you to pass through the gates of time and access the past, future, or parallel worlds, or to become invisible. A powerful mosyazhni is also believed to protect the wearer from arrows, bullets, or any kind of blow.

---

105. S. P. Boyan and N. Bayurchak, "Mol'fary Ukrayins'kykh Karpat: Typolohichnyy Analiz," *Halychyna* 27 (2015): 45–51.

106. Johns, *Baba Yaga.*

### *Totemy/Talismans*

Talismans made of fur, bones, horns, teeth, or feathers connect the molfarka with the spirits of special guardian animals. With these *totemy*, a molfarka can evoke her spirit-assistants in important or challenging moments. These talismans are always in the service of the molfarka and assist her in communication with these animal spirits.

### *Kaminchyky/Stones*

Stones have been around for millions of years, and as such, they are believed to be imprinted with information about the creation of the world. A molfarka understands stones as living creatures with their own character and behavior and uses them to heal illness and banish negativity.

A molfar or molfarka can take a big, round, smooth gray stone to the top of a mountain, raise their hands to the sky, and toss the stone from one hand to another while reciting the following incantation:

> *This stone I'm holding,*
> *I place all illnesses on it.*
> *Let the stone take the pain,*
> *so it will save me!*

They then throw this stone far away. If someone picks it up, the illness will be transmitted to them. To avoid this, a molfarka could alternatively bury the stone with the words "accept this, Mother Earth!"

Stones from the base of waterfalls are also quite powerful. A stone that has had water falling on it for centuries or longer has absorbed the energy of the water and now contains that great magical power.

### *Trembita/Horn, Drymba/Jaw Harp, Sopilka/Flute*

A molfarka or molfar may use musical instruments for invoking altered states or trances so that they can travel to the lower, middle, or upper worlds. The *trembita* is a long horn similar to an alphorn, which creates a sound that can carry across long distances in mountainous regions. The *drymba* is a jaw harp that is held against the teeth and rhythmically plucked to create a droning twang that can lead to altered states of consciousness. The *sopilka* is a wooden shepherd's pipe that is played to imitate the sounds of birdcalls and whistles. With these sounds, the molfar can hypnotize people, conjure spirits, or charm animals. The sounds from these musical instruments also have a calming effect on the mind, purify the elements, and connect one to the animals, the elements, and other parts of nature.

## Creating Your Own Molfa

To create a sacred tool, begin with any durable object—the more mundane, the better. Choose something that is unassuming, inexpensive, and unremarkable. Go for a walk in nature and look for special sticks, stones, and bones. To make a molfa, you need something that will last for years and perhaps even be handed down to a grandchild or protégé, so ephemeral things like flowers or leaves are not a good choice for this kind of magic.

If you go on your walk with your inner knowing turned on, you may find that a very average-looking item stands out for you, or there may be an out-of-the-ordinary interaction with nature, like separating a snake and a frog, that empowers the object with magic. Bring this object back home with you and begin working with it: hold it in your hands, whisper to it, place it on your altar.

Likewise, you may already have an object at home that you can charm: a ribbon, a ring, or a necklace, for example. Either way, communicate with your potential molfa as it sits on your altar or carry it with you. Let it tell you what it can be used for magically. Speak your words of power, your zaklynannya, over it. See if it grows more enchanting to you or if you lose interest in it. Invite it to participate in and empower your spell work. Burn a candle next to it, hold it close to your heart, envision imbuing it with radiant light, put it out in the moonlight or under the sun. Magical tools become empowered with use and intention. Give it a name. Develop a relationship with it. The more you work with your molfa, the more powerful and useful it will become.

## The Way of the Vidma

What is Baba Yaga? Is she a knowing vidma? A powerful chaklunka? A mystical molfarka? Or is she all of these? One of the things I love about Ukrainian witchcraft is that there are so many choices of how to identify yourself, and all of them are magic. As you move on your spiritual path, at some point you may want to give a name to what you do. Are you a *voroshka* who has the gift of foretelling the future, or a baba sheptukha who uses her words to dispel disease and empower objects? Are you a molfarka who has the power to control the elements, or a znakharka with special skills in using herbs? Learn the different magical techniques that Baba Yaga brings to you throughout this book, and you may find that formerly hidden magical talents come to the surface. You are more powerful than you think you are.

# CHAPTER 10

# YIZHA: THE ENCHANTED FOOD

Baba Yaga laughed and laughed, "Ah ha ha!" She slapped her thigh, she held her skinny waist and bent over even further as she cackled, trying to regain her composure. She took a deep breath, and then, as she still chuckled to herself, "She wants to know Baba Yaga, oh ho ho!" She wiped away her tears of laughter.

When she finally composed herself, she looked Vasylyna up and down again. "You are a little one ..."

She picked up Vasylyna's wrist and measured it with her gnarled fingers. "And skinny, too."

She dropped her wrist in disappointment and disgust. "You wouldn't make half a meal for a polecat."

And then she stumped over to the clay oven and opened the metal door to throw another log on the fire.

"Sit down at the table, girl," she said without looking over her shoulder. "First, I will get you something to eat, then I will make up a bed for you on the bench. Sleep tonight, and then we can see about knowing Baba Yaga tomorrow. Hmph." She snorted and shook her gray head.

Vasylyna did as she was told and sat down on the bench at the table. The old woman bustled around the pich muttering to herself, and with a long wooden paddle, she pulled a warm circle of braided bread from the oven. She set a small bowl of salt in the center of the loaf, picked it up with an embroidered rushnyk, and brought it over to the table. She placed it in front of Vasylyna, who looked up, not knowing whether she should eat the bread or not.

"Well," Baba Yaga said, "are you going to spill the salt on the floor? Go ahead! Eat!"

*Vasylyna tore off a piece of the bread and gently dipped it in the salt before taking a bite.*

*"Hmph," said Baba Yaga, and she went back over to the cupboard and poured some sweet, sticky uzvar into an earthenware cup and placed it before the girl. Then, she unfolded some soft woolen blankets and went about making a comfy bed on the unoccupied bench next to Vasylyna.*

*While Baba Yaga was busy with the tucking and folding of the blankets, Vasylyna snuck a pinch of bread and a sip of the uzvar to the motanka in her pocket, then broke off another piece of the loaf for herself. She was so hungry, and the sweet, soft bread and honeyed fruit juice were the best she had ever tasted. Before she knew it, she had eaten and drunk her fill.*

*Baba Yaga cleared the table, and Vasylyna, filled with the warm bread and exhausted from her travels, got ready for bed. She slipped under the thick blankets that Baba Yaga had set for her on the bench, tucked her motanka next to her, and, with the pokut' above her head, she soon closed her eyes and fell asleep.*

## Baba Yaga Shares the Wisdom of Yizha

So, you thought that as soon as you met me, it would be all about flying spells and commanding whirlwinds. Nobody wants to learn. They all want to get to the finish line. Without walking the road, there is no destination.

I hear that whiny voice in your head: "But Baba Yaga, food is so boring, so mundane. I want to get to the *good* stuff."

What? You didn't know I could read your thoughts? Hmph. What kind of vidma would I be if I couldn't read a thought as obvious as that?

"The good stuff." Food *is* the good stuff. It is everything. You know the saying "you are what you eat"? If you want to be a vidma, you have to *become* magic. If you want to *be* magic, you need to *eat* magic. The food you take in, the food you give to others, the food you offer to the spirits—it can all be imbued with your spells, your incantations, your magic. And the more often you recognize this and work in this way, the more witchy you will become.

All the magic that is created by Mother Earth—the seeds, the grains, the herbs, the roots; everything that is given to us by my daughters, the animals—the milk, the eggs,

the honey; every element that you add—the water, the air, the fire; and every step of the process—the work of your hands, the words of the incantations—they all come together in our food. Sometimes the simplest things truly have the most power.

The znakharka, the molfarka, and the baba sheptukha know that one of the best methods of casting a spell, one that goes back to the oldest times, is to whisper incantations over food or drink. Speak your intention into something you will take into your body, and you will create profound changes—clear curses or bring blessings, create potions that can empower you or charm another person. It is all within your power.[107]

Food and drink can also charm the spirits. Remember whom you've met on your journey so far. Every time you touch the world of the spirits, you make an offering. The motanka, the Domovyk, the Lisovyk, the Rusalky—they are not obliged to help you, but if you offer them something delicious, they may be inclined to do so. Offering food to these wild spirits builds a relationship with them. It connects you to them and them to you.

All meaningful interactions with our beloved ancestors also involve offering them food and drink. We set kutya and uzvar, wheat porridge and fruit juice, at the pokut' to connect to our loved ones who have passed on and to help them on their way. We leave *khlib* and krashanky, bread and dyed eggs, at their gravesites to let them know we miss them and haven't forgotten them.[108]

We also extend hospitality to people who are in the world of the living, too. Whether a familiar face or a newcomer, powerful or humble, a guest is treated with honor. There is an ancient tradition of welcome where we offer bread and salt to those who come into our home. Bread is the sacred gift of grain from our Mother Earth, our Maty Zemlya, and salt is that once-rare seasoning that gives flavor to life. We give the gift of blessed food to our guests, presenting them on a magical rushnyk.[109]

A person receiving this bread tears off a piece, dips it in the salt, and eats it. This transaction builds a friendly link between the one offering and the one receiving. Bread is also what we give to our loved ones who must travel, not just so that they can eat, but so they are protected with the love that we put into the bread we have made for them.

---

107. Ryan, *The Bathhouse at Midnight*.

108. Svitlana Kukharenko, "Traditional Ukrainian Folk Beliefs about Death and the Afterlife," *Folklorica* 16, no. 1 (December 2011), https://doi.org/10.17161/folklorica.v16i1.4209.

109. Hubbs, *Mother Russia*.

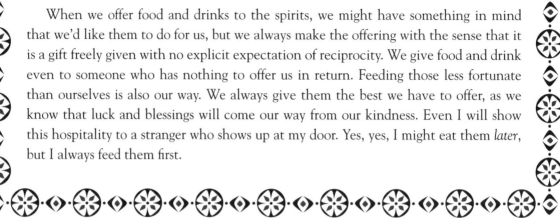

When we offer food and drinks to the spirits, we might have something in mind that we'd like them to do for us, but we always make the offering with the sense that it is a gift freely given with no explicit expectation of reciprocity. We give food and drink even to someone who has nothing to offer us in return. Feeding those less fortunate than ourselves is also our way. We always give them the best we have to offer, as we know that luck and blessings will come our way from our kindness. Even I will show this hospitality to a stranger who shows up at my door. Yes, yes, I might eat them *later*, but I always feed them first.

## Madame Pamita Teaches the Magic of Yizha

Growing up, whenever I would bring friends over to the house, my mother would bustle about in the kitchen and make something for them to eat. "Here, I made these cookies," or, "Would you like a root beer float?" Of course, my friends loved it, but as I got to be a teenager, I would get so embarrassed by what I thought of as my mother's fussing.

Whenever she hosted a holiday party, she would always make a huge spread: three different main dishes, four different salads, and dozens of side dishes. Often these would include Ukrainian comfort food like stuffed cabbage called *holubtsi*, potato dumplings called *varenyky*, garlicky pork sausage called *kovbasa*, and cooked buckwheat called *kasha*. We always laughed and said that if she was expecting five people, she made sure she had enough to feed fifty. I always thought overserving food was my mother's special quirk, but as I got to know other Ukrainians, I realized that food and hospitality are truly intertwined deep in the Slavic psyche. Whenever someone comes over, you always offer them hospitality through something to eat or drink.

There is a spiritual part of this hospitality that my mother expressed fully—food is only tasty if it has the secret ingredient of being made with love. So much of magic is about intention. If you are embroidering, your mind must be clear. If you are making a motanka, you must have a light heart. And with food, it is the same. Whether it is whispering into a piece of garlic to create a charm or baking a loaf of bread filled with wishes of health and happiness for your loved ones, food is the perfect substance to imbue with your magical intentions.

## Yizha Today

Food is intertwined in so much of Ukrainian folklore, including some of its oldest recorded magical practices, with good reason. Ukraine itself has been called the bread-basket of Europe because of its fertile fields of rich black soil that are able to grow vast amounts of grain and other foods. So many people of Ukrainian descent can trace their family lines back to people who worked closely with the land, and so there are many magical practices connected to food. From the growing and harvesting of crops to the preparation of meals, there are numerous ways that people infuse food and drink with spiritual power.

Every holiday has its special foods that have magical significance. For example, there is an ancient Pagan winter solstice practice that has been preserved as part of the *Sviaty Vechir*, the Christmas Eve celebration. On Sviaty Vechir, or holy night, Ukrainians prepare an elaborate twelve-course meal. Each of these different foods has a special meaning and represents a blessing for the twelve months ahead.

There are even more ways that Ukrainians use food for magic that have nothing to do with eating it: washing in water that has been imbued with the power of a magic herb, scattering seeds to provide protection. The power of these magical ingredients has been passed down through the generations and is intricately woven into the spiritual life of people even today.

## Creating Enchanted Yizha

It is such an ingrained custom to provide hospitality for guests that even a wild spirit such as Baba Yaga serves food and provides a bed to all who come to her hut. The foods that she provides, however, are the same meals that are served to the ancestor spirits, food for the dead. And the bed that she makes for her guests places their head at the pokut', just as the bodies of the dead are positioned during a wake.

All foods are magical, blessed, and holy, but there are some key ingredients that seem to have extra magic in them. These seven special foods amplify intention and have long magical traditions: grain, honey, garlic, poppy seeds, mushrooms, eggs, and salt.

Magic can be found working closely with these foods and putting your own energy into them. For example, instead of buying a loaf of bread, make your own bread. Grow your own garlic. Buy honey from beekeepers and eggs from chicken farmers or keep your own bees and chickens. Cook from scratch. Eat with mindfulness. And, of course, share these intentional foods with others.

## Zerno/Grain

Grain is emblematic of the relationship of exchange between humans and the spirit world. The magic of grain is very old. There is archaeological evidence that the Trypillian people were performing magic and ritual in their granaries seven thousand years ago. Grain and bread were believed to absorb both solar energy and the power of the earth. Even today, there are echoes of these ancient beliefs in the ritual breads that are baked in a round shape symbolic of the sun.[110]

Grains show up in so many of the foods that we use to connect to the spirits. For instance, the wheat porridge called kutya is made with wheat berries, honey, and poppy seeds, three very magical ingredients, and is eaten on holidays and offered as food to the ancestors.

With grains being so important, there is a natural reverence for khlib, bread. There is a Ukrainian saying that expresses this perfectly: "Bread is the head of everything." Bread is not just food. It also has rich meaning as a symbol for hospitality, prosperity, happiness, long life, health, well-being, and protection in the afterlife. It is considered an insult to Mother Earth to throw away a piece of bread. Even crumbs are collected from the table and shared with birds and animals or thrown into the air as an offering to the spirits. It is believed that if any bit of bread is thrown out, then wealth and luck will be thrown out, too. Bread is never tossed into the trash because it can be used by your enemies to cause you harm. If a piece of bread accidentally falls to the ground, it isn't thrown away; it is kissed and lifted up to heaven to be cleansed of all harm and then eaten.

Bread is honored in song and is sworn on when making agreements. It is included in rituals for the construction of a new home, for marriage, for welcoming newborns,

---

110. Pysarenko and Harmash, "Etnohrafichni Osoblyvosti Ukrayins'koho Narodu Ta Yikh Rol' u Stvorenni Ekoposelen' Na Terytoriyi Ukrayiny," 83–88.

and for seeing loved ones off to the afterlife. Bread is also used in spells for healing and getting rid of prychyna.

Before baking bread, it is appropriate to ask for a blessing from the spirits and to never disrespect the grain by swearing or cursing while making the bread. To do so is to invite poverty and famine.

### Bread Divination

If you bake your own bread, you have a wonderful opportunity to do a household divination. Breads were traditionally baked once a week on Saturday, and it was believed that breads that turned out well, especially ritual breads, brought luck, health, and wealth to a home, while breads that flopped were a sign that misfortune and troubles would come to the family. Even the detailed state of your bread was believed to predict what was to come for the family that week:

- **Light and flavorful:** Happiness in the home. Good outcomes without much effort.
- **Flavorful but heavy:** Kindness and wisdom in the home; however, challenges might arise due to the people around you.
- **Light but unappetizing or flavorless:** Greed and laziness. Someone in the home is taking advantage of a situation.
- **Tough and chewy:** There is a lack of logical thinking by someone in the family, and their stubborn resistance might create trouble.
- **Dry and hard:** Distractions and secrets; something is off. Someone may have a secret obsession, or there may be a troublesome spirit in the house.
- **Cracks on the surface:** If there are many unusual cracks in the bread, it is a warning of danger. Stay vigilant and take extra precautions to avoid trouble.
- **Burned:** Quarrels and spite. Burned bread sends a message that happiness can be brought back if one is willing to make some positive changes.

### Med/Honey

Honey is a sacred talisman considered to be the food of the gods. Traditionally, farmers blessed their livestock by smearing a cross of honey between their eyes. Even today, people wash their faces with water and honey to magically enhance their beauty and eat honey with a prayer to make their lives just as sweet.

Honey's special magic lies in its long-lasting and sticky qualities. Any spell done with honey will last a long time, even a lifetime, so care should be taken, as it can be challenging to undo these spells. Honey is both a healer and an aphrodisiac. It shines in spells for passion and love and brings sweetness to spell work, but it is quite powerful, too. It is believed that any target who eats enchanted honey will subordinate their thoughts and will to the spellcaster.

There are many old rituals surrounding beekeeping and the collection of honey. Bees are considered to be messengers from the heavens, and killing a bee is a crime against the divine. Traditionally, beekeeping was the job of the *didy*, the grandfathers and older men of the community, and the most skilled ones were called *pasichnyk-charivnyk*, beekeeper-magicians.[111]

### Empowerment Spell with Honey

Spells and incantations for honey are numerous—to bring love, money, or a new home, for example. Since honey contains the condensed energy of the sun, you can charge your honey for spells in this traditional way. Leave a jar of honey in the sun at noon. Open it, bring it to your lips, and whisper these words into the jar:

> *As honey is very sweet and gets sweeter in the mouth,*
> *so let my power come to me.*
> *No one opens their mouth to this honey.*
> *This honey's sweetness warms only my soul and heals only my body.*
> *So be it!*

The ritual is to be carried out in secret, and the jar must be closed and hidden in a secret place where no one else can find it and take your power.

Four days after speaking the incantation, begin taking one teaspoon of this honey on an empty stomach every day before breakfast. You will immediately feel a surge of strength and vigor.

---

111. Ulyana Movna, "The Ritual Complex of Traditional Beekeeping of Ukrainians of Nadsiannia," *The Ethnology Notebooks* 147, no. 3 (2019): 608–621, https://doi.org/10.15407/nz2019.03.608.

### Reconciliation Spell with Honey

If you quarrel with someone, you can reconcile with the help of honey. Add a spoonful of honey to tea and whisper the following charm over the brew: "Calm anger, remove old memories." Serve the tea to the person, or, if the argument caused the two of you to not be on speaking terms, you can sprinkle this tea on their property.

## Chasnyk/Garlic

Since ancient times, garlic has been used in spells and rituals for banishing and protection from evil spirits and people with bad intentions. People with malevolent designs are frightened of garlic, and so it is worthwhile to be on guard when encountering people who refuse to eat garlic. If a stranger or an unpleasant person comes to your home, put a couple of cloves of garlic on the table. It will neutralize the negative mood of any enemy or ill-wisher.

### Personal Protection Spells with Garlic

There are many quick spells that can be done with garlic to protect yourself from jealous glances. Rub a piece of garlic over your body, thread a clove of garlic and wear it as a charm around your neck, or carry a garlic clove in your pocket. You can hang a clove over a cradle to protect an infant from the evil eye. If you are bothered by evil spirits, wearing garlic around your neck or at your waist during the day and placing some under your pillow at night will keep them at bay.[112]

### Home Protection Spell with Garlic

Having garlic in the house protects the family from outside problems. A braid of garlic tied with a red string and hung next to the door can protect the home from evil people and spirits. However, garlic from this protective braid should never be eaten, as it has absorbed negativity. Another way to cleanse the home is to place a garlic clove in each room overnight and throw them away the next morning by scooping them up with paper, making sure not to touch them with your hands.

---

112. Ryan, *The Bathhouse at Midnight*.

### Strength and Healing Spell with Garlic

Because of its "bite," garlic is used in spells to increase physical strength. Those who want to increase vigor and health eat raw garlic at the winter solstice holiday celebrations to stay strong and healthy throughout the following year. When eating garlic and bread, you can say the following incantation to protect yourself:

> Garlic, protect me from all evil:
> from injury, from the evil eye,
> from disease, from weakness.

### Garlic Spell to Get Rid of Bad Neighbors

If you want to banish troublesome neighbors, face the west and put three bay leaves, three black peppercorns, three dill seeds, and a head of garlic in a glass bottle. Whisper the words "connect these as a whole and stock up on strength." Shake the bottle three times, and then hide it in a secret place on their property.

## Nasinnya Maku/Poppy Seeds

Poppy seeds are also a powerfully protective talisman that can reverse negativity and protect against evil. They are often included in offerings for the ancestor spirits but can be used in other ways besides eating them. If these seeds are sprinkled on a pathway, it is believed that no evil spirit can pass them until they have collected and counted them all.[113] They find the seeds irresistible, so, while they are busy counting, people can attend to their everyday activities without interference. Poppy seeds are poured in front of the threshold of the home so that enemies are not able to pass through the door. Shaking the seeds directly from a dried field poppy is thought to be especially powerful.

### Reversing Spell with Poppy Seeds

To reverse negativity that has invaded a home, sprinkle poppy seeds in cracks, gaps in the floorboards, at the baseboards, in window frames, or in any other nooks and crannies where they cannot be removed. Start at the entrance and move around the

---

113. Ryan, *The Bathhouse at Midnight.*

perimeter of the home clockwise. Scatter the poppy with three fingers of the right hand and whisper the following incantation:

*I sow poppies as I wish, and everything will be as I wish.*
*If someone has cursed me, let them try to collect these poppy seeds.*
*It is time to remove the scattered poppy seeds,*
*and it is time to remove all curses from me.*

### Uncrossing Love Spell with Poppy Seeds

Poppy seeds are also used in love spells, particularly if you sense that your loved one has had a charm put on them by someone else. If that is the case, sprinkle poppy seeds around the home of your lover and whisper this charm:

*When you, the villain [name of your rival],*
*has found each seed,*
*collected them and put them back in the package,*
*only then will my beloved [name of your loved one] leave me.*

### Poppy Seed Spell to Return Lost Love

Poppy seeds can also be used in spells to return a lost love. For seven days in a row, whisper the following zaklynannya over the poppy seeds:

*I will prepare a feast for you, [loved one's name],*
*and you will obey my command.*
*You will not move away from me,*
*you will follow me at my heel.*
*You will love me as you did on the first day,*
*and will not look for a replacement for me.*
*You will only look at me, and not look at anyone else.*
*Eat this food and you will never reject me,*
*and you will forget anyone else.*

On the seventh day, bake cookies or buns with the poppy seeds. Give your loved one the pastries to eat at least once. After you feed them, resist the temptation to initiate a meeting or communication of any kind. If they reach out to you, the ritual has been successful.

### New Love Spell with Poppy Seeds

Poppy seeds can also be used to attract a new lover who is known to you. Arise every morning at dawn for seven days. Imagine the person you want to enchant. Over a bowl of poppy seeds, recite the following incantation as the sun rises:

> *As soon as the dew on the poppy petals dries up, dries up,*
> *[name of your target] remembers me.*
> *Let them love me more than life,*
> *let them follow me as if on a leash.*
> *All their thoughts aspire to be with me,*
> *all their feelings for me wake up.*
> *I bind this spell with words,*
> *I bind our souls forever.*

After doing this for seven days, you need to add the poppy seeds to your loved one's food without their notice. If it isn't possible to offer them food, scatter the seeds where they can step on them.

## Hryby/Mushrooms

Mushrooms are one of the most emblematic foods of Baba Yaga. They can be delicious or deadly. Just as you take your chances when you encounter Baba Yaga, the unwary person who goes mushroom picking also risks losing their life if they are not alert and humble. Baba Yaga is not only associated with edible mushrooms, but also with fly agaric, *amanita muscaria*, or mukhomor, the alluring fairy tale red mushroom with white spots. This toxic toadstool is known for its hallucinogenic properties and was used as an entheogen in spiritual ceremonies by the ancients.[114]

However, mushrooms of all kinds are considered special and provide a link to the lower world. They are neither plant nor animal; they are truly otherworldly. Circles of mushrooms, popularly called fairy circles in English, are known as *vid'myne kil'tse*,

---

114. Greg A. Marley, *Chanterelle Dreams, Amanita Nightmares: The Love, Lore and Mystique of Mushrooms* (White River Junction, VT: Chelsea Green, 2011).

witch's rings, in Ukrainian. These circles were believed to indicate the places where witches gathered for their rituals, and the mushrooms found in these circles were thought to be enchanted.

Collecting edible mushrooms has long been a part of life for those living in mountainous regions like the Carpathians. Even in modern times, mushroom hunters take to the forest from June through October to find these delectable tidbits under the pines, firs, oaks, and birches. Once they get them home, they can be dried for use throughout the winter. In folklore, these magical fungi are thought to be the creation of the Lisovyky, and so much of the magic surrounding mushroom hunting involves the Lord of the Forest. Should you have the opportunity to go into the forest with an experienced mushroom hunter, you can perform these small rituals to ensure success.

### Offering to the Lisovyk for Mushroom Hunting

Because mushrooms are found in the domain of the Lisovyk, many people bring an offering to the Master of the Woods before they begin their search. A loaf of bread or another appropriate offering is left for him and an incantation is spoken to ensure a safe and fruitful hunt.

> As I go to collect mushrooms,
> I will say this spell in order not to be poisoned by mushrooms,
> and to return with a full basket. Let it be so.

### Mushroom Hunting Rituals

A small divination ritual can also be performed before mushroom hunting. Take your gathering basket and throw it into the air and say, "Lord of the Wood, give me a full basket!" If your basket falls to the ground upright, you'll have a good day of picking, but if it falls upside down, you will have a hard time finding mushrooms that day.[115]

Since finding good mushrooms requires luck as well as skill, there are other charms that assist in having a successful hunt. Having a cheerful attitude may mean the difference between finding mushrooms or coming up empty-handed. There is a proverb: "If

---

115. Ryan, *The Bathhouse at Midnight*.

you're happy, you'll go mushroom hunting. If you're unhappy, you'll go for a walk in the woods."

Mushrooms are shy and like to hide under the leaves, so one should walk quietly through the forest, not speaking too loudly or singing. If you find good mushroom picking spots and gather a good harvest, you should never brag about your success. Someone's envy might drive away your luck, or they'll find your bountiful secret mushroom spot and get there before you do next time.

### Honoring the Ancestors with Mushrooms

Because mushrooms traverse between the worlds, they are used for medicine and healing by wise women, featured in dishes shared with the ancestors, and served at memorial dinners. The winter solstice meatless meal that is shared with the ancestors includes mushrooms as one of the dishes.

### Ritual for Creating a Mushroom Hunting Stick

There is a magical game that is part of the winter festivities. In the old days, hay was sprinkled on the floor under the table at the Christmas Eve meal, and dried mushrooms—or, later, more enticing candies—were hidden in the hay for the children of the family to hunt and find. They looked for the treats and shouted, "Here's a mushroom!" whenever they found one. A stick could be used to find these "mushrooms," and when true mushroom season began, this same stick, now imbued with extra mushroom-finding powers, could be taken out to bring more success in a real mushroom hunt.

## Yaytsya/Eggs

Eggs are sacred magical objects to be treated with special reverence. In folklore, it is believed that each egg yolk is a small image of the glowing holy sun. Humans were only able to look up at the sun from a distance, but birds are messengers who were able to fly up to the sacred sun. There, they were handed a gift: a piece of the sun's magic, a symbol of light and warmth, to carry in their eggs. They brought these back down to Earth in their bellies and laid them in their nests for us to eat.[116] A beautiful love letter from the sun to humanity.

---

116. Dixon-Kennedy, *Encyclopedia of Russian and Slavic Myth and Legend*.

### Traditional Yaytse Cleansing

The power of the *yaytse* can be used for more than just eating. They can be used for cleansing away vroki. A traditional egg cleansing is done by a magical practitioner on someone else to remove any negativity, illness, or curse.[117] If you'd like to do this practice, use a fresh, fertilized egg with a white shell. If you want to be very authentic, you can use an egg that has not been refrigerated and was not purchased. It must be collected directly from a hen or given to you as a gift from someone who owns chickens.

Begin by preparing your ritual space during the day. Open all windows to let in fresh air and all curtains to let in as much light as possible. Wash the egg you will be using with spring water or rainwater before you begin.

When you are ready to perform the cleansing, light a beeswax candle and have the subject you'll be cleansing sit in a chair. Stand behind them and hold the egg in your right hand. Whisper words of prayer or intention to remove the negativity and move your hand holding the egg in a clockwise circle around their body. Make two circles around the head, two around the neck, and two around the torso. Then, holding the egg with your fingertips, roll it directly on the subject's body from the right shoulder toward the chest, over the abdomen, down the left leg, and to the left foot.

Break this egg into a clear glass of water for a divination to see if there are any remnants of negativity. Threads of egg white indicate the presence of vroki, or the evil eye. Red or black dots indicate the presence of a curse. If this is your first time interpreting a cleansing egg, you may want to break an unused egg in another glass of water before starting the cleanse and then compare the two. If you note any unusual signs, repeat the cleanse again with a new egg until you get an egg that appears normal.

Good or bad, the broken eggs and the water should be buried where no one will step on them or, alternatively, flushed down the toilet. As you ritually dispose of your egg, say the following incantation: "Water, take away all curses, negativity, and illnesses."

### Simple Yaytse Self-Cleansing

You can also do a simple egg cleansing on yourself. Break an egg in a clear glass of spring water. As you do so, say these words: "Take all negativity away from me." Place this glass on your nightstand next to your head overnight while you sleep. In the morning,

---

117. Hanchuk, *The Word and Wax.*

examine the egg for changes. If there are any negative signs, as described above, repeat each night until you get a normal-looking egg.

### Spell for Wealth and Luck Using a Yaytse

Take a fresh, fertile egg and hold it at the top and bottom with your index finger and thumb. Visualize your luck and wealth as you hold it for several minutes. When your visualization is complete, say the following zaklynannya:

> *I will go out from door to door, from gate to gate.*
> *Away from my house, away from my city.*
> *I will go to seek my happiness in ways I do not know.*
> *Winding paths, on all four sides, I will go without turning.*
> *My happiness is hidden, hidden deep and strong, not to be found.*
> *It is not hidden in a strong chest,*
> *it is not hidden behind a heavy door.*
> *It is found within the shell of an egg from a chicken.*
> *I find my happiness and will not break it,*
> *I do not break it on the road,*
> *so I do not lose it to anyone and do not give it away.*
> *Chickens lay eggs and raise chicks, and I live in wealth.*
> *Key. Castle. Words. It is so.*

Wrap the egg in a black cloth and hide it in a safe, secret place where it will not get broken and no one will find it. One year later to the day, retrieve your enchanted egg and bury it in the ground. Immediately after that, wealth and luck will follow.

### The Amulet of the Yaytse

Eggs appear again and again in Ukrainian magic, as offerings to the spirits, as tools for divination, and as symbols of protection. Whole eggs are such an incredibly powerful magical tool that they are used as talismans as well. In chapter 13, you'll learn about krashanky and pysanky—the decorated egg amulets—and how they are used in magic.

## Sil'/Salt

Salt is a potent tool for protection from negative people and vroki, the evil eye. Many people carry small bags of blessed table salt as a talisman to ward off evil. There is a well-known counter-curse, "Salt into your eyes!" This is said to someone who is perceived to be jealous.

Regular salt is quite protective, but there is a special blessed salt called *chetverhova sil'*, Thursday salt. Due to the syncretism with the Christian calendar, often this salt is made on Holy Thursday, but its origins are much, much older and can be tied to the spring holidays. Thursday salt can be made at any time but is especially powerful if made around spring equinox.

### How to Make Thursday Salt

As with the creation of any magical tool, you should begin by calming your mind and making your thoughts light and peaceful. On the night before spring equinox, grind a blend of magical herbs with a mortar and pestle. Choose your own blend from among the herbs listed in appendix I.

As you grind the herbs in your mortar and pestle, speak a blessing for your intention. Blend these herbs with coarse rock salt in a ratio of five parts salt to one part herbs and add a slice of crumbled rye bread, preferably bread that you have baked yourself. There are two methods for cooking the salt.

Method 1: Mix all ingredients together in a cast-iron skillet and bake in a low oven (250 degrees Fahrenheit/130 degrees Celsius) overnight. The salt will turn black after baking. At dawn the next morning, remove from the oven and allow to cool.

Method 2: Mix all ingredients together and place them in a cast-iron skillet. Cook on top of the stove over medium heat. Stir as you cook the salt mixture until it turns black.

With both methods, cooking the salt mixture will be smoky, so it's a good idea to use a fan or other ventilation as you are making it. Once your salt has cooled, pulverize it in a mortar and pestle as you speak the following incantation:

> *Salt of all salts. Protect me, [name], from evil.*
> *Protect my house from enemies whose names I do not know.*
> *Stop those who think badly of me,*

*shut the mouths of those who would speak evil of me.*
*As a leaf falls from a tree, so my enemies and all evil fall from me.*

Thursday salt prepared in this way can be wrapped in a piece of linen or placed in a linen bag and left outside overnight to absorb the power of the moon and the stars. Place this linen bag in the pokut' and the salt can be used throughout the year until the next spring.

### Working with Thursday Salt

As with many magical ingredients, you can store your Thursday salt in the pokut' for use throughout the year. Thursday salt can be used for many protective purposes. If you've had a quarrel with your partner, you can put a small bag of it under their pillow so that reconciliation happens quickly. A small charm bag of this salt in a car, suitcase, or backpack will ease travel and protect against trouble. Any magical tools can be cleansed and blessed by placing them in or on a bowl of Thursday salt.

### Protection Spells with Thursday Salt

Thursday salt can also be used to preserve the health of the people living in your home. Placing a little salt under your child's pillow ensures that they will not get sick and protects them from bullies. Bathing in water with a little Thursday salt will preserve beauty and bring health and happiness. You can also add a tiny pinch of Thursday salt to drinking water to spiritually protect your health.

### Home Protection with Thursday Salt

Sprinkling Thursday salt in front of your door will prevent people with evil intentions from entering your house. A small bowl of Thursday salt can be set in the middle of the table as a talisman to attract happiness, luck, and abundance. Little bits of this salt can be scattered in the corners of the house to guard against evil spirits and unwelcome people and banish sorrow or strife from the home. Thursday salt can be added to water for washing floors after a visit from someone with bad intentions or sprinkled on their footprints after they have left to ensure that they don't return.

## The Magic of Yizha

In nearly every story of Baba Yaga, there is an element of enchanted food. Whether she is making it and serving it to the strangers who come to her door or having them cook food to satisfy her voracious appetite, food is integral to her witchcraft. She truly is the keeper of the knowledge of how to make the mundane magical. Imbuing your food with your intentions and incorporating these ingredients into your spiritual practice will awaken you to the magic that is in everything.

# CHAPTER 11

# PICH: THE OVEN

The next morning when Vasylyna woke up, she smelled the scent of a delicious wheat, honey, and poppy seed porridge and saw that Baba Yaga was already awake and cooking breakfast.

"Get up, girl. The day is short and the chores are long."

As Vasylyna sat down to eat the porridge, she took a pinch and put it in her pocket to share with her motanka. Baba Yaga sat down across from her and sipped from a cup of hot herbal brew.

"So, I ask you again, do you come of your own free will or are you coming on someone else's errand?"

At first, Vasylyna equivocated, but finally she confessed.

"My stepmother sent me to steal fire from you," Vasylyna admitted, "but I would rather earn an ember than steal one. What can I do to get some fire to take back to my stepmother?"

"Fire is precious, and an ember comes dear. The fire that comes from my pich is no ordinary fire, girl. It is a powerful magical tool, not to be given out except to the most worthy."

Baba Yaga looked her up and down.

"And it remains to be seen if you are worthy. However, I might have a few little chores around the home that you can do for me."

Baba Yaga snatched up Vasylyna's hand in her own bony one with the scraggly nails, brought her face down to look closely at the girl's palms, and smiled.

"Hmph. I can see in your hands that you are hard-working, but let's see if you are clever as well."

She went back to holding her cup and inscrutably drinking her brew.

*"You want some fire to take home, yes? But, my pich is so very hungry. And you might have noticed that my fence post is missing one lantern, too. So, how about we play a little game. I will give you a few small tasks to do. If you complete them, you will get a reward. However, if you fail, I will feed you to the pich and fill in that last lantern on my fence."*

*There was no way Vasylyna could return to her stepmother without an ember, so, as intimidating as Baba Yaga was, what choice did she have except to agree to Baba Yaga's game?*

## Baba Yaga Shares the Wisdom of the Pich

Ah, the pich—my pich. You might be wondering if the old woman is cracked, being so adoring of her oven. Has she lost her mind? Not even close! Everyone who lives here in the mountains adores their woodstove. We have a saying here, "the pich is our own dear mother," and it's true. Without the warmth the oven gives us, we would be as helpless as babies left in the forest on a winter's night.

Remember the pich from back when Vasylyna was taking care of her mother, and her encounter with the Domovyk? Back in the old days, everyone had a big clay oven that took up half the space in their khata. The pich is more than just a place to cook our food. It's also where we do our laundry; it's the place where we can dry our grain, herbs, and mushrooms; and it provides warmth for us all winter long.

The nook above the stove also provides a safe, warm sleeping spot for our youngest ones and our oldest ones. It's the place where a woman gives birth when it's cold and where we place the newborn babies after they are born. We put our loved ones who are sick on it so that they will get well.[118] We even have a small cubbyhole beneath the stove where our chickens can snuggle up during the winter so they don't freeze. The pich is also the place where our house spirit lives: the Domovyk, the lord of the house, the guardian of the home, and the embodiment of our ancestors.[119] So, you can see why the pich is practically a full-fledged character in this story.

---

118. Johns, *Baba Yaga*.

119. Musya Glants and Juri Toomre, *Food in Russian History and Culture* (Bloomington, IN: Indiana University Press, 2014).

Whenever a baby was born too soon—"premature," is that what you call it?—we knew they came out of the oven of their mother's belly before they were ready, and so, to strengthen them, we would gently wrap them up in a thin layer of dough, put them on the bread shovel, and dip them into a slightly warm oven to "bake" them. Symbolically, we would kill off the weakness and rebirth them as a strong and healthy child. Ah, so maybe now you understand why you've heard stories of me putting small children into the oven. They were unformed, incomplete, and they needed to be reborn whole and powerful.[120]

We treat our pich with a deep reverence, not just for what it provides to us, but because we honor the element of fire. And why shouldn't we? Fire is transforming. Fire is passion. Fire is power. Anything put into the fire is an offering to our departed loved ones, to the Domovyk, and to the spirit of fire itself, so we never throw trash in the fire. Instead, when we sit down to eat, we give the pich the first and best bite. At harvest, we give a sheaf of grain to the fire to feed it and thank it for its hard work. We even put a pot of water in there overnight for the fire to drink and bathe in, for it is known that the spirit of the fire washes itself at night while everyone is asleep.

We never swear when we are lighting a fire or working with the pich for fear of offending these spirits. The stove also protects the house from arguments. Whenever someone says a harsh word, we remind them, "The pich is in the house!" Yes, we really do![121] And we respectfully ask for its help: "Lord of the fire, burn for us, not so that we can smoke tobacco but so that we can cook our porridge." Although, truth be told, I use the pich to light my pipe more than I cook porridge, but then again, my pich indulges me.

When we move, we carry a bit of the fire and the Domovyk from the old home to the new one. We can carry the Domovyk on a baking shovel; at the same time, the fire is raked out of the old stove into a pot, and we carefully transfer them both to their new oven, saying, "Welcome, grandfather, to your new home!" Our home fire is so precious that we avoid lending it to anyone else. To lend fire might mean giving away your good fortune. So, you can see why I need my visitors to prove themselves before I part with a bit of my own sacred fire.

120. Andrey Toporkov, "'Perepekaniye' Detey v Ritualakh i Skazkakh Vostochnykh Slavyan," *Fol'klor i Etnograficheskaya Deystvitel'nost'* (1992): 114–118.

121. Hubbs, *Mother Russia*.

## Madame Pamita Teaches the Magic of the Pich

I love a fire. Give me a campfire, a chiminea, a bonfire, and I am here for it. I am fortunate to have an old fireplace in my house, the house where I grew up. My mother loved a fire, too, and even though we lived in Southern California, when the nights got a little chilly, we would get some logs together and enjoy the crackle and warmth of the fire. Although nowadays I go to the firewood stand to buy a half cord of firewood to burn over the winter, my mother didn't believe in paying for wood. Whenever she saw trees being cut down, she would pull over, and together we would hoist the logs into the back of the station wagon and haul them back home. She would let them season for a few months, and then we would burn them over the winter. Burning logs in the fireplace of my childhood always brings back so many beautiful memories of my mom and her magic.

We used to do so many little witchy things at the fire. We would ask questions about the future and then listen to what the crackle and pops of the burning wood had to tell us. Our method would be to ask a yes/no question, and if the fire was quiet, it meant no, but if the fire made noises, it meant yes. The louder and more frequent the pops, the bigger the affirmative.

These days, I do much of my magic at the hearth. On the mantle above it, I have an ancestor altar filled with meaningful symbols of my mixed Ukrainian, English, and Scots heritage. I have a statuette of a Domovyk up there and even some little figurines of Baba Yaga. As I meditate on the flames, I imagine my mother, my father, and all my ancestors and spirits gathering together around the crackling blaze, enjoying its warming glow in companionable silence.

## The Pich Today

Today, many people heat their homes with gas or electric heat, but in Ukraine, about a third of the population, mostly those in the countryside, still heat their homes with coal or wood.[122] The pich remains the powerful center of life-sustaining heat throughout the bitterly cold winters, and many of the beliefs honoring fire still remain.

In traditional homes, there is still a practice of embellishing the pich by whitewashing and painting it with beautiful symbols. Those pretty adornments of fruit, birds,

---

122. "Cold at Home," EnAct, accessed May 14, 2021, http://www.coldathome.today/cold-at-home.

flowers, symbols, and shapes are actually powerful talismans meant to bring in blessings and distract and confuse evil, should it enter the home through the portal of the pich.

## The Home of the Ancestors

From around 3000 BCE, the ancient Trypillians practiced cremation, and so all fires were viewed as an entrance to the spirit world. In the generations that followed, the stove itself became an altar and the most important place in the home, a portal to this world of spirit.[123] Later, some of the spiritual responsibilities of the pich transferred over to the pokut', but the woodstove still plays an equally important role as a place where our ancestors reside.

Even today, fire symbolizes lineage and family. Because of this, there is a belief that you should never spit into a fire, for doing so would be "spitting in the eyes of one's dead ancestors." Not only that, but the ancestors might teach you to have better manners by giving you blisters on your lips and tongue. You should also never poke at the fire to break up embers in the pich, for to do so might cause your ancestors to fall into oblivion.

## The Living Fire

In times past, the pich was burning day and night, all year long. It was the belief that as long as there was a fire in the stove, poverty would not be able to enter the house. So, the old ones never let the fire in their pich go out completely, except for once a year. Like any hardworking member of the family, it was thought to need a rest and reset. At the winter solstice or Christmas Eve, the family would cook kutya for their beloved ancestor spirits, and then for the next twenty-four hours, they would let the fire die out naturally. The following day, they would light a new "living fire" in the oven with twelve sacred logs, representing the lunations of the coming year.

What's living fire? Well, fire itself is sacred, but living fire, that is the most powerfully magical of fires. In the oldest times, with no lighters or matches, people had to work hard to get a fire started by rubbing two sticks together. At one time, even whole villages would gather to create a bonfire through the friction of rotating a tree trunk. These fires, large or small, were called living fire. The necessary skill of creating fire

---

123. Andriy Dorosh, "The Phenomenon of a Ukrainian Pich (Stove)," Dorosh Heritage Tours, February 11, 2019, https://doroshheritagetours.com/the-phenomenon-of-a-ukrainian-pich-stove/.

through friction was passed down from parent to child, and because living fire was so hard-earned, the family had a sworn and sacred duty to protect it.

## Working with Living Fire

Living fire can be a powerful tool for a magical practitioner. It heals, it purifies, it transforms. Witches were closely identified with the pich. The stove symbolized a liminal place of transition from the ordinary world to the world of spirit, so it was thought that witches used the oven's chimney to fly to their gatherings. The tools near the fire—the poker, the fork to pull out the heavy pots, and, of course, the fire broom—were all seen as objects for a witch to fly on. In a more mundane sense, the pich was also where a wise woman would prepare her healing potions.

If you would like to use the power of living fire and have access to a fireplace, a woodstove, an outdoor chiminea, or a firepit, you can perform these rites. While it might not be practical or safe to leave the fire burning for an entire year as the old ones did, you can still create living fire for your most special spells. There are so many beautiful rituals that can be performed with the magic of fire.

## Making Living Fire

To create your own living fire, you will need a fire-starting method, and there are several to choose from. A hand drill is a thin, straight stick spun between your palms to "drill" into a wooden board to create friction and heat. A bow drill is similar to a hand drill, but it has the added feature of a bow with a cord moving the spindle back and forth instead of your hands. A pump drill is a variation of a bow drill but with a coiled rope and a cross-member of wood that is pushed down to spin the spindle. A fire striker is made up of two pieces of iron pyrite or marcasite struck together to create sparks over tinder. Quartz, jasper, agate, or flint can also be struck against high-carbon, nonalloyed, hardened steel to create sparks. A solar fire-starter concentrates sunlight with a lens, such as a magnifying glass or a concave mirror, to start a flame.

Choose one of these methods to ritually start a fire in a fireplace or woodstove, to light a candle or incense for special spiritual work, or to burn paper for a spell. Use the cleansing power of living fire to banish, cleanse, or empower your workings.

### Fire Spells to Relieve Pain

Fire can be used to relieve emotional or physical pain. If you would like to restore well-being, you may sit with the spirit of fire and ask it to remove your pain with a request such as this one:

> Dear Lord of the Fire,
> be gentle and kind to me.
> Burn away all my aches and pains, tears and worries.

If you have a certain part of the body that is suffering from illness, you can create a small clay model of that body part and throw it into the fire to support healing and relief. Another method is to wipe the affected area with a piece of clothing from that part of the body and then throw that piece of clothing into the fire to destroy the illness.[124]

### Consecrating Ritual Items with Fire

Like all the elements, fire is seen as a purifier. Ritual items that are firesafe, such as those made of stone or metal, can be consecrated with fire by passing them through the flame. Use tongs and quickly pass the item through the fire, envisioning all unwanted energies being burned away and the fire blessing it with power, energy, and life. Be sure to place the item on a heatproof surface and let it cool before touching it.

### Working with Ashes

Even the ashes of a living fire can be used for magic. Ashes can be mixed with water to create liquid fire and can be used as a blend of fire and water in magic. Ashes can be applied to ritual objects that can't take direct contact with fire or to body parts that need the blessing of living fire.

### Obkuryuvannya or Censing

Dried herbs can be lit with fire and used for obkuryuvannya or censing a person or a space for protection, healing, or cleansing. The smoke of any wood fire is useful for

---

124. P. Y. Len'o, "Vykorystannya Vohnyu u Narodniy Medytsyni Ukrayintsiv Zakarpattya (Na Osnovi Suchasnykh Pol'ovykh Materialiv)," *Naukovyy Visnyk Uzhhorods'koho Universytetu: Seriya: Istoriya*, no. 2 (2014): 123–126.

casting out general negativity, but different herbs can be used for particular spiritual situations.

If the dried herbs are cut, they can be placed in a small dish, cup, or shell where they can gradually smolder. If the dried herbs are in a bundle, they can be held in your hand and either lit with a match or lighter or lit from the living fire of the fireplace or woodstove. If you are cleansing the home, smoke from the herbs should be wafted throughout each room. If the smoke is to be directed to a specific location, such as an object or body part, then it should be fanned toward that location.

If you are censing another person, you should hold the smoldering herbs and let the individual bring the smoke to themselves by scooping their palms, as if carrying water and pouring it on themselves. They can follow the ritual formula of first directing the smoke to their heart, then their head, then their feet.

Smoke was used to drive out fear, as well as negative spirits and disease. If an animal or bird frightened someone, they would use a tuft of fur or a feather from the animal or bird, light it, and fumigate the person to remove their fear. If a loved one had a fever, the healer would take a snip of the sick person's hair and burn it over them to assist in banishing the illness.[125]

## The Living Fire Portal

The living fire of the pich is essential to Baba Yaga's magic. What appears in fairy tales as simply a place for an ogress to cook some unwary children actually contains hidden messages about who Baba Yaga originally was. With the understanding of the fire being the representation of the ancestors and the pich being the portal to the otherworld, we can see that she was there as the gatekeeper to the land of the spirits.

When you have had the experience of making fire from nothing more than the friction of wood, you, too, will feel how precious and magical fire can be. Begin to appreciate the magic of the flame and view fire as a portal to the world of spirit. Perform divinations with fire, do your spells of banishing and healing, and begin to deeply connect with the magic of Baba Yaga's pich.

---

125. Len'o, "Vykorystannya Vohnyu u Narodniy Medytsyni Ukrayintsiv Zakarpattya (Na Osnovi Suchasnykh Pol'ovykh Materialiv)," 123–126.

<br />
<br />

<br />

# CHAPTER 12

# VERETENO: THE SPINDLE

Baba Yaga picked up a basket and began bustling around the khata, packing up this and that. As she did, she gave some directions to Vasylyna.

"Do you know how to spin hemp fibers?" she asked.

"I do," said Vasylyna.

"Good. I must attend to my business out in the world today. While I'm gone, I want you to spin my hemp into thread. Can you do that?"

"I can try," said Vasylyna.

At that, Baba Yaga picked up a wooden spindle and a distaff and handed them to Vasylyna. She then pushed aside the big wooden chest, and there was a little door Vasylyna hadn't noticed before. Baba Yaga unlatched it and pushed it open to reveal an entire room filled floor-to-ceiling with bundles of hemp fibers.

"I will return at sundown," she said matter-of-factly. "See to it that all of this fiber is spun into fine thread by the time I come back." And with that, Baba Yaga left the khata, locked the door behind her, and left Vasylyna alone with the room full of hemp. The poor girl took one look at the mountain of unspun fibers and felt her heart sink to the floor. Then, she felt a rustle in her pocket as the motanka pulled at her sleeve. She brought out the doll and wiped the tears welling up in her eyes and said, "Dolly of mine, what do I do? If I spun all day every day for a year, I couldn't spin all of this hemp."

<br />

<br />

<br />

<br />

<br />

<br />

<br />

<br />

<br />

<br />

<br />

<br />

<br />

<br />

<br />

<br />

<br />

<br />

<br />

<br />

<br />

<br />

<br />

<br />

<br />

<br />

<br />

<br />

<br />

<br />

<br />

<br />

<br />

<br />

<br />

<br />

<br />

<br />

<br />

<br />

<br />

<br />

<br />

<br />

<br />

<br />

<br />

<br />

<br />

<br />

<br />

<br />

<br />

<br />

<br />

<br />

<br />

<br />

<br />

<br />

<br />

<br />

<br />

<br />

<br />

<br />

<br />

<br />

<br />

<br />

<br />

<br />

<br />

<br />

<br />

<br />

<br />

<br />

<br />

<br />

<br />

<br />

<br />

<br />

<br />

<br />

<br />

<br />

<br />

<br />

<br />

<br />

<br />

<br />

<br />

<br />

<br />

<br />

<br />

<br />

<br />

<br />

<br />

<br />

<br />

<br />

<br />

<br />

<br />

<br />

<br />

<br />

<br />

<br />

<br />

<br />

<br />

<br />

<br />

<br />

<br />

<br />

<br />

<br />

<br />

<br />

<br />

<br />

<br />

<br />

<br />

<br />

<br />

<br />

<br />

<br />

<br />

<br />

<br />

<br />

<br />

<br />

<br />

<br />

<br />

<br />

<br />

<br />

<br />

<br />

<br />

<br />

<br />

<br />

<br />

<br />

<br />

<br />

<br />

<br />

<br />

<br />

<br />

<br />

<br />

<br />

<br />

<br />

<br />

<br />

<br />

<br />

<br />

<br />

<br />

<br />

<br />

<br />

<br />

<br />

<br />

<br />

<br />

<br />

<br />

<br />

<br />

<br />

<br />

<br />

<br />

<br />

<br />

<br />

<br />

<br />

<br />

<br />

<br />

<br />

<br />

<br />

<br />

<br />

<br />

<br />

<br />

<br />

<br />

<br />

<br />

<br />

<br />

<br />

<br />

<br />

<br />

<br />

<br />

<br />

<br />

<br />

<br />

<br />

<br />

<br />

<br />

<br />

<br />

<br />

<br />

<br />

*But the doll replied,*

*Have courage, Vasylyna dear.*
*The help you need is standing near.*
*While it's true two hands could never spin it,*
*four hands can finish in a minute.*

*The doll picked up the distaff and, with her tiny, rolled hands, began pulling out the fibers for Vasylyna. Vasylyna took the fibers from the motanka and began twisting them as she spun the spindle. Vasylyna was amazed at how fast the doll could work, but as fast as the doll was, Vasylyna found that her own hands could spin just as fast. The two of them pulled and spun and wound the fine threads into skeins and stacked them up one by one as they finished them. As the day went on, they found a rhythm to their work that allowed them to spin even faster, and together they wound up the last skein just as the sun was beginning to set.*

## Baba Yaga Shares the Wisdom of the Vereteno

Come here, come here. I want you to see what I have behind this little door. I know my hut appears to be just a single room, but I am not bound by your earthly problems of physical space. Far from it! Come let me unlock this door and hold up this lamp so you can see what I keep inside. Do you see what it is? Ha! I see the disappointment in your face. It is hemp. A room full of hemp fibers. Hmph! Hemp that must be spun into threads.

You don't know how to spin? Oh, my child! Spinning is magic itself! The threads we spin in the physical world imitate the invisible divine threads that stretch between the worlds. They mimic the mysterious universal attraction that connects all things. The threads that tie the stones, the plants, the trees, the animals, and the people together. They represent the thin invisible thread that is the oldest symbol of human life and destiny.

Let's begin at the beginning, then. Let me hand you this spindle. Yes, a spindle. Not a spinning wheel. No, that invention came much, much later, merely a few hundred years ago. To tread the path of the spinner, you need to know spinning as it was done

for the thousands and thousands of years before that, with a simple weighted stick and a distaff holding the unspun fibers.

It's so different nowadays. Back even a few generations, every woman knew how to spin. All our people had a spindle in the home, often more than one. Women grew their own flax and hemp, sheared their sheep, and spun their yarn. Each item of clothing, each blanket, each rushnyk was made from cloth that was woven from threads that were spun in the home. So, you can see how important it was to possess this skill. Each thread, spun with love and intention, became part of the magical garment that protected and blessed our loved ones.

I have a close relationship with spinning.[126] Some even say that my khatynka stands on a spindle, that the hen's legs were simply supports for the four corners and that the center of the house was fixed on a spindle rotating around and around.[127] Others say that I spin the thread of life from the bones and entrails of the dead.[128] Though you might not see a spindle under my house or me trying to make thread out of intestines, I won't say they're completely wrong.

When you begin to create yarns yourself, you will understand the magic of spinning: the transformation that occurs as fluffy fibers tighten into useful thread, the spiral of the yarn mimicking the strands of DNA. It's not for nothing that in Greece they depicted the Fates as spinners, that the Rusalky are spinners and weavers,[129] that Paraskeva P'yatnytsya (Saint Friday) was a spinner, and that the old mother goddess Mokosh spins one's life destiny.[130] Spinning is the act of creation itself.

And don't forget that the *pavuk*, the spider, is one of our ancient sacred weavers, the collector of the threads of life. Let me remind you that you should never kill a spider, because if you do, there will be no happiness in your home. A spider coming down from the ceiling carries good news. In our old magic, we used the symbol of the spider and asked her for help when we were doing spells to link or even bind something—to create a connection from nothing.

---

126. Matossian, "In the Beginning, God Was a Woman," 325–343.

127. Johns, *Baba Yaga.*

128. Hubbs, *Mother Russia.*

129. Gray, *Mythology of All Races Volume 3.*

130. Patricia Monaghan, *Encyclopedia of Goddesses and Heroines* (United States: New World Library, 2014).

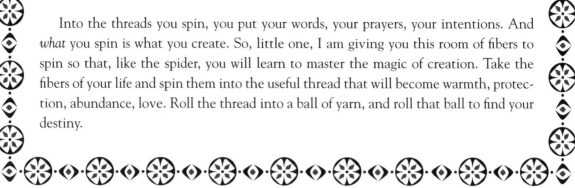

Into the threads you spin, you put your words, your prayers, your intentions. And *what* you spin is what you create. So, little one, I am giving you this room of fibers to spin so that, like the spider, you will learn to master the magic of creation. Take the fibers of your life and spin them into the useful thread that will become warmth, protection, abundance, love. Roll the thread into a ball of yarn, and roll that ball to find your destiny.

## Madame Pamita Teaches the Magic of the Vereteno

It wasn't until I began my devotion to Baba Yaga that I learned to spin. For many years, I had watched as good friends created beautiful handspun yarns and used them for knitting, and I always admired the way that with a gentle spin of the wrist and a twist of their fingers, they could instantly transform tufts of wool into beautiful yarn, and those yarns into cozy hats and sweaters and scarves.

I never thought I could learn this skill. However, I knew that if I wanted to deeply understand Baba Yaga's magic, I would have to begin spinning myself. I was overwhelmed. Where would I begin? I texted my friend Queta and asked her advice on what kind of spindle to get and what fibers to use. I video chatted with my friend Cloven so he could watch me work with my drop spindle and teach me how to improve my technique. I practiced on my own, slowly twisting the fibers as I chatted with friends on video conferencing calls. My first attempts ended with a clumsy but charming roll of lumpy yarn that varied wildly between thick and thin. But I kept at it, and my fingers began to get used to giving just the right tug on the fibers and the perfect twist of the spindle. Eventually, I was able to make a yarn that was of an even thickness. It wasn't machine-made perfection, but it was something I was proud of enough to place as an offering on my Baba Yaga altar. As I placed that ball of yarn next to her figurine, I realized that when Baba Yaga challenges us to a seemingly impossible task, it's because she knew all along that we were capable of doing it.

## The Vereteno Today

While using a spindle to spin thread might seem like technology from the Middle Ages, drop spindles were a normal tool in Slavic households even just a couple of generations back. It's still quite easy to find rustic antique spindles that look like beautifully turned wooden wands or purchase polished replicas that can be used for spinning fine threads.

Spindles show up over and over again in Ukrainian myths and fairy tales and are ingrained in the oldest practices of magic, a fact that is not surprising, considering that spinning itself has been practiced for at least twenty thousand years. In story after story, we see Baba Yaga associated with the tools of the spinner as well.[131]

After decades of being a nearly lost art, hand spinning has made a resurgence in recent years. While most of us will never hand spin and weave our clothing from scratch, we can learn the art of spinning to create yarns that can be used quite powerfully in magic. We can use them to knit special clothing imbued with intent, create charms from knotted threads, or simply feel the power that we hold as creators of our destiny.

## Vereteno Magic

If you've never spun before, making yarn from fiber is an excellent way to show devotion to Baba Yaga: to meet with her, to understand her ways, and perhaps even to earn her begrudging approval. To begin with, any spindle that you intend to use in magic should first be used for spinning. Ritual spinning can be done to affect a person's fate, either cursing or blessing them, depending on the intent of the spinner. An adept vidma can use a spindle to correct and untwist someone's bad fate, foretell the future, cure illness, remove hexes, attract love, and even change the weather.

You can purchase a spindle to begin this work, but if you are fortunate enough to inherit one from a relative or friend who put their own positive energy into it, then you have a magical tool, indeed. A spindle is both a wand and a scepter, a symbol of the power of the vidma that allows her to weave the fabric of the universe. Like the pavuk, the spider, the person who spins sits at the center of the universe. Like Baba Yaga, spinners can create and destroy.

---

131. Małgorzata Oleszkiewicz-Peralba, *Fierce Feminine Divinities of Eurasia and Latin America: Baba Yaga, Kālī, Pombagira, and Santa Muerte* (New York: Palgrave Macmillan, 2015).

When we touch a spindle, our collective unconscious remembers. The rhythmic, repetitive motion can become a meditation. If we turn our thoughts and intentions toward the beautiful life we wish to spin for ourselves and our loved ones, we can imbue the yarn or thread with that powerful transformative energy.

## Choosing a Vereteno

If you are just learning to spin for the first time, you may want to start with a top whorl drop spindle, as you will gain skill and confidence in your spinning faster working with this type of spindle. As you progress, you may want to graduate to the type of spindle Baba Yaga uses: the elegant wandlike drop spindle. There are many different kinds of spindles unique to each culture, and finding the type that your ancestors used is a special way to connect to your family line.

When purchasing a spindle, you can choose a specific kind of wood that will support your magical work. Refer to appendix I for a list of magical woods used for making spindles.

To begin spinning, you should start with an easy-to-spin long-staple fiber. Wool roving, hemp sliver, Acala cotton, and Pima cotton fibers are all suitable for hand spinning. When spinning yarn for a magical result, you can choose fiber dyed a color that supports your intention. See appendix II for a list of colors and their magical correspondences.

## Beginning with Your Vereteno

Before you begin spinning, take a moment to close your eyes, center yourself, and envision the magic you want to create. Thank the spirit of the fiber and the spindle for their assistance in your magic before you start and after you finish for the day.

If you start a tuft of fibers, spin it until it is complete. Leaving unspun fibers can invite mischievous spirits to spin your destiny for you. Always leave your spindle wrapped with some spun threads. There is a saying, "A spindle should never go hungry." If you are finished spinning and putting your spindle away, you can break off a length of yarn and wrap it around the spindle nine times to keep it "fed."

## Spinning Divination

Practice spinning nonmagical threads before committing to spinning your magical ones. When spinning these magical threads, you can do a divination for yourself by paying attention to what your thread tells you about your immediate future:

- **Smooth thread with no knots:** Smooth, peaceful, and uneventful times.
- **Tangled and knotted thread:** Eventful times and experience gained.
- **Even thread:** Riches and good health.
- **Uneven thread:** Care should be taken to improve finances and health.

## Making Nauzy with Spun Yarn

Once you've spun some yarn, you are now ready to turn it into a magical charm by creating *nauzy*. Nauzy are knots tied in yarn to create a very old-style amulet. Magical workers for millennia have crafted talismans by simply taking a piece of yarn, string, or thread and uttering incantations over it as they knotted it, symbolically locking in their spells.[132] These knots were used in binding magic, to protect the wearer from spiritual harm, and to maintain health, wealth, happiness, and success. Nauzy were worn on the wrist, arm, leg, waist, head, or chest. The circles formed around the body with these magical talismans symbolized eternity, connection with the divine, and unity with the ancestors. They were also empowered by the energy of the sun, whose symbol is also a circle. In times past, nauzy were also signs of initiation, and so they could be bestowed to signify an achievement or a new status.[133]

Wool was typically used to make nauzy, but any natural fiber you spin is suitable for your own knot magic. Complex woven decorative knots can be created, but even a single thread tied with simple knots from fiber that you have spun can be a very potent charm. If you would like to bring in more than one intention, you can weave or braid threads of different colors together, following your own intuition or using the color magic guide in appendix II.

---

132. Ryan, *The Bathhouse at Midnight*.

133. V. P. Kotsur, *Slovnyk Symvoliv Kul'tury Ukraïny* (Kyiv, Ukraine: Milenium, 2005).

With any knotted charm, if the thread breaks, there's no need to panic. It means that you were protected against a great misfortune. Burn the old amulet, thank it for protecting you, bury the ashes or scatter them in the wind, and make a new one.[134]

### Creating Nauzy

Ideally, nauzy should be made by yourself to ensure that your positivity and focus go into the talisman. As with all magic, when making nauzy, you should be sure your feelings are calm and your thoughts are empowered and positive. Before starting to make nauzy, focus on your goals. You may also want to create them at a time that aligns with your intentions. Create attracting nauzy during a waxing moon phase and binding or banishing nauzy during a waning moon phase.

### Wearing Nauzy

Nauzy can be worn, carried in a pocket or purse, or placed somewhere in the home or workplace. If worn, they can be wrapped around your wrist, ankle, neck, or waist. They can be worn on your left side for protection and your right side for attraction. Your knot charms are for you alone. Avoid bragging about or showing off your nauzy to others or explaining what the talismans are for. When you tie your nauzy on your body, finish by saying, "It is to be as I wish!" or, "My word is strong!"

### Simple Red Thread Spell for Protection

On the full moon, light a white beeswax candle. Take red wool that you have spun and wind it into a ball, repeating the following incantation:

> *A red ball of yarn was rolling across the field, across the woods.*
> *It stopped at my doorstep to make my path easy.*
> *Red ball of yarn, take bad luck away from me,*
> *and protect me from any misfortune.*

Once the ball has been wound completely, tear off a piece of yarn long enough to tie around your wrist, saying the following incantation:

---

134. Bosyy, "Svyashchenne Remeslo Mokoshi," 39–40.

*Ball of yarn, give me a piece of thread,*
*to protect me and help me in all matters.*

Take the enchanted thread and tie it to the wrist of your left hand with three knots. With each knot, speak your wishes. Wear the thread without removing it. If it breaks, you can bury or burn it and make a new one with the same process.

### *Nauzy to Attract Money and Luck*

Nauzy can be created to bring in continuous prosperity. Make seven knots in a simple red wool thread and tie it to your right wrist to attract money and luck into your life. When the thread breaks, ritually dispose of it and craft a new one.

### *Nauzy to Achieve an Immediate Goal*

To achieve one goal, take a red thread, yarn, string, or ribbon and tie three knots in it. Whisper an affirmation for that goal and repeat it as you tie each knot. Carry this amulet with you for three days and then burn the nauzy and scatter the ashes in the wind.

### *Nauzy for Three Wishes*

Create a talisman for three wishes. Choose yarn of a color that aligns with your intentions and loosely tie one knot for each of your three wishes. Carry this talisman or place it on your home altar. As each wish comes true, untie the corresponding knot. When all the wishes have come true and you have untied all three knots, you can burn the yarn and scatter the ashes in the wind to seal your spell.

### *Nauzy for Power*

If you'd like to attract more respect and feel more self-empowerment, take a long piece of red yarn. Wrap it around your right wrist three times and tie the ends in three knots. When it breaks, you may burn it or bury it and make a new one.

## Other Forms of Vereteno Magic

Spindles can be used in other kinds of magical workings outside of spinning. Whether you are using your spindle for spell casting or spinning magical thread, you should never let another person use your spindle. At best, letting someone touch your magical *vereteno* will weaken your connection to it; at worst, they can unintentionally or even intentionally infuse it with negative energy. If that happens, it will need to be spiritually cleansed. There are a few methods of purifying your vereteno.

### Cleansing Your Vereteno

If your vereteno does need a deep cleanse or a freshening up before you work with it for the first time, you can purify your spindle by fumigating it with the smoke of cleansing herbs (obkuryuvannya), washing it in blessed water, or putting it on a dish of Thursday salt overnight. You can also cleanse your spindle by passing it through a candle flame (as long as you're careful not to scorch it). After it is purified, it should rest for nine days, ideally on your home altar or pokut', and then it will be recharged and ready for use.

### Baba Yaga's Special Vereteno Blessing

Spindles and staffs have long had a connection with snakes, as has Baba Yaga herself. If you'd like to consecrate your spindle and increase its magical power for spell casting, you can do so by gently stroking a snake with the sides of the vereteno. The ideal is to please the snake, not harm it, so never poke at it with the tip of your spindle or harm it in any way. If the snake responds positively to the loving touch of the wood, it is a good sign that it is sharing its power and blessing your ritual tool.

### Vereteno Spell for Invoking or Banishing

You can use a spindle for simple invoking and banishing. While you can use any type of spindle for most of the workings, this method seems to flow best with the wandlike drop spindle.

Set the heaviest part of the spindle on a table and spin it as you would a top, keeping your fingers in constant contact with the top end of the spindle. Spin clockwise as you whisper incantations or affirmations for things you want. Spin counterclockwise as you speak incantations or commands for things you are banishing.

### Casting a Circle of Protection

If you are doing divinatory work or working in liminal areas, you may want to create a circle of protection around yourself before you begin. A vereteno can be used as a wand for creating this circle. Wands are used to focus energy, so using your beloved spindle can be an exceptionally powerful way to create your circle of safety.

Grasp the spindle at the large end and use the point of the slender end for creating circles of protection before doing your magical work. Drag the point clockwise on the floor around you to delineate your circle or point the spindle straight out at arm's length and spin slowly in a clockwise direction to create a spiritual boundary.[135]

### Using a Vereteno for Healing

A blessed spindle is so powerful that it can be used on its own to banish illness. If you want to help heal someone, you can seat them in front of you, stand behind them, and move a spindle around their body in a counterclockwise direction as you whisper incantations to remove their sickness.[136]

### Vereteno Weather Spell

Past generations were dependent on the weather for good crops, and so a spindle spell could be done to bring nourishing rains. Nowadays, with global warming, we may want to invite rain to prevent devastating droughts. By placing a spindle in a glass of water, you can perform an old ritual to encourage gentle showers to water the land and replenish Mother Earth.

### Vereteno Pendulum

A pendulum is a tool for divination or contacting the spirit realm. Any weighted object hanging on a thread or a chain that can swing loosely can be used as a device to get yes/no answers to your questions. Hang your spindle by a thread that you have spun and allow it to swing back and forth freely. Ask your vereteno pendulum to show you *yes* and note the direction it is swinging. It could be circling in a certain direction or swinging back and forth. Do the same for *no* and note the different direction it is moving. Once you have established what *yes* and *no* are, you can invite your helpful spirits to give you answers to your questions.

---

135. Bosyy, "Svyashchenne Remeslo Mokoshi," 39–40.

136. H. I. Hrymashevych and Yuliya Vasyl'chuk, "Povir'ya, Zvychayi Ta Obryady, Pov'yazani z Tkatstvom," *Student·S'ki Linhvistychni Studiyi* 2 (2011): 39–46.

*Directional Divination*

If you want to do some directional divination, ask questions such as these: "Where should I travel?" "Where will my future lover be coming from?" You can lay the spindle on its side on a table and spin it, much like playing spin the bottle. Whatever direction the slender end stops in is the direction you should be looking toward for your answer.

## The Legacy of the Vereteno

Spindles seem like archaic throwbacks to the past, something completely unnecessary in our modern world where you can purchase clothing straight off the rack, but the vereteno is more than a tool for spinning fiber. It connects us to the spirit realm: to our ancestors, to the ancient mother goddess Mokosh, to the playful Rusalky, and to the deep mystery of Baba Yaga herself. By incorporating this old technology in our modern life, we can cultivate mindfulness, create ancient charms, and build a relationship with a powerful magical tool.

# Chapter 13

# Krashanky I Pysanky: The Decorated Eggs

*J*ust as Vasylyna and the doll were winding the last skein, they heard a rustling at the lock. Quick as a weasel popping back into a burrow, the motanka jumped back into Vasylyna's pocket and out of sight. Vasylyna froze where she stood with the last skein in her hands.

Baba Yaga flung open the door and stood holding her heavy basket with both hands as a few stray black feathers fell from her shoulders.

"Oho!" she cackled triumphantly.

But then she raised her eyebrows in surprise when she saw that not even the tiniest piece of fiber remained and that all the hemp had been spun and stacked in neat skeins against the wall.

She set the basket on the table, stumped over to where Vasylyna was standing, and took the skein of hemp from her hands. She stretched out a thread to inspect it, pulling it tight, holding it up to the light, running her fingernail over it and bringing it up close to her eye, like a jeweler inspecting a rare piece of amber.

"Hmph," Baba Yaga said finally as she examined the smoothness of the thread. "Not bad, girl. Not bad at all."

She went over to the skeins and one by one picked them up and handled them with begrudging approval. Finally, she set the last one down and stamped her way over to the pich, patted its warm sides, and sighed. "Ah, my dear pich, I'm sorry to tell you that today is not your day."

She turned back to Vasylyna. "Well, girl, you accomplished one task and you did it passably well. So, for tonight, my pich goes hungry, but you and I shall eat."

*And with that, Baba Yaga reached into her basket and began to pull out eggs one by one, small and large, but all a glossy, rich red color. She picked up one, rapped it against the table, and began to peel the shell off its hard-boiled interior. She carefully placed the shells in a little bowl and began to eat the egg as Vasylyna watched.*

*"Go ahead, girl. Eat!" said Baba Yaga.*

*Vasylyna sat at the table and picked up one of the boiled eggs, feeling the warmth of it in her hand. Like Baba Yaga, she placed the shells in the bowl as she peeled hers, and when she bit into the soft yellow yolk, she felt a surge of power within her, as bright and glowing as a daz-zling summer sun. With each mouthful, she savored the gentle heat of the egg as it slid down into her belly.*

*When they had both had their fill, Baba Yaga scooped the remaining eggshells that had fallen onto the table into the bowl, placed the remaining eggs on top, put on her warm, shaggy coat, and picked up the bowl and her walking stick. She stopped and stared at Vasylyna.*

*"Put on your shawl, girl. We don't have all night."*

*Vasylyna wrapped herself up and followed Baba Yaga out the door.*

*They went out the bone gate, past the bone fence, and down a path through the forest. As they stepped out under the bright moonlight, they made their way down the path until they came to a small clearing with a circle of aspen trees. Vasylyna stood shyly at the edge of the grove while Baba Yaga went in and laid the eggs at the base of the trees, whispering something under her breath as she did.*

*She quickly turned and continued walking, and Vasylyna scampered to keep up, following her through the grove and down the path until they reached a small stream.*

*Here, Baba Yaga knelt by the stream and whispered to the eggshells as she placed a handful in the water. Vasylyna watched as they dipped below the surface and tumbled into the flowing water like tiny pieces of rare red coral glistening in the moonlight.*

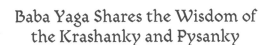

## Baba Yaga Shares the Wisdom of
## the Krashanky and Pysanky

When it comes to magic, *yaytsya*, our eggs, are as precious as jewels. And like jewels, we like to polish them, embellish them, and decorate them to make them even more magical. Yes, we can use them for our spells naked as they are, but why not dress them up in something special? We have done this for millennia, with krashanky that are dyed a single color and eaten, and also with pysanky, which are made as amulets and decorated with intricate designs—talismanic symbols for health, wealth, love, luck, and protection.

Don't ask, "Which came first, the chicken or the egg?" It's a dead giveaway that you're a ninny. Of course the egg came first. Before there were any eggs, before there was anything at all, there was the night sky and the stars. And from the stars, the World Egg was born. Each of the seventy-seven Sister Stars took turns brooding over the egg, nestling against it, turning it over, gently warming it until, one day, it hatched. And from the egg was born the sun, the moon, the earth, the World Tree, the plants, the animals, the spirits, and the first people.

The spirits were allowed to live where they wished. Some chose the upper world of teaching and guidance. Some chose the middle world to live close to the humans with their chaos and creativity. And some chose to live in the lower world, close to the animals living in its mystical landscape. The ones who chose to live there were called the *Rahkmany*, the blessed ones. It was the place where animals, plants, water, rocks, and trees could all speak the human languages, where the pale light of the full moon always shone, and where magic flowed the most freely. There was always plenty to eat and drink, so there was no need to work, the weather was always warm and balmy, and the creatures all lived in harmony.

The beings there had just one problem. Time did not exist in the lower world. The good part about that was that they would never age, but the sun never rose, the moon was always full, and it was always the most verdant part of summer. There was no sense of days, there was no sense of seasons, and there was no sunlight. The spirits of the lower world felt that everything was perfect except for this one thing, and so they asked the people of the middle world for their help. They sent a message to the seers and asked for

them to send the sun to them. The mystics of the middle world saw that if they sent the shells of blessed eggs once a year, the Rahkmany would have a day of sun and so could mark that time that passed.

So, each spring equinox, the beginning of the ancient new year, we remember our spirits and drop red krashanky shells into flowing water. These shells travel for twenty-five days to the lower world, and as they travel, they reassemble themselves. When they arrive on Rahkmany shores, the spirits receive them as bright and beautiful whole red eggs, full of the life force of the sun. They open these eggs and eat them. They don't need much. One red krashanka feeds twelve Rahkmany for a year. And on that one day, the day that they receive this mystical gift, the sun shines in their beautiful land, and they celebrate the new year and mark the passage of time in the middle world. This beautiful ritual allows those in the middle world to connect with those in the lower, to remember our loved ones and blessed spirits who have chosen to live there, and to share a gift with them.

Blessed krashanky are powerful talismans that can be eaten to take the power of the sun within yourself. When you eat them, save the shells, carry them to a river, and drop them in the water. The shells will float down the river to the Rahkmany to give them this gift from the sun and will connect you to the spirit world so that you can receive messages back from their realm.

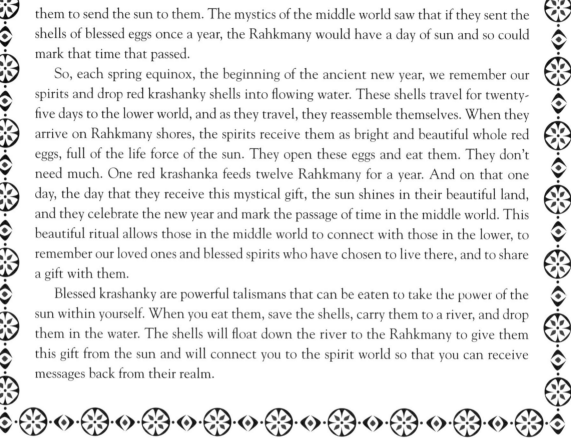

## Madame Pamita Teaches the Magic of the Krashanky and Pysanky

Every Easter was a special time in my house growing up. We had a magical mix of American Easter egg hunts blended with the spiritual richness of a traditional Ukrainian Easter, our table overflowing with delicious dishes. My mother would pull out her special Easter rushnyk embroidered by her own mother and create a basket filled with breads, ham, sausages, and, of course, the krashanky I had dyed with the egg coloring kits we bought at the supermarket. With these, we would play the egg knocking game, seeing whose eggshell was the toughest. My mother would also perform the ritual of blessing one of the eggs, peeling it, and popping a piece of it into the mouth of each family member to bless them for the year.

As a girl, I was fascinated by the book that we had on our bookshelf about pysanky, the intricately decorated eggs made with the wax resist method. I was mesmerized by the stories my mother told me about her mother creating these eggs in the early spring, and I longed to make them myself. However, we didn't own the simple tools needed for writing pysanky, so all I could do was admire the photos in the book and imagine making them. It wasn't until I was an adult that I was able to procure the dyes and the tools and begin writing my own pysanky for invoking the magic of the coming spring.

I marvel at the perfection of the timing of my magical knowledge. Although writing pysanky is simple enough for an older child to do, the meditative and mindful spiritual nature of this practice would have been lost on me when I was young. As an adult, I am able to fill these beautiful talismans with my magical intentions and feel the connection to my ancestors as I heat the wax and write the lines over the smooth surface of the egg.

## Krashanky and Pysanky Today

Eggs in general are powerful talismans that are revered. Yaytsya, plain eggs, are used in cleansing rituals for removing jinxes, hexes, and the evil eye, as described in chapter 10. Krashanky are hard-boiled eggs dyed a single color and are meant to be eaten to unlock their magic. Pysanky are intricately decorated talismanic eggs that are placed in the home to bring their protective magic. Although these decorated eggs are one of the most identifiably Ukrainian crafts, different variations of these beautiful talismans can be found in every country and culture of Eastern Europe and even in some Central European nations.

During the twentieth century, the Soviet regime forbade creating pysanky as it was considered to be religious and in defiance of the state-imposed atheism. Those who made them were treated with contempt, ridicule, and even punishment. In all but the most remote Carpathian villages, the crafting of pysanky ceased. However, diaspora Ukrainians brought the art with them to their new homelands and kept the folklore and techniques alive during this time. After Ukrainian independence in 1991, interest in the creation, traditions, symbols, and history of pysanky had a huge resurgence, with museums, collections, and serious scholarship being dedicated to this ancient magical tradition. Nowadays, pysanky are created and celebrated all over the world as magical talismans and beautiful art pieces.

## The Power of the Krashanky

Whenever an egg is used magically, it invokes the energy and the vitality of the sun, abundance, and, of course, fertility of all kinds. To eat an egg is to take the power of the sun into one's body. While you can find modern chemical egg dyes in any color, you can empower your egg magic even more when you dye the eggs with plant dyes, imbuing them not only with the energy of the colors but with the life force of the plant itself.

In the days before artificial dyes, people dyed krashanky with onion skins to make rich terra-cotta-colored eggs. These deep red eggs represented the life-giving blood of the mother and amplified the vitality of the sun's magic.[137] As the community gathered, piles of these beautiful red eggs would be blessed and imbued with good wishes for all and then distributed back to each member of the village.

Spring is the most traditional time of year for making red krashanky, and the new spring sun imparts the greatest power to them. However, you can perform rituals with these eggs at any time of the year to invite strength, healing, luck, and blessings.

### *Creating Red Krashanky*

Creating krashanky can be a ritual in itself. Imbue your eggs with extra energy by focusing on your intentions of protection, love, and vitality as you dye your eggs. It can be quite powerful to envision or whisper your incantations as you peel off the onion skins, stir them in the pot, and add your eggs to simmer.

### Ingredients
- Onion skins from about 12 yellow onions
- 4 cups of water
- 3 tablespoons of white vinegar
- 12 large white eggs
- Olive oil or other edible oil

---

137. Dixon-Kennedy, *Encyclopedia of Russian and Slavic Myth and Legend.*

**Instructions**

1. In a medium stainless-steel saucepan, combine the onion skins, water, and vinegar and bring to a boil.

2. Turn heat down to low, cover, and simmer for at least 30 minutes. The longer you simmer, the richer the dye will be.

3. Scoop or strain out the onion skins, add the eggs to the onion skin dye, and simmer for 10 to 15 minutes.

4. Using a slotted spoon, remove the eggs from the pot and gently put them into a jar, bowl, or crock.

5. Let the dye liquid cool slightly and pour it over the eggs in the jar to cover them.

6. Make sure that the dye liquid is covering all the eggs. If not, you can add extra water.

7. Place the jar in the fridge and let the eggs soak overnight. The longer they soak, the darker they will be.

8. The next morning, remove the eggs from the dye with a slotted spoon and allow them to dry on a wire rack or egg carton.

9. When the eggs are dry, use a few drops of olive oil and a paper towel to polish them.

10. Keep the eggs refrigerated until ready to bless and eat, up to one week.

### Creating Krashanky in Other Colors

While red krashanky are the oldest and most traditional, krashanky can be dyed with other natural dyestuffs to make beautiful eggs of almost every hue. You can use the color guide in appendix II to select colors that correspond to your spells and wishes.

### Natural Kranshanky Dye Recipes

Follow the method for dyeing red krashanky above, but substitute the following items for the various colors. For pastel colors, only soak a short time. For richer colors, soak overnight in the refrigerator.

- **Pale Yellow to Rich Gold:** 3 tablespoons of turmeric
- **Tan to Dark, Rich Brown:** 1 quart of strong black coffee

- **Light Pink to Deep Magenta:** 4 cups of chopped beets
- **Light Blue to Royal Blue:** 4 cups of chopped red cabbage
- **Pale Green to Medium Green:** 2 cups of spinach
- **Pale Blue-Violet to Deep Violet:** 2 cups of grape juice
- **Pale Silver to Dark Gray:** 2 cups of blueberries (fresh or frozen)
- **Pale Teal to Jade Green:** Skins of about 12 red onions
- **Gray-Brown to Black:** 9 walnut husks

### Blessing and Empowering Your Krashanky

Once the eggs are made, you are ready to have the sun bless and empower these talismans. Place your eggs in a basket, and just before dawn, bring your basket outside to catch the first rays of the sun. As the sunlight begins to break, hold your hands over the basket with your palms down. Visualize your wishes and whisper words of power over the eggs.

After the eggs have been blessed, they can be eaten right away or kept in the refrigerator and eaten up to a week later. As you eat your krashanka, be sure to mindfully meditate on the blessings you wish to bring in or eat in communion with your loved ones in a joyful celebration to increase health and happiness for all. And don't forget to save the shells to use in your rituals.

### Luck and Beauty Krashanky Spell

Once the red krashanky have been blessed, there are lots of magical ways to use them. On the night before your springtime celebration, place a krashanka in a bowl of water with a copper coin. Whoever awakens the earliest the next morning gets the lucky coin and the krashanka and will be blessed with luck and beauty for the year.

### Family Blessing Ritual with Krashanky

For springtime blessings for the entire family, place three red krashanky in a basin of water. Each member of the family washes their face with this holy water blessed by the krashanky and dries with a new face towel. If this towel is a rushnyk embellished with magical embroidery for the occasion, all the better. The youngest member of the family washes their face first, and the oldest member goes last. As each person washes their face, they are symbolically cleansing away old cares and beginning anew. With each person, the old water is ritually disposed of at the base of a tree, and new, fresh water is added.

### Krashanky Breakfast Blessing

When you settle in for your springtime breakfast celebration, have one member of the family break open a krashanka to be shared by all. Pop a small piece of egg into the mouth of each family member with a blessing for health and happiness and gratitude for the return of spring.

### Krashanky Egg Battle

Since you have a pile of krashanky left to enjoy, start an egg battle. Have two people tap the tip of their eggs together until someone's eggshell breaks. That person is out of the game and the krashanka can be eaten. The winner can challenge another person and either crack or be cracked. When the last egg has survived the egg-knocking battles, that person is declared the winner, and that egg can be buried in the yard or in a potted plant for extra blessings of strength and abundance throughout the year.

### Blessing Animals with Krashanky

Naturally dyed krashanky shells can be ground to a powder and fed to your pets or farm animals to bless them. This krashanky powder is full of calcium, as well as magic, and can be safely added to your cat, dog, rodent, or bird food, your chicken or farm animal feed, or even a human smoothie for imbuing the body and bones with health and strength. Say an incantation over the powder with the intentions that you wish your loved ones to receive.

### Other Magical Ways to Use Krashanky

Krashanky shells can also be saved and burned in a fire or over charcoal to smoke out a fever. And, of course, they can be buried in a field, your garden, or even a potted plant to bless your land and bring in bountiful abundance. No matter what way you use them, the shells should never be carelessly discarded. To heedlessly step on the shells of a krashanka is thought to bring bad luck.

### Krashanky Offerings for the Spirits

Springtime is also a time for communing with the ancestors. Eggs have been placed in tombs and on graves since before recorded history as a symbol of life and rebirth. In the spring, we connect with family—our living family, and also those who have passed on to the spirit world.

As the sun warms the earth, take a picnic lunch to a cemetery and enjoy a meal with your beloved family members, living and dead. Be sure to bring some krashanky for the ones who have passed on. Arrange the krashanky on the graves for them to enjoy and leave them overnight. Come back the following day and take a look at the krashanky. If they are still in the formation that you placed them in, your family member is resting in peace. If the eggs have been disturbed in some way, your loved one is telling you that there is some unfinished business that needs to be taken care of.

Finally, krashanky make beautiful gifts for the spirits of the middle world as well. Leave a whole krashanka in the forest for the Lisovyk, on a riverbank for the Rusalky, or at a crossroads for the Mavky. These potent magical charms will be appreciated by these spirits.

## The Magic of Pysanky

Pysanky are intricately decorated eggs that are shared at Easter, spring equinox, or other springtime celebrations. While there are many variations on decorated eggs, there are three defining features that make an egg a pysanka: it must be created with the wax resist method, traditional symbols are used, and the egg is not cooked or eaten.

### The History of Pysanky

Ancient Ukrainians worshiped the sun as it was seen as a source of all life. Eggs decorated with nature symbols became an integral part of spring rituals, serving as benevolent talismans. Springtime was the beginning of the new year and the celebration of the return of the sun and its life-giving warmth. Archaeologists have discovered Bronze Age Trypillian pottery and ceramic eggs decorated with designs that are still in use today.

When Christianity arrived in 988 CE, the old symbols and meaning of the pysanky were subsumed into Christian mythology. Older Pagan traditions of all kinds coexisted with the newer Christian beliefs, and pysanky that were once a talisman of spring and the sun god became a part of Easter celebrations.

### Legend of the Pysanka

The Hutzuls, an ethnic group who live in the Carpathian Mountains of Western Ukraine, believe that the fate of the world depends upon pysanky. They believe that there is a dangerous monster named Pekun who is chained to a cliff. Every spring, Pekun sends his minions out into the world to count how many pysanky have been created. If the number is low, his chains get loosened, and he is free to roam the earth, causing havoc and destruction. If the number of pysanky is higher, the chains get tighter, keeping the world safe so that goodness can triumph over evil for another year. As long as there are people making pysanky, the world will exist, but if people stop making them or forget how to make them, the world will be destroyed.

### Writing Pysanky

The word *pysanky* comes from the Ukrainian word *pysaty*, to write. Decorating pysanky is called "writing" pysanky, and when we inscribe the symbols on them, we are, in essence, writing out our wishes and desires.

### Ingredients and Equipment for Pysanky

Up until the twentieth century, pysanky were always made with fresh whole eggs. Fertile eggs were used, as they had the power of life, and for an extra powerful talisman, the first fertilized egg laid by a young hen was selected. Infertile eggs were avoided because it was believed that they would block fertility in the household—crops and livestock as well as people. After the pysanka was created, the inside of the egg was left to slowly dry up over time, leaving a hollow pysanka with a small, dried yolk that rattled around inside.

A more recent innovation has been to use eggs that have a small hole in one or both ends where the raw egg yolk and white can be blown out. This avoids the occasional whole egg that breaks open as it's drying out, but it makes it more challenging to submerge the egg and keep the dye from seeping into the holes.

### Egg Dyes

The old ones took the magic of pysanky seriously and would use "living water" collected from the first spring rain for making their dyes. Living water was felt to have powerful magic, and this energy could be transferred to the pysanka. Back then, dyes were made from plants with all their magical attributes, but today, most people create pysanky with brighter aniline dyes.

When you create your own pysanky, you can choose whichever type of dye is more appealing to you. If you are working with natural dyes, you can follow the directions for creating the krashanky dyes, but you will use them after they have cooled. Aniline pysanky dyes are sold as powders in paper packets. Follow the directions printed on the packet for making liquid dye. Usually this involves dissolving them in boiling water and adding a tablespoon of vinegar to colors other than orange.

### Kistka

The *kistka* is the stylus used to apply wax onto the egg. The traditional kistka is a small copper funnel wrapped with wire to attach it to one end of a small wooden dowel. Today, there are kistky with high-temperature plastic handles and even electric-heated kistky. To write on the egg, you scoop some beeswax into the funnel and then heat the kistka by holding the funnel next to a candle flame. Once the wax melts, you draw the funnel across the egg to make a line of beeswax that will preserve the color underneath.

### Candle

A taper candle is used to heat the kistky and to melt the wax off the egg once the pysanka is complete.

### Beeswax

Beeswax is used to create the wax resist inscriptions on the egg. Black or dark-colored beeswax is often used, as it is easier to see when writing on the white egg.

### The Pysanky Process

Pysanky are written on and dyed in a certain order. First, wax is applied to the white egg in all areas that you wish to remain white. Then the egg is dipped in yellow dye. Once this is done, the egg is dried, and then wax is applied again to all the areas that you want to be yellow. Then it is dipped in orange dye. To use the most traditional colors, you repeat this process, applying wax and dipping the egg in dye, going from yellow, to orange, to red, and finally to black. Once all the dye has been applied, hold the egg next to a candle flame and gently heat. Wipe away the melted wax to reveal the beautiful multicolored design beneath.

### Pysanky Symbols

Similar to the embroidery on vyshyvanky, the symbols on traditional pysanky have meaning and magic. The oldest symbols are geometric and nonrepresentational, such as wavy lines, circles, spirals, dots, crosshatches, and lines. Some of these can be found echoed in Trypillian pottery that is more than seven thousand years old, and so we know their magic is very ancient. Though we may never be sure of the specific meanings these symbols held for the old ones, they are viewed as iconography of protection in modern times.

Meandering lines and spirals in particular are seen as safeguards against malicious entities. Evil spirits who come near them are said to get trapped in these shapes, where they are unable to escape and harm anyone. In general, however, the symbols on *pysanky* are not meant to be read individually; the pysanka itself is seen as a talisman to guard the family, the home, and the property.

### Pysanky Traditions

Pysanky were created after Stritennya (February 2/February 15) up until just before spring equinox, or the old New Year, or Easter. In times past, pysanky were created primarily by women and were written at night after work had been done and the children were asleep. Like other talismanic objects, it was and is important to have a positive state of mind when writing a pysanka, for the emotional state you are in is inscribed into your talisman.

### Pysanky Spells of Protection

Pysanky were seen as expendable magical talismans because new ones would be made each year, so they would be placed around the home and farm for protecting the family, home, livestock, and beehives. A bowl of pysanky would normally be found in every house, often near the pokut' or home altar, to enhance household protection.

### *Working with Broken Pysanky Shells*

If a pysanka accidentally broke, its shell pieces could be used by ill-wishers to curse the family, so they were never carelessly thrown away. Instead, they were either ground up and fed to the animals (if they were dyed with natural dyes) or thrown into running water. Like krashanky, broken pysanky shells could also be burned and the smoke used to banish disease.

### *Pysanky as Talismanic Gifts*

The egg symbolizes life and the return of the sun, and the designs and colors on a pysanka have deep meanings of protection and good fortune. Pysanky are often given as gifts to loved ones and respected members of the community, with eggs being customized with special symbols and colors for different individuals. Even those who had passed on were gifted with these talismans. Pysanky were placed in coffins to protect loved ones traveling to the afterlife, and they were and are placed on gravesites as offerings to those who are buried there.

## The Magic Egg

When it comes to objects of power, don't let looks deceive you. That something as simple as an egg could be treasured, embellished, and valued as a powerful spiritual tool is emblematic of Ukrainian magic. An egg may seem unremarkable to most people, but when its power is understood, it becomes a forceful ally for spells of abundance, cleansing, and protection. The same can be said of Baba Yaga. Behind the exterior of a cranky old woman—one who looks as fragile as the shell of an egg—lies the formidable vidma of legendary knowledge, skill, and power. Those who know can see beyond mere appearances to the truth within.

# CHAPTER 14

# TKATS'KYY VERSTAT: THE LOOM

*T*he next morning, Vasylyna woke up to the scent of honeyed porridge and saw that Baba Yaga was already awake and cooking breakfast.

"Get up, girl. The day is short and the chores are long."

Vasylyna tucked her motanka into her pocket and then sat down to eat the bowl of porridge Baba Yaga had set down for her. She took a pinch of the grains and put it in her pocket to share with her doll before Baba Yaga turned around and sat down to drink her tea.

"Do you know how to weave, girl?" Baba Yaga asked Vasylyna.

Vasylyna nodded and said, "Well, I helped my mother weave many times."

"Good, for today you are going to weave the hemp that you have spun. If you can weave all this thread into cloth by the time I get back from my errands, I will give you a reward." She set her cup down on the table. "And if not, I will give you as a reward to my pich."

And with that, Baba Yaga got up, gathered her things, went out the door, and left Vasylyna to finish her breakfast alone. Vasylyna took one look at the big loom and the room full of the thread that she had spun and she lifted her motanka out of her pocket.

"Dolly of mine, what am I to do? I know how to spin but I've never worked a loom on my own. My legs can barely reach the treadles and my arms are too short to move the shuttle back and forth." The doll replied,

> Weaving takes a lot of skill,
> but you can do it, if you will.

*All you have to do is ask,*
*and I can help you with this task.*

So Vasylyna quickly finished her porridge, cleaned the dirty dishes, and went over to the loom. The doll directed Vasylyna to pull the shaft and work the treadles, while quick as a darting bird, the little motanka pushed the shuttle between the threads. Vasylyna moved her hands and feet quickly, but the doll flew back and forth across the warp threads even faster, so fast that she looked more like a blur than a doll.

They worked and wove as the sun rose higher and higher in the sky. And they continued to work at the loom as the sun began moving lower toward the mountains in the distance. They wove all day without stopping, and by the time the sun was dipping down behind the mountains, they had woven every last thread. They took the cloth off the loom and folded it into a neat pile just as Baba Yaga was unlocking the door.

## Baba Yaga Shares the Wisdom of the Tkats'kyy Verstat

Weaving: something you folk know nothing about these days. You go to a store and you buy a piece of clothing that a machine has made out of fibers that have never seen a living day. You call that clothing? Pah! What can it do but cover your body, and probably not even *that* very well. The clothing *we* made had life, had magic.

The fact that I have a *tkats'kyy verstat* in my khatynka is nothing remarkable. In the past, every house had a loom. No loom, no clothes. And no clothes? You're going to be a little cold in the winter, that's for sure. But a loom does so much more than make clothing. We make blankets. We weave tablecloths. We create the magical rushnyky that we use to bless our homes and protect our loved ones. Weaving is the magic of mastering creation.

This art is something we have been doing since we were living in caves. From practically the beginning of time, we were the magicians creating something from nothing. So many of our spirits and goddesses are spinners and weavers. Naturally, I am an exceptional weaver, but the goddess Mokosh, Saint Paraskeva P'yatnytsya, and the Rusalky are, too.[138] The Rusalky sing and spin their yarn and hang it on the trees. They weave

---

138. Johns, *Baba Yaga.*

their cloth, wash it in the river, and lay it on the banks to bleach and dry it. That cloth is not only beautiful but powerful; so powerful that if a person should tread on it while it's drying, they would be unable to walk again.

We had our special seasons for making cloth. In the winter, when we were all tucked in our homes anyway, *that* was the time for weaving magic, after the sun had gone down and everyone had been fed. We would go to our wooden looms that were carved with magical symbols of protection, get out our homespun, and begin by singing.

The singing? That's an important part of weaving. We sing to make ourselves happy, and if you've been paying attention, you know that you need to be in a happy state before you begin to create anything magical. We sing as we work to weave our incantations into the fabric. What we sing is bound into what we make each time we draw a thread through the warp and beat it down into cloth. Weave with pure thoughts and a light soul, otherwise you may end up with a broken thread. What's the problem with a broken thread? Well, we saw it as a very bad omen indeed. A broken thread could mean bad luck of all kinds, changing a good destiny to a bad one.

When you learn the art of weaving, ah, that's when you learn how to create your own destiny. The thread of your life is reflected in the thread you weave. So, if your life is not to your satisfaction, you can weave yourself a better one.

## Madame Pamita Teaches the Magic of the Tkats'kyy Verstat

One of my deep spiritual practices is an act I call "mindful appreciation." In mindful appreciation, we think about all the layers of genius, inspiration, and skill that go into everyday objects.

Take, for example, the clothing that you wear. The shirt you are wearing was first just a fashion designer's idea, then they sourced the fabric to make it. To make that fabric, a fabric designer had to come up with materials, colors, and textures. Cotton, linen, or some other material had to be grown from the land and processed. Dyes had to be invented. Tailors had to cut and assemble the piece. Shippers had to transport it. Sellers had to sell it. When you contemplate it, the list of people who conspired to create the simple piece of clothing you are wearing is like a long, beautiful thread. They all worked together so that you could cover your skin in a way that feels good to you. When we think about Mother Earth and the people all along the way who provided for us, our clothing can be imbued with deep appreciation, enjoyment, and a profound sense of wonder.

I have a small collection of antique vyshyvanky. As I look at these gowns, I think about the women like my grandmother and great-grandmothers who grew the hemp or flax, beat it, spun it by hand, wove it by hand, sewed it together, and then embroidered it with delicate threads of red and black. I don't know the women who made these exquisite garments, but I imagine them and bless their spirits as I touch their handiwork, so lovingly created.

As I began my own journey to meet Baba Yaga, I knew that I not only had to learn how to spin, but that I also had to learn how to weave. I began with something small and doable: a *krayka*. A krayka is a woven belt that is wrapped around the waist and tied. I bought a small loom for band weaving and began to weave my first belt. At first it was uneven, but as I learned to pull the shuttle with just the right amount of tension, I could see, even within that one weaving, my technique getting better and better.

Like spinning, weaving has a meditative, rhythmic quality that allows you to drift into that magical liminal space where you can commune with the spirit world. Each time I weave, I imagine riding the thread of time back to my grandmother and great-grandmother, who wove their own cloth at home, back to their mothers and grandmothers. Back and back and back I go until I am weaving beside the first weavers, the ones who discovered the magic of making cloth.

## The Tkats'kyy Verstat Today

Cultures all over the world and throughout history have recognized that the process of weaving has deep spiritual significance. The thread is a symbol of destiny and life. The patterns that we weave with that thread can affect our physical condition and the direction that our life takes. The ancients understood the magic of transforming a tangle of fibers into cloth, the act of creating beauty from chaos. This profound transformation echoes magic itself, where we take nothing and create something to our will.

Like vyshyvanky and the decorations on pysanky, each village had their own patterns and colors that were used in their weaving. Today, weaving for most people may not have the deep mystical significance that it did a few generations ago, but interest in reviving the traditional styles, methods, and techniques has had a renaissance. Because spiritual symbolism is such an integral part of weaving, even the most casual weavers are familiar with the magic of the handwoven artifact.

### Weaving in One Day

The ultimate magic of weaving is seen in a powerful village ritual from back when every home had a loom and all women were weavers. If the fields needed rain or the community needed protection from disease, war, famine, or some other evil, the women of the village would gather before sunrise, each bringing bundles of flax fibers. In complete silence, they would spin the flax into threads, set up a loom and weave a cloth. Just like a task given by Baba Yaga, this talisman had to go from flax fibers to finished cloth in one day. Once it was woven, it could be brought to a sacred well to invite needed rain, fastened across a road at the entrance of the village to keep out disease, displayed over a cross set up at a crossroads, or used in a ritual where it was held aloft so that each member of the community could pass beneath it and have any negativity lifted from them. This magically woven cloth was used as a portal to the supernatural world. Once the ritual was completed and contact with the liminal had been made, the artifact would be burned and destroyed.[139]

### Weaving Throughout Life

Not all woven talismans are destroyed. In fact, the vast majority of them are kept for a lifetime and even handed down through generations. When a child was born, they would be wrapped in a piece of linen. This cloth would then be made into a wedding rushnyk when that child grew up and got married, and it would be put into their coffin when they died. Cloth is a symbol of a life that has been protected and blessed from birth to the grave.

## The Magic of the Krayka

While rushnyky were and are worn on the body for special life events such as births, weddings, and funerals, there were other woven talismans that were worn on a daily basis: the woven sash or belt called the krayka. The krayka was a talisman that was worn throughout

---

139. Johns, *Baba Yaga.*

life, from childhood on. In the old days, belts held sacred meaning, representing a circle: perfection, infinity, and the cycles of time. If the body is a personal replica of the World Tree, then the belt delineates the middle world, protects the wearer in this reality, and defines them as a living human.[140]

Belts were seen as a spiritual necessity, and a simple rope or cord of leather would do in a pinch. However, even people of modest means could weave a krayka of colorful wool, flax, or hemp. As a magical tool, the weavers would fashion symbols in the weaving to enchant them and add to their protective powers.

The krayka was also a symbol of initiation. From the earliest days when the child was introduced into society, to the initiations into professions and guilds, to marriage, and to death, the krayka accompanied a person through all their important life changes and initiations. It also symbolized the umbilical cord that connects the individual to their lineage. The belt was seen as a magic circle that constantly surrounded the individual, giving them protection from unseen spiritual forces. The krayka itself is protective, but it can be amplified by tucking wormwood, lovage, or other protective herbs at the waist.[141]

### To Be Unbelted

To untie your krayka or to not wear a belt at all was considered scandalous and compromising. A person who behaved dishonorably was called unbelted, or, if they committed an outrage, it was said that they "took their belt off." It was considered indecent to be seen outside the home without a belt, for it meant that you were discarding the one thing that centered you in the middle world and connected you to your family and society. Going without a krayka was seen as a sure sign that you were associating with the spirit world. The spirits themselves would give away their identities because they did not wear belts. For example, Rusalky, Lisovyky, and Mavky could be identified by the fact that they did not wear belts.[142]

Magical rituals necessitated opening the door between the seen and unseen worlds, and so they often required that the person doing the magic do something transgressive.

---

140. Ryan, *The Bathhouse at Midnight*.

141. Bosyy, "Svyashchenne Remeslo Mokoshi," 39–40.

142. Gilchrist, *Russian Magic*.

Loosening hair or clothing, having wide sleeves, going barefoot, and, of course, removing your krayka were considered signs that you were traversing to the lower world. To be able to travel freely—whether in magical dances, divination, spell casting, or in rituals such as calling rain, controlling the weather, or banishing epidemics—you had to be willing to release your personal protection.

For modern-day vidmy who no longer have the social requirement of wearing a belt every day, a krayka can be worn when you feel the need for some extra protection from negative spirits. Making one from scratch will imbue it with all your intentions and magic.

### Making a Krayka

To create a woven belt, you can work with any variety of loom. The ancient ancestors used warp-weighted looms, but there are other possible looms from cultures all over the world that can be used for weaving your krayka. A backstrap loom is a compact, inexpensive, and mobile loom made of sticks, rope, and a strap that is worn around the weaver's waist. An inkle loom is a simple-to-use table loom that allows you to weave long bands such as a krayka. A Swedish band loom is a larger and more expensive floor-standing loom that is quite easy to use. Though any kind of weaving will connect you to the cloth-making spirits, if you'd like to make a krayka, choose a loom that allows you to do "band weaving."

### Types of Yarn for Creating a Krayka

For the best success in making a krayka, you need to begin with a sturdy, firmly twisted yarn. Any of the following will bring you great results.

- Perle cotton (also known as mercerized cotton) in size 3/2 (thicker) or size 5/2 (finer)
- Embroidery floss
- Cotton rug warp
- Linen yarn
- Firmly twisted wools
- Hemp yarn

### *Weaving Your Krayka*

Before you get started, make your krayka plan. Your krayka should be long enough to wrap around your waist twice (or more) with some extra to hang down several inches when tied. Traditionally, women's belts were anywhere from one to six inches wide (two to fifteen centimeters) and men's were two to eight inches wide (five to twenty centimeters), but you can choose a width that suits you. Choose colors for your krayka based on the magic you wish to bring into your life. The magical properties of colors can be found in appendix II.

Before you begin weaving, be sure that you are feeling calm and happy. Your mood will influence your weaving, and you're creating a talisman that will carry that energy. Put on some music that you can sing along to. Traditionally, the women weaving would sing old traditional folk songs with incantations in the lyrics, but you can sing songs in your own language that have sentiments you wish to imbue your work with. Positive, empowering songs are your best choice for bringing those qualities into your life.

### *Wearing Your Krayka*

Wearing a krayka can be seen as an expression of the magic you wish to do. You can view your belt as a magical tool that you wear on special occasions, or you can wear it every day. For example, a slender krayka can be worn under your clothes on a daily basis to provide protection from negative spirits.

Think of your krayka as a tool you might want to wear before performing divination and magic. Wear it during the day before you start your rites and rituals to gather energy, marshal your resources, and protect yourself from negativity. When you begin your ritual, spell casting, or divination, you can take off your krayka to symbolically allow yourself to traverse the world of spirit. When your ritual work is done, tie the krayka back on for the rest of the day to gather and integrate the work that you have done.

## Weaving as Magic

The act of taking threads and creating something from them is a powerful physical metaphor for the act of magic itself. It's not surprising that many of our spiritual descriptors have textile references, such as "spinning a spell" or "weaving a web of enchantment." There are goddesses and spirits of many cultures who are weavers, including Baba Yaga. Challenge yourself to weave cloth or simply weave a potholder on a homemade cardboard box loom in devotion to her, and you will gain a deep understanding of the power of will and creation.

CHAPTER 15

# VOLOSSYA: THE HAIR

**B**aba Yaga laid her sack down on the table and went over to the room filled with cloth. She inspected the stacks of neatly folded fabric that Vasylyna and the doll had made.

"Hmmm…" She ran her wrinkled hands over the cloth. It was as soft and finely woven as the finest silk. She unfolded it, pulled it, stretched it out, and even sniffed at it.

"Hmph," she said. "Not bad, girl, not bad. I suppose my pich will have to wait another day to be fed." And with that, Baba Yaga began to pull herbs, mushrooms, a cabbage, and some beets out of her bag. She cleaned them off, chopped them up, and added them to a pot of broth that had been simmering over the fire all day.

While they waited for the soup to cook, Baba Yaga lit her pipe, picked up an old comb made of animal horn and a bowl of lovage water, and sat down next to the pich.

"Come here, girl," she said, "I need you to comb my hair."

Vasylyna took one look at Baba Yaga's matted, greasy hair and was repulsed. She didn't want to touch it, let alone get the tangles out. Nevertheless, she took the comb from Baba Yaga's hand.

"I might have a knot or two in my hair, so be careful," said Baba Yaga. "I have a very sensitive head, so you must be very gentle. If you cause me pain, well, then I will add you to the soup tonight."

Vasylyna took the comb in one hand and a matted piece of Baba Yaga's hair in the other and began carefully untangling each knot. Section by section, she gently worked the comb through her hair, untangling the greasy strands and washing them with the herbal infusion. As she worked her way up, she spotted lice on Baba Yaga's scalp, and these she picked out with the comb and crushed between her fingernails.

Baba Yaga sat there and smoked her pipe and closed her eyes as if taking a nap, while Vasylyna gently combed and cleaned.

Finally, when she had combed out her hair completely, rinsed it with the lovage water, and dispatched all the lice, Vasylyna began to braid Baba Yaga's thick silver hair, as she had done with her mother's hair so many years before. Baba Yaga opened her eyes and slapped Vasylyna's hands away.

She stood up to her full height, turned toward Vasylyna, and her hair shone like a radiant silver halo around her face.

"Did I ask you to braid my hair, girl?" she said sternly.

She snatched the comb from Vasylyna's hand and began combing it through her own locks. As she did, bright sparks of silver crackled in the air around her.

"Hmph," she said. "You were very mistaken about trying to hide my hair in a braid, and for that alone I should throw you in the pot. But, on the other hand, my hair is quite magnificent now, and I didn't feel a pull or a pinch. I suppose you did the job well enough, and for that I guess you have earned the right to be eating soup instead of being the soup tonight."

She went over to the pich and ladled out two bowls, one for herself and one for Vasylyna. She set down a basket of warm bread, and together they sat down to eat.

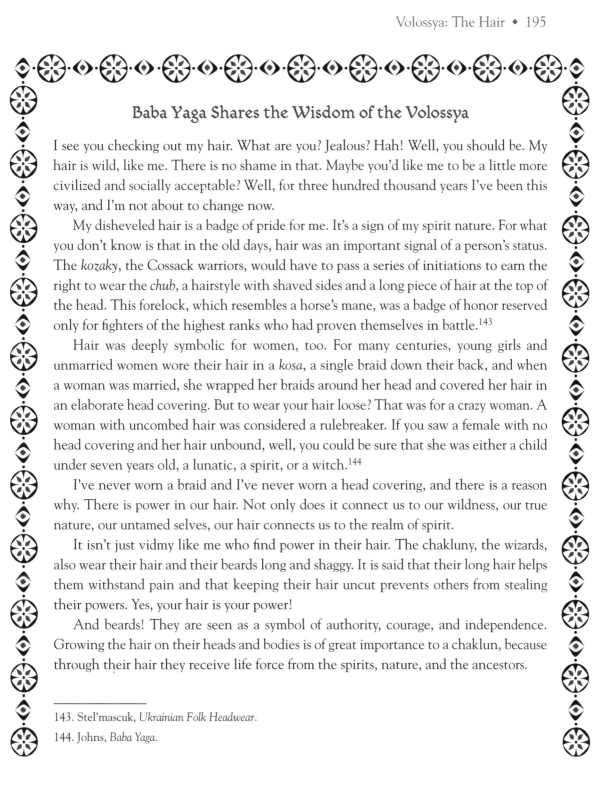

## Baba Yaga Shares the Wisdom of the Volossya

I see you checking out my hair. What are you? Jealous? Hah! Well, you should be. My hair is wild, like me. There is no shame in that. Maybe you'd like me to be a little more civilized and socially acceptable? Well, for three hundred thousand years I've been this way, and I'm not about to change now.

My disheveled hair is a badge of pride for me. It's a sign of my spirit nature. For what you don't know is that in the old days, hair was an important signal of a person's status. The *kozaky*, the Cossack warriors, would have to pass a series of initiations to earn the right to wear the *chub*, a hairstyle with shaved sides and a long piece of hair at the top of the head. This forelock, which resembles a horse's mane, was a badge of honor reserved only for fighters of the highest ranks who had proven themselves in battle.[143]

Hair was deeply symbolic for women, too. For many centuries, young girls and unmarried women wore their hair in a *kosa*, a single braid down their back, and when a woman was married, she wrapped her braids around her head and covered her hair in an elaborate head covering. But to wear your hair loose? That was for a crazy woman. A woman with uncombed hair was considered a rulebreaker. If you saw a female with no head covering and her hair unbound, well, you could be sure that she was either a child under seven years old, a lunatic, a spirit, or a witch.[144]

I've never worn a braid and I've never worn a head covering, and there is a reason why. There is power in our hair. Not only does it connect us to our wildness, our true nature, our untamed selves, our hair connects us to the realm of spirit.

It isn't just vidmy like me who find power in their hair. The chakluny, the wizards, also wear their hair and their beards long and shaggy. It is said that their long hair helps them withstand pain and that keeping their hair uncut prevents others from stealing their powers. Yes, your hair is your power!

And beards! They are seen as a symbol of authority, courage, and independence. Growing the hair on their heads and bodies is of great importance to a chaklun, because through their hair they receive life force from the spirits, nature, and the ancestors.

---

143. Stel'mascuk, *Ukrainian Folk Headwear*.

144. Johns, *Baba Yaga*.

Some say that a woman with her hair bound up can't do magic, but I would say that for some people, there is a time for hair being bound and covered and a time to let your tresses fly. When you need to get on with the mundane aspects of life, it's useful to have your hair pulled back and tied up. If you want to get on with your business and keep things "under your hat," keeping your hair tied up will keep you from being distracted.

However, when you want to be your authentic self, let your locks flow freely. With your hair loose, you can connect to the wild divine. You have the ability to draw up the power of Mother Earth, Maty Zemlya, call down the power of the Sister Stars, and connect to all that is out there. The more you let your hair be free, the stronger your connection with the cosmos, the universe, and the other realms. Think of your hair as an on-off switch: bound hair for control, and loose for freely exploring all the worlds.

Those who practice magic know that if they lose even a single hair, they will lose their power, so they guard their hair jealously. If you ever encounter a shape-shifter of any kind and want them to appear in their true form, snip a bit of their hair or a tuft of their fur, and they will appear to you as they truly are.

Hair is sacred to the spirits. If you want to make an offering to the weaving goddess Mokosh, showing her that you trust her to protect your destiny, leave her a piece of your hair overnight so that she can weave your fate. The beings of the spirit realm—the Rusalky, the Mavky, and even Paraskeva P'yatnytsya, the goddess whom some have converted into a saint—wear their long, flowing hair loose.[145] Some of the spirits even appear naked, with only their long hair covering their bodies. In a world where women were required to keep their hair under control, these spirits are the ones who really know how to let loose.

Hair is always important in magic. Some people even say that the broom I use in my nightly rounds is made of human hair. Well, I won't deny it. And is it my hair, or someone else's? Who's to say?

145. Dixon-Kennedy, *Encyclopedia of Russian and Slavic Myth and Legend*.

## Madame Pamita Teaches the Magic of Volossya

I have always had a sense that hair was magical. I think most of us do. When we grow our hair long and then experience a sense of shock when we cut it short, I think that is more than just insecurity about a change in our looks. I believe it is our spirit experiencing a profound change in some way. Yes, it will grow back, but that first look in the mirror always seems to come with a destabilizing jolt, no matter how good the new cut looks.

For most of my life, I have kept my hair long. When I began my journey with Baba Yaga, I began to understand the power of hair and began braiding it in the morning rather than just always throwing it into a messy ponytail. As I cross the three strands one over the other, I speak words of empowerment and intentions for my day ahead, binding those wishes to myself to gird me for what lies ahead.

### Volossya Today

In Ukrainian folklore, hair is seen as a link to an individual and something to be used magically. Using a strand of hair to get someone to fall in love with you or to cross someone up is something that we see in many magical systems, not just Slavic magic. However, there is special attention paid to hair, with magical herbal remedies and, in recent years, a revival in wearing the kosa and the chub as a sign of Ukrainian identity and empowerment. Hair is, was, and always will be perceived as something magical and powerful.

### Volossya Magic

It is said that the fate of the individual resides in the hair. Hair is one of the most intimate parts of our body. Do you let just anyone touch your hair? No, because instinctively you understand that your hair is part of your magic. People who are spiritually aware pay attention to what happens to their hair when it is cut. Hair can be used in sympathetic magic for strongly connecting an object to an individual. This can be done for positive magic as well as negative, so those who want to spiritually protect themselves guard their hair.

### Kosa Rituals

In times past, there were many initiation rituals involved with women's hair in particular. At a young age, girls would get their first kosa, signifying that they were leaving their infant state and entering into childhood and then young womanhood. The braiding of three strands had ritual significance, combining the vital forces of the three worlds: the lower world, the middle world, and the upper world. As the hair was braided, the mother could weave positive spells and incantations for her child into this braid.[146]

Braids were a talisman and a source of not only beauty, but also strength and health. When a young woman was about to be married, there was a ceremony where incantations were sung as her single braid was unbound by either her mother, her bridegroom, or the members of his family. Her hair was then braided into two braids and wound around the head, symbolically giving her strength not only for herself, but also for her future children. She then covered her hair with a large wrap or scarf to protect her hair and her power from vroki, or jealous looks.[147]

In the past, even some men experienced the magic of the braid. For a kozak, the one long lock at the top of the head could be braided and woven and imbued with protective and strengthening power.

There is a power in what we do with our hair on a daily basis. Hair contains energy. Think of braiding and loosening hair being like locking up or opening a door. Sometimes, it's useful to keep your door locked, and at other times, it's better to let it open. So, at times when you wish to conserve magical power and protect yourself, bind your hair in a braid. Braiding incorporates the magic of knots and weaving and so can be viewed as a way to bind good things to you and protect from negativity. At times when you want to project magical power, take your hair out of its braid. This action will allow you to freely traverse the realms of spirit. If you have very short hair or don't have hair, you can still practice this magic. Tie a cloth on your head to conserve energy and ritually untie it when you wish to cast your spells.

---

146. Zajvoronok, *Oznaky Ukrayins'koyi Etnokul'tury.*

147. Kononenko, *Slavic Folklore.*

### Volossya Trimming Rituals

Although growing hair is done to increase one's power, cutting hair can be done to transform your conditions, shaking things up to make an abrupt change. If things are not going well for someone—for example, if they are ill—trimming hair can cut the disease and give their health a fresh start. Trim the ends of the hair on the new moon to cut ties with the disease, and then burn the hair to banish the illness completely. You may also give the cut hair to a stream or river so that any illness or negativity is washed away. You might also combine these two methods by cutting the hair, baking it into a cookie, crumbling the cookie, and throwing it into a running stream or river. This ritual brings in the cleansing power of both fire and water, breaks the hold the disease has, and cleanses the body.

Many vidmy, chakluny, and other people who perform magic do not cut their hair, both to preserve the power in their locks and to prevent someone from stealing their essence through a piece of their hair. They believe that if hair is cut, it should be burned to avoid falling into the wrong hands. Even a mouse or a bird taking a piece of hair can cause the hair's owner to have a headache.

### Timing Volossya Cutting Rituals

If you are trimming hair to remove unwanted energies, there are different days of the week and times of the month that will support your intentions.

### Days of the Week

- Monday: To remove any negativity that has accumulated in recent days.
- Tuesday: To relieve depression, fatigue, and low vibes.
- Wednesday: To bring novelty and excitement into your life, such as making new friends, traveling to new places, and experiencing new positive life events.
- Thursday: To attract success, become a confident person, and improve relationships with loved ones.
- Friday: To radically change appearance and lifestyle, a trim on this day will not only change your look, but your life.
- Saturday: To rejuvenate, recover, and remove ancestral negativity.
- Sunday: Not recommended for haircutting, as a trim will cut your luck, destiny, and prosperity.

### Times of the Month

The effectiveness of hair cutting can also be enhanced by the time of the month when the hair is trimmed. If you wish hair to grow back thicker and fuller, cut it during the waxing moon phase, particularly closer to the full moon. It is not recommended to cut your hair during the waning moon phase, especially close to the new moon. It is believed that if you do, you will have problems with your hair, such as slow regrowth, split ends, thinning, or even hair loss. And getting a haircut on the night of the new moon is believed to deplete strength and health, so it's advisable to wait at least a day so that you are cutting in the waxing moon phase.

### Volossya Washing Rituals

There are many old methods of washing hair. Apart from plain water, hair can be washed or rinsed in magical herbal decoctions to impart it with beauty and infuse it with magic. A decoction is simply steeping fresh or dried herbs for fifteen to sixty minutes in boiling water, just as you would an herbal tea. Decoctions of burdock, chamomile, lovage, mint, or nettle can feed the hair and empower it magically. This wasn't just for women—the kozaky would wash their hair with decoctions of chamomile, wormwood, hazel leaves, and willow.[148] If you'd like to create some infusions for your own hair, check out appendix I for the magical properties of these herbs.

There are rituals that you can perform as you apply these potions to your hair. Rub the decoction into the scalp and comb it through your hair with the following incantation:

> *I will make my hair healthy and thick, like a lion's mane!*
> *It will be beautiful and brilliant!*
> *I will give my hair the power of mountains,*
> *the health of forests, the brilliance of rivers!*
> *I conjure it with the sun, I fix it with the earth.*
> *As I have said, so shall it be!*

### Hrebinets' as a Magical Tool

*Hrebinets'*, or the comb, is considered a traditional magical tool, as its sharp "teeth" are seen as protective against negative magic. In many of the stories of Baba Yaga, an

---

148. Anatoli Pasternak, *Kozats'ka Medytsyna* (Ukraine: Optyma, 2001).

enchanted comb can be thrown on the ground so that a forest sprouts up around the protagonist, protecting them from an evil force.

Combing your hair before a ritual can not only be part of getting ready but can be a spell in itself to mentally and spiritually prepare to do magic. Dedicate a special comb as your ritual tool. A ritual comb can be used in spells of all kinds, but it is particularly helpful in spells to change your own emotional or mental state or cleanse or purify the self. Comb spells can also be done to enhance beauty, attract love, affect someone's thoughts of you from a distance, or generally increase personal magnetism. Combing rituals can also be done to remove agitated thoughts, calm the mind, or help you fall asleep.

Combs made of natural materials such as bone, horn, or wood have a positive effect on the hair, the body, and the spirit. It's possible to choose one that has a special significance for you, connecting you to a certain animal or wood for your magic. It goes without saying that you should always choose a material that is renewable and never choose a comb made from an endangered species. If you'd like to work with a wooden comb for specific magic, refer to appendix I for the spiritual correspondences of woods.

### Choosing and Storing Your Hrebinets'

To select a comb to work with, you should trust your own intuition. If you find a comb that is visually appealing, simply hold it in your hands, or touch it to your hair. If doing this brings a pleasant feeling, then the comb is the right one for you to work with.

When not in use, a ritual comb should be wrapped in a soft cloth and kept away from the prying eyes of those who might be jealous. A comb used ritually should never be shared with another person. Using another person's comb or allowing them to use yours opens you up to potential magical mischief.

### Volossya Combing Ritual

It is thought that if you want to attract a new and passionate love, you should not comb your hair regularly after dark. While there are special occasions, such as performing combing divinations or nighttime rituals that require you to comb your hair at night, doing it simply for grooming is believed to remove sexual attraction. However, if you don't want to be bothered with suitors, then combing your hair after dark will dampen their ardor.

Combing the hair can become a sacred ritual, during which you touch the cosmic currents and physically feel streams of life force. Using your ritual comb, comb your hair in the morning as a magical rite. Whisper an affirmation or visualize your intentions with each stroke. For example, if your goal is to get in better physical shape, sit or stand in front of a mirror, look into your own eyes, and start combing your hair rhythmically. Imagine that with each stroke, you are getting fitter and fitter. Do this on a daily basis. You should notice that you are reprogramming yourself and your habits and that your body responds to this attention by making fitness enjoyable and effortless.

### Volossya Combing Divination

If you are single and would like to see your future lover, you can perform a divination rite with a comb and a mirror. After dark, preferably on a Monday or Friday, stand in front of a large mirror in an unlit room and let your hair down. Your hair needs to be long enough to cover your face or at least your eyes. Start combing your hair over your face and eyes, mentally focusing on your future love and looking through your hair into the mirror with your eyes partially unfocused. As you do this, you will enter a trance state. Continue to comb, and eventually images will appear in the mirror. Among them, you should see the image of your future lover. Do not focus your eyes too closely on the mirror, otherwise the image will disappear.

### Hrebinets' Attraction Spell

If you want to attract your true love, perform this ritual each night before going to bed. Tie a piece of your hair to a comb and hang your comb from this hair outside your bedroom window. Invite your lover to come by chanting this charm: "My betrothed, come and comb your hair!" Do this each night until you see a new piece of hair on the comb indicating that your lover has combed their hair while you were sleeping. The color and texture of the hair on the comb will give you a hint as to who your admirer is.[149]

---

149. Ryan, *The Bathhouse at Midnight.*

### *Volossya Combing Passion Charm*

If you would like to deepen the passion and increase the affection between you and your lover, comb each other's hair before going to bed. Before beginning, hold the comb and bless it with your intentions for your loved one. Take turns combing each other's hair and whisper your incantations and prayers during the combing process, or think them silently as you comb. This act is quite intimate and very soothing and relaxing at bedtime.

### *Volossya Love Spell*

Hair can be a powerful tool for influencing another person, and if you have a piece of hair from your beloved, you can perform this coercive love spell. This spell will require some courage, as you may have to eat a small amount of ashes and beeswax.

#### Ingredients

- A piece of your beloved's hair
- A plain uncolored beeswax taper candle (natural yellow or white)
- A circular saucer with no chips or cracks
- Matches or a lighter
- A glass of water
- A wooden box large enough to hold the candle—a cigar box is ideal

#### Instructions

1. Melt the bottom of the candle and affix it to the saucer.
2. Place the piece of hair on the saucer to the left of the candle.
3. Light the candle and meditate on the flame.
4. Visualize yourself and your target being in love and happy.
5. When the visualization is vivid and you feel the happy emotions of what you see in your mind's eye, you can begin the ritual.
6. Pick up the hair and light it in the fire, letting the ashes of the burned hair drop into the pool of wax.

7. Recite the following incantation:

*Your hair burns with a bright flame.*
*So you [name] come to me [name] with a passion that does not go out.*
*As the flame burns, so your passion burns,*
*so I, [name], burn and melt your heart.*
*From now on and forever you will burn for me, [name].*

8. Once the hair is burned into the wax, pull the taper off the saucer. Drip the wax and the hair ash into the glass of water while reciting the following incantation:

*As water takes, so it hides, so I, [name], have taken your love forever.*

9. Snuff the candle out and place it in the wooden box by itself. You may light this candle again if you would like to do additional influence spells on the same target.

10. Thank the fire, water, and wax for their assistance.

11. Ideally, you should drink the glass of water, and then chew and swallow the wax and the ashes from the burned hair. Alternatively, you can dig a hole at the base of a tree and pour out the water and bury the wax, or you can pour the water and wax into a running stream or river.

### *Love Binding with Volossya*

Because hair is an artifact that contains the DNA code of the individual, it is a powerful tool for sympathetic love magic. To keep your loved one faithful to you, you can perform this simple ritual. Stand under the moonlight of a full moon with a strand of your hair and a strand of your lover's hair. Tie your hair around your lover's hair and knot it three times. While you are making the knots, imagine your lover being faithful and devoted to you. Keep this magical talisman hidden in your home as long as you want this person's love, and they will think only of you.

### *A Spell to Grow Volossya*

To do spells with hair, it's useful to have a healthy mane. To make your hair thick and lush, make a magical ritual of rubbing the nails of one hand against the nails of the other every day for five to ten minutes while visualizing luxurious hair on your head.

## Baba Yaga's Volossya

As a vidma, Baba Yaga is quite aware of the power of hair. On the one hand, she would appear to be careless about her hair, letting it become a greasy, tangled home for lice. However, she knows the power of her *volossya* as well, letting it grow long and keeping it uncovered so that she is fully engaged with the spirit world and all her powers are at their peak. Tune in to the power of your own hair, whether on your head or on your body, and use it to create magic and attune to the spirits.

CHAPTER 16

# STUPA: THE MORTAR AND PESTLE

The next morning, Vasylyna woke up to the scent of wheat and honey porridge on the stove and Baba Yaga humming a song as she stirred the pot and ladled out two portions into bowls.

"Get up, girl. The day is short and the chores are long."

Vasylyna got up, tucked her doll into her pocket, took the bowl of kutya that Baba Yaga offered, and sat down to eat with her. As she ate, she took a pinch of the porridge and reached into her pocket to give it to her doll.

Baba Yaga pulled a poppy seed from her porridge.

"Do you know what this is, girl?"

"Yes," said Vasylyna. "It's a poppy seed."

Baba Yaga took a wheat kernel from the bowl.

"And do you know what this is?"

"Yes, babusya," said Vasylyna. "It's a grain of wheat."

"Good, good," said Baba Yaga. "Then finish your breakfast and we'll get started with the day's work."

Vasylyna was excited because she knew how to cook and was looking forward to impressing Baba Yaga with her skill.

When they finished their meal and Baba Yaga had put the dishes in the wash bucket, she got up, but to Vasylyna's dismay, the old woman moved over to the door of the small room and opened it. Vasylyna dreaded to see what was inside, but look she did, and what she saw made her stomach drop. The cloth was gone, and instead, a mountain of seeds was piled on the floor, reaching up to the ceiling.

"I have some poppy seeds and wheat that are mixed together. If you can separate them into two piles by the time I get back from my chores, I will give you a reward. If not, well, my poor little pich hasn't eaten in days and is getting very hungry." And with that, Baba Yaga gathered her things and left Vasylyna in the house.

Vasylyna sat down next to the pile of seeds and grains and put her face in her hands. Then, she remembered her motanka and took her out of her pocket.

"Dolly of mine," she said. "What am I to do? Each task that Baba Yaga gives me is harder than the last one. And this one is totally impossible. Even with your help, I will never be able to separate all those grains, and Baba Yaga will throw me into the pich." She looked at the doll's hands that were little balls of cloth, hands that could never begin to sort through the seeds, and she sighed. "And I don't think even you can help me this time." But the doll leaped up and said,

> We need to sort through grain and seed.
> I know the very thing we need.
> Vasylyna, don't despair,
> I'll call my cousins of the air.

The doll directed Vasylyna to open the door. When she did, the motanka began to sing a song that sounded like the call of a songbird, and seventy-seven magpies flew into the house. At the doll's command, they began to sort the seeds with their beaks into separate piles of wheat grains and poppy seeds. Vasylyna joined in and helped, and the doll directed the birds. As the sun moved across the sky, they sorted seed after seed, grain after grain. Just as the sun was beginning to set, Vasylyna placed the last seed in its pile. The birds flew out the door, Vasylyna shut it behind them, and the motanka jumped back into Vasylyna's pocket. A moment later, Baba Yaga stepped into the khata, stamping the dirt from her straw shoes and setting her sack on the table.

"Well, little pich," she said to the oven. "Do you get your reward today?" But Vasylyna opened the door to the room and showed her the pile of wheat and the pile of poppy seeds. Baba Yaga stamped her way into the room and looked each pile up and down.

"Hmph," said Baba Yaga. She pushed at the poppy seeds and poked at the pile of wheat, looking for one grain that was out of place, but there was not one that was not in its correct pile.

"Hmph," she said again. "I don't know how you did it, girl, but you did as I asked." She flicked off a poppy seed that had gotten stuck to her finger.

"Very well," she sighed. "I suppose today you will get some dinner and my poor little pich will get none." And with that, Baba Yaga began to set about making the evening meal for the two of them.

After they had eaten their fill, Baba Yaga stood up.

"Come, girl. Put on your shawl and follow me." And Baba Yaga put on her shaggy coat, picked up an old wooden mortar and pestle and the fire broom she used to sweep out the pich, and stepped outside. Vasylyna put on her own shawl and headscarf to keep herself warm, felt to make sure that her dolly was in her pocket, and followed Baba Yaga out into the night.

When she stepped outside, she stopped short and was astounded to see that the mortar and pestle had become as big as a small boat. Baba Yaga was standing inside and settling the pestle at the edge of the bowl.

"Come, come! Hurry!" said Baba Yaga. "We have much to do!" Baba Yaga extended her hand, and Vasylyna shyly stepped forward. With incredible strength, Baba Yaga pulled Vasylyna up and into the mortar. Then she took the pestle with both hands and shoved it against the earth beside them.

With one push, they were off, skittering over the ground as quickly and as effortlessly as a flat stone over the surface of an icy pond, pushing over trees in their path like bending blades of grass. Baba Yaga took out her broom and gave one sweep behind them, and the trees righted themselves as if they had never been touched. She gave another push with the giant pestle, and the mortar flew even faster, bumping and skipping over the ground.

## Baba Yaga Teaches the Magic of the Stupa

Ah! The *stupa*. My magical mortar and pestle. I'm known for riding through the forest in my mortar. Some say on the ground, pushing myself along with the club of my pestle and sweeping away my tracks with my fire broom. Others say I fly through the air, creating whirlwinds as I go.[150] Who's to say I can't do both?

I know what you're thinking: "Why can't you just ride on a broom like other witches? Why do you have to be so *extra?*" My dear, in case you haven't figured it out by now, the whole point of being Baba Yaga is that I do whatever I want, and I don't care what anyone thinks. Ponder on it for a second: It's a cold winter night. You are an old woman. Do you want to fly around with your legs dangling in the winter wind, or do you want to be in a nice, cozy container, flying in style? I know which one I prefer. Baba Yaga only flies first-class.

The mortar is a special tool in any witch's cabinet, whether you can fly in it or not. Such a humble thing. Like all my tools, it's something that was common, found in every peasant's khata. You might just think it's a useful tool for crushing up herbs, or pulverizing powders, or making potions, and it is, but it's also something ritually symbolic. You know, at one time, friends would gift a bride and a groom a mortar and pestle and also give them a nudge and a wink. The pestle moving around in that mortar, grinding away—it's kind of sexy, no?

To imagine me, Baba Yaga, flying around in a mortar, you must know about what life was like in past times. Every house had a small stupa, but if you were grinding grain into flour and you tried to use that little stupa, it would take you the entire day to grind enough for just a loaf. No one has time for that. So, in villages, they would sometimes have a community millstone so that everyone could have a turn grinding their grains quickly. However, not every village was rich enough to have a mill, and those who couldn't afford it would have a *khata stupa* instead: a mortar house. This little building would have a huge stupa carved from the fat trunk of a big oak with another log serving as the pestle. This stupa, used by all the families in the community to grind their grain,

150. Johns, *Baba Yaga*.

was large enough to hold a person. So, the idea of me flying about in a stupa doesn't seem so outlandish, after all.

We used these large mortars to grind our grains and pound flax and hemp to prepare them for spinning. These acts are paradoxically both destructive and constructive at the same time. When we crush up a kernel of rye, we are destroying the grain but creating flour. We destroy the flax stem and create a fiber for weaving. When you want to do magic to get rid of one situation and bring in a new and improved one, well ducky, you can't beat a mortar.

Now think about me. Everyone nowadays seems to focus on the fact that I destroy, but they have forgotten that I also bring rebirth and renewal. As I push through the forest, I knock over trees, but I sweep to bring them back again. Anyone who willingly goes into my oven, they see that the fire of my pich doesn't consume them, it transforms them. The mortar and pestle are your tools of transformation, changing something from one state into a new state. And we all know that change is good.

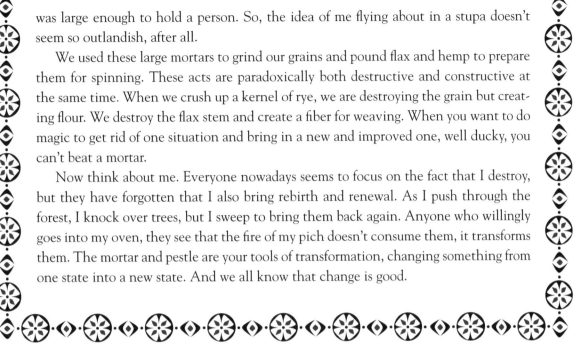

## Madame Pamita Teaches the Magic of the Stupa

I have always had a fascination with mortars and pestles. As a little girl, I used to wonder how they worked and what they were used for. I knew about Baba Yaga using a giant mortar for transportation, pushing herself along with her clublike pestle, but I suspected that mortars had some other use as well.

When I began to learn witchcraft, I saw how powerful a mortar and pestle could be, not only for the practical matter of grinding herbs and resins, but as a tool to imbue your ingredients with magic. Each pound or grind would transform the herb, changing it from a leaf to powder or paste, and each of those important moments of transformation could be used to imbue your ingredients with intention. The mindful and meditative qualities of the rhythmic pounding become almost like the hypnotic beating of a drum, allowing you to step out of time and into the liminal world of spirit.

# Stupa Magic Today

At one time, a mortar and pestle were part of every home. People of even a few generations ago would have to grind herbs, grains, and other edibles to prepare food or medicines. Today, they are still used in gourmet cooking and mixology but are also a primary tool of magic. Because they are found across all cultures going back at least fifty thousand years, they connect us back through our family line to our early ancestors. When you are doing spells to transform and change, a mortar can be your go-to tool, and when you need to pulverize an herb or resin to make a potion or incense, this low-tech approach can allow you to add your energy to your magical concoction.

### Choosing a Stupa

When choosing a mortar and pestle set, you want to take some things into consideration. While finding one that appeals to you visually is important, it's equally important to find one that is functional.

### Size

While a teeny-tiny mortar and pestle can be cute, a small mortar will only allow you to grind up a tiny amount of herbs at a time, and a doll-sized pestle won't allow you to get the force and pressure necessary to grind harder woody stems and pods. Ideally, you'll want a mortar that's about four to six inches in diameter and heavy enough that it won't move around too much while you are pounding.

### Shape

While there are mortars that come in a range of shapes for various purposes, one with a wide mouth and a steep side will be easier to use and will keep whatever you're grinding from spilling out.

### Texture

In most cases, grinding will be easier if the inside of the mortar and the end of the pestle have some texture and are not too slick. Very rough textures will grind faster but are a little trickier to clean up. Smooth-textured ones will be easier to clean but will take more effort to grind. Finding one that is neither too smooth nor too rough will allow you to grind and to not have to spend too much effort in the cleanup.

## *Material*

Mortar and pestle sets can be made out of any number of materials. Each material has its own advantages and disadvantages. To be safe, most witches choose to have at least two different sets: one for edible herbs, and the other for inedible herbs and resins.

### Wood

*Advantages:* Can be less expensive. You can choose a wood aligned with your magical goals.

*Disadvantages:* Wood absorbs oils and juices. Smoothness may make grinding difficult.

### Porcelain/Ceramic

*Advantages:* An unglazed interior makes it easier to grind.

*Disadvantages:* Unglazed parts may get stained by oils and colors.

### Stone

*Advantages:* Heavy, so they are easier to grind with.

*Disadvantages:* If the stone is soft or rough and the mortar unseasoned, you could get tiny chips of stone mixed with your herbs. Some light-colored stones, particularly marble, can get stained by herbs and resins.

### Metal

*Advantages:* Easiest to clean, great for working with resins. Sturdy and indestructible.

*Disadvantages:* Some can be too smooth, and grinding can take longer.

## *Seasoning Your Stupa*

If you have a new stone or wood mortar and pestle, it's a good idea to season it, both to get some practice grinding and to wear down any rough spots before you pound your first herbs. Put a few tablespoons of dry white rice and coarse salt in the bowl and pound and grind away until the rice and salt are completely pulverized. If you have a colored stone, wood, or finished metal, you may see the powder turn the color of your mortar and pestle. This is normal. Dump this powder into the trash and repeat at least three times or until the powder comes out white.

### Cleaning Your Stupa

A mortar and pestle can absorb colors and odors, so it should never be washed with a scented soap. Instead, use plain water and either scrub with a stiff brush, rinse out, or wipe down.

To remove sticky resin residue from a metal, ceramic, or stone mortar and pestle, pour rubbing alcohol, perfumer's alcohol, or inexpensive high-proof vodka or other spirits into the mortar. Place the pestle in the mortar and soak for ten to fifteen minutes to dissolve resins. Wipe out with plain water.

### Stupa Technique

There are two techniques to using a mortar and pestle for grinding herbs. The first is to pound the plant matter, and the second is to grind the plant matter by moving the pestle in a circular motion. Both work well, and depending on the texture of your herbs, one or the other will feel more natural and be more effective. Be sure to only grind a few tablespoons at a time. Adding more than that will work against you when you try to grind. Grind or pound small amounts, dispense them into a jar or container, add a few more tablespoons, and repeat.

### Stupa Spells

Mortars and pestles have some clear advantages over other more modern technology for pulverizing herbs. With each pound or grind, you are putting your energy into the herbs. It is through your effort and will that you are changing the state of the matter, just as your effort and will create magical changes of any kind. Like Baba Yaga, the mortar and pestle represent death and birth, destruction and creation.

Before you start working with your mortar and pestle for a spell, think about what it is that you want to accomplish magically. Create a visualization or think of a short affirmation or incantation that reflects what it is that you wish to manifest. The actions you make as you work with the mortar and pestle can empower your magic. If it is something that you wish to bring in, you can grind your herbs in a clockwise motion. If it is something that you want to get rid of, you can grind your herbs in a counterclockwise motion. If you would like to infuse your herbs with force, you can pound the herbs with a rhythmic beat and speak your spell words with every beat of the pestle.[151]

The mortar can be used for things other than grinding. Traditionally, people saw the mortar and pestle as having erotic symbolism, so before a wedding, they would offer the couple a mortar wrapped in a small skirt and a pestle with tiny trousers. They would push the pestle into the mortar and sing racy songs. If you'd like to invite more passion and chemistry into a relationship, you can use the mortar and pestle for some sympathetic magic. Envision the sensual scene that you'd like to enact and mimic that with the mortar and pestle or put some edible love herbs, such as poppy seeds or lovage root, into the mortar and grind them with the pestle. Mix these into food that you serve to your beloved as an aphrodisiac.

## The Stupa as a Tool of Change

Along with the house on chicken legs, the stupa is the most iconic of items associated with Baba Yaga. This may seem like a random attribute until you realize that the mortar and pestle perform the same function as Baba Yaga: destruction to create something even better or more useful than what was there before. This is all part of initiation—the death of the old life to awaken into the new. Working with the stupa will give you a chance to meditate on the nature of change, and reflecting on Baba Yaga's associations with transformation will deepen your spiritual practice with the mortar and pestle.

---

151. Raven Grimassi, *Old World Witchcraft: Ancient Ways for Modern Days* (San Francisco, CA: Weiser Books, 2011).

# Chapter 17

# Maty Zemlya: Mother Earth

**B**aba Yaga pushed the ground with her pestle, and the two of them bumped and bounced and shoved their way through the forest until they stopped at a tiny clearing.

A sliver of moonlight shone down from between the branches of the big spruces onto a large flat rock sticking out from the ground. Baba Yaga whispered some words and rapped her broom on the stone three times. As she did, the broom seemed to soften and bend like a candle next to a fire. As it bent down, it turned shimmery and shiny and began undulating gently. The broom turned into a snake, beautiful and as black as ebony polished with beeswax. Baba Yaga bent down to release the snake as gently as she would place an egg in a nest. The snake slid under the rock and out of sight. Baba Yaga lifted the edge of the rock like a trapdoor, revealing a tunnel underneath.

"I need you to follow that snake, girl. My children are down there, and I need them to come home. Don't come back out until you have all of them. Fetch them and I will have a reward for you. But if you come back and have not brought every single one of them with you, well, then you will finally become a well-deserved morsel for my pich."

The tunnel looked cramped, damp, and dark and Vasylyna was scared. But she could hear her doll whisper to her.

> Don't be afraid, Vasylyna dear.
> In Mother Earth there is nothing to fear.
> Into the tunnel you must go,
> to find the children down below.

And so Vasylyna took a step and went down into the damp, earthy tunnel. It was dark, and as she felt her way along the moist walls, her fingers touched roots and stones and animal bones *compacted in the earth. As her eyes adjusted to the dark, she could just make out the shimmer of the snake as it slithered ahead of her.*

*Finally, the tunnel widened into a chamber that faintly glowed with a luminescent golden light. Vasylyna could make out the slimy walls dripping with moisture, but there were no children down in the hole. Perhaps Baba Yaga had tricked her, and Vasylyna was going to be trapped down here forever. She sat down on a stone, and a tear trickled down her cheek, but in a moment, she felt her doll in her pocket, once again tugging at her skirt. She lifted the dolly out and held her close to her heart.*

*"Dolly of mine, what do I do? Baba Yaga has trapped me and led me down into this hole and there are no children here. She has left me here to die." But the doll replied, "Sing, Vasylyna. Sing, and the children will come out."*

*So, even though Vasylyna was afraid, she began to sing, her voice echoing off the walls. She sang the songs that she had learned from her mother, songs about doves and falcons. Songs about roses and poppies. Songs about oaks and birch trees. Songs about the moon and the stars. And as she sang, the walls began to glow a little brighter, and she felt a little less afraid.*

## Baba Yaga Shares the Wisdom of Maty Zemlya

As the old saying goes, "Don't look up at the heavens—there is no bread there. As you get closer to Earth, you get closer to bread." If you really want to meet the divine, you don't need to look up to the sky. The earth beneath your feet is alive and all-knowing. *Zemlya Svyata Maty*, Holy Mother Earth. We don't think of Mother Earth as a goddess walking around, no. The actual ground you tread on is our Holy Mother. She falls into a deep slumber in winter and wakes up each spring to adorn herself with flowers and greenery. She benevolently spreads life, strength, and abundance. Grasses, flowers, bushes, and trees are her lush hair; boulders, stones, and rocks are her bones; the twisted roots of the trees are her veins; the water that bubbles up from the springs is her blood. Eternally, she receives seeds, becomes pregnant, and gives birth to a new harvest.[152]

152. Hubbs, *Mother Russia*.

When we speak of her, we are as emotional and full of love as if we are talking about our human mother. In the days when we all farmed the land, no one could strike the earth with a plow before her birthing time at *Kolodiy*, Shrovetide, the holiday that marks the end of winter. At this time, bread was buried for her to eat, and beer or wine was poured on the earth for her to drink.

At any time of the year, anyone spitting on the earth had to beg her forgiveness. Property disputes were settled by calling on Mother Earth to witness the justice of the claims. Oaths and marriages were confirmed by swallowing a small clump of earth or holding it on the head.[153] We kissed her before setting out on a journey, and then again at journey's end. And prior to death, one was expected to ask the earth's forgiveness, for if she was not honored, she would lie heavily on one's coffin.

How do I know so much about her? Ah, young one, I know her intimately. Not only do I have my home in the forest, I have a home in the lower world. Unlike regular mortals who only go into the earth when they die, I can travel freely back and forth between my homes deep in her belly and above ground in the forest. Is it the land of the dead? Yes, if you think of death as being change and transition. Her belly gives birth to all living beings: she feeds the living, and she receives the dead. She does it all. Womb to tomb, over and over again.

So, I am mistress of the forest *and* of the lower world, a place of initiation. Deep in my forest, you'll find the portal to enter. A flat rock or a boulder that I lift aside. Come with my permission, and you'll find a deep cavern of sacred mysteries. You'll learn the ways of life and death, the secrets of transformation. A quiet and meditative place where you can discover the answers to your deepest questions, back in your mother's womb.[154]

It might be a challenge for you to squeeze into this spot on your own, but not for me. Oh, I must have forgotten to tell you that I am gifted in the art of shape-shifting. Not only can I turn my broom into a snake, but I can also easily assume the form of a serpent myself—as small as a newly hatched grass snake, or as large as a dragon. It's one of my prouder accomplishments. Instead of describing me with my one good leg and my one bony leg, some say I have only one leg, and in my snake form, they would be correct.[155]

153. Gilchrist, *Russian Magic*.

154. Warner, *Russian Myths*.

155. Johns, *Baba Yaga*.

What? You don't like snakes? As far back as ten thousand years ago, we looked upon snakes with much respect and even affection.[156] We domesticated them in our houses and honored them as household guardians by making them offerings of milk, eggs, and cheese. Snakes sometimes do us good service, both in keeping away the pests and in aiding us in rapidly growing rich, and they require nothing in return but simple offerings. It's a happy omen if a snake takes up its quarters in a cottage, and we gladly set out offerings for it. To kill such a snake would be a very great transgression. However, should you find one that has died a natural death, there is much healing power found in the heads and skins of snakes.

Snakes can be more than just allies, they can be teachers. One of the paths of the molfarka is to learn to communicate with animals and plants. As you can imagine, these lessons from the spirits can take years to master. However, there is a legend of a girl who fell into a pit and lived underground, where she was taught to understand the language of the animals and the plants by the Queen of the Snakes.[157]

When they talk about the Queen of the Snakes, I have to chuckle. When I choose to fly through the sky in my fiery mortar with my burning broom, I often take the form of the Fiery Snake, a dragon. In that form, I also guard the springs of the "Water of Life" and the "Water of Death," the waters that cure wounds and restore the dead to life. So, am I the Queen of the Snakes, the Ruler of the Underworld? Well, I'll just let you figure that one out.

## Madame Pamita Teaches the Magic of the Zemlya Svyata Maty

I remember that whenever we would travel long distances and come back to our home, my mother would kiss the ground in our yard. I used to think it was just a quirk of hers. I thought that even though she seemed happy and eager to travel, she must have been

---

156. Nadiia Kotova et al., "Microscopic Examination of Mesolithic Serpent-Like Sculptured Stones from Southern Ukraine," *Antiquity* 92, no. 366 (2018), https://doi.org/10.15184/aqy.2018.249.

157. V. F. Yatchenko, *Ukrayins'kyy Shamanizm* (Kyiv, Ukraine: Milenium, 2011).

harboring some secret anxiety and was kissing the ground in a gesture of being back on terra firma after flying or sailing. It wasn't until I learned about Ukrainian spiritual practices that I learned that kissing the ground is and was a magical tradition—a way of honoring Mother Earth and your place on the land.

## Maty Zemlya Today

Ukrainians today have what can only be described as a deep reverence for the land—not just geographic designations, but for the earth itself. Ukraine is one of the most fertile places on the planet, possessing 25 to 30 percent of the world's reserves of black earth, the richest in organic matter.[158] This awareness of the life-giving force of the land generates a deep sense of pride and at least the subconscious awareness of the power of Maty Zemlya. People instinctively turn to her for a sense of connection and grounding.

In traditional ways, the earth is never personified as a goddess, but is herself respected as righteous, holy, and divine. There is an old saying, "We hold on to the earth, because the earth holds us." People are willing to defend Maty Zemlya to their last breath, because they know that she is the source of all life and *their* life.

### Gestures to Honor Maty Zemlya

The simplest way that you can connect to the divine through Mother Earth is through the act of kissing the ground. Kissing the earth is considered a sign of the greatest respect for Mother Earth and will ensure that you receive her bountiful blessings. In times past, a warrior, upon returning home, would first climb a high hill, bow to each of the four directions, raise their hands to the sky in prayer, and then kneel and kiss the earth.

### An Earth Amulet

A small clod of earth, collected from under the threshold of your home, yard, field, village, or settlement, is a powerfully protective amulet when you travel far from home into the world of strangers. Your native Maty Zemlya will protect you anywhere you go and allow you to return home safely. In the old times, they would give bread, salt, and

---

158. "Ukraine Adopts Land Reform," Official Website of the International Trade Administration, September 30, 2020, https://www.trade.gov/market-intelligence/ukraine-adopts-land-reform.

a handful of earth wrapped in a rushnyk to a loved one going on a long journey. They believed that those who did not take a handful of their native land with them when setting out would never see their homeland again.

Kozaky were said to carry a pouch of their native soil wherever they went, as well. This ensured their safety at any place abroad. Should they die in a distant land, then this clod of familiar earth would connect them to the land of their ancestors when they were buried. When in distress, they were able to take that pouch, touch the earth in it, and even kiss it to show their love for Mother Earth and ask for her help. If they had to stay in a foreign land, they could pour out the earth from this amulet, step on it barefoot, and say, "I walk on my land," and the new land would become their own.

Today, you can feel the protection of Maty Zemlya by carrying a clod of earth from your own home. You can wear it in a leather pouch around your neck, a sack attached to your belt, or a small cloth or handkerchief placed in your purse or luggage for protection while traveling.

### Healing Yourself with Maty Zemlya

Mother Earth's energy may be used when performing rituals for healing physical wounds, increasing beauty, restoring strength, and mending bones. She is called on for tranquility, to release troubling thoughts, to invite peaceful sleep, and to protect our possessions.

If a person is ill and nothing seems to be helping, they may stand in an open field at sunrise or sunset for three days in a row and ask Mother Earth for her forgiveness. Turning clockwise and bowing to each of the four directions, they say the following appeal three times:

> Holy Mother Earth, help me, forgive me if I did something wrong.
> Return me to the way I was before.

If you fall outdoors and get bruised or broken in some way, you should lie down on the ground at the same spot where the injury occurred and ask Mother Earth for forgiveness, so that your injury heals quickly. Speak the following request:

> Forgive me, my own native soil, Moist Mother Earth!

Poultices made with damp earth are also used to cure headaches with the following incantation:

*As the earth is well, may my head be well.*

### Healing Someone Else with Maty Zemlya

Kozak sorcerers, called *kharaktérnyky*, used earth from the homeland as a healing tool. They stanched bleeding wounds by applying poultices made from the victim's native earth soaked in spit. As they applied this concoction, they would say, "As the earth is healthy, so you will be healthy."

If you want to invoke Maty Zemlya for healing someone else who cannot leave their sickbed, you can create a healing wash with water and earth. First, pick up a handful of dirt with these words:

*Moist Mother Earth with your little children,*
*bless me to take some strength.*
*Not for exploitation, not for wisdom, but for good health.*

This blessed earth is sewn into a cloth pouch and carried by the spellcaster as a charm for three days. After which, the pouch is put into a cauldron full of water and heated until boiling. The resulting water is cooled and then poured over the sick person, and any dirt remaining in the pouch is returned to the same spot where it was taken from.

### Earthy Footprint Magic

A footprint left in earth is a powerful tool both to help and to harm. The harshest curse of death can be performed by collecting the dirt from the footprint, piercing it with nails and pins, and burning it in the oven. Dried mud stuck to someone's feet or shoes could be collected in a pouch and charmed into a protective amulet for that person. It can also be used for divination. A talented vorozhka could foretell the future by reading the dirt accumulated under one's left shoe.

### *Sealing an Oath*

In times past, Mother Earth was often called upon to witness promises and contracts. Just as nowadays people say, "I swear on my mother's grave," people in those days would make a solemn vow, saying, "Let Mother Earth cover me forever, if I lie!"

Earth was considered so holy that serious oaths could be taken while holding a clod of soil. Placing a handful of soil on one's head before taking a vow made the promise inviolable, for Mother Earth could not be cheated and would not forgive one who did not keep their word.

Oaths of brotherhood or sisterhood could be made with earth as well. If two people of different families wanted to create a sibling bond, they would make a small cut on their fingers, mix their blood and exchange handfuls of their native soil to seal their new relationship.

## Feeding Maty Zemlya

The beliefs about Maty Zemlya were that she went to sleep over the winter and woke up again in spring. Food offerings of bread, beer, or wine or sacred offerings of bones or eggshells, particularly painted kranshanky and pysanky, were given to her in the spring after her long sleep. Offerings and objects left for Mother Earth were buried, left on the ground, hidden inside hollow logs, or tied to tree branches. At a home altar, Mother Earth would be honored by a dish of earth, herbs, twigs, moss, or stones collected from a power spot.

At harvest time, to protect the earth as she slept through the winter, people would honor her by facing in each of the four directions and pouring a few drops of hemp oil on the ground, saying, "Moist Mother Earth, banish anything that is cursed by hexes, foul touch, or evil deeds." This simple gesture protected the land from extreme winter weather: winds, blizzards, and hail.

More elaborate invocations can be made in each of the four directions to protect Mother Earth as the weather gets colder and more unpredictable. Face in each of the four directions and say the corresponding incantation:

*Toward the east:* "Mother Earth, subdue every evil and unclean being so that they may not cast a spell on us nor do us any harm."

*Toward the south:* "Mother Earth, calm the winds coming from the south and all bad weather. Calm the moving sands and whirlwinds."

*Toward the west:* "Mother Earth, engulf the unclean power in your boiling pits and in your burning fires."

*Toward the north:* "Mother Earth, calm the north winds and the clouds, subdue the snowstorms and the cold."159

### Invoking Curses with Maty Zemlya

Mother Earth is considered the final judge because she gives birth and accepts in death. She produces, destroys, transforms, and gives birth again. It is believed that if someone lived a worthy life, the earth would gently receive them, but if they were evil, the earth would not accept them, and their body would not rot, and they would become an *upyr*: a ghoul or a vampire, wandering the lands in distress. There are serious curses that can be flung at wrongdoers regarding this matter: "May the holy land not receive you!" or "May the earth swallow you up!" implying that Mother Earth would not take you lovingly or gently and that you would become a restless spirit.

### Listening to Maty Zemlya

There is a method of communication with Mother Earth that is unique to Slavic ways. By digging a small hole into the earth with a stick or your fingers, you can create a channel of communication. You can release your burdens, cleanse yourself, ask for blessings, or beg forgiveness of Mother Earth by whispering into this hole. Speak your question or desire into the hole and then put your ear to the hole to listen for Mother Earth's reply. The response that you get may be a feeling, a visual impression, or words heard through your "mind's ear," or you may actually be able to make out words in the whispers coming from the ground.

---

159. Kenneth Johnson, *Slavic Sorcery: Shamanic Journey of Initiation* (St. Paul, MN: Llewellyn Publications, 1998).

### *Power Places to Connect to Maty Zemlya*

While Mother Earth is everywhere, there are power places where it is easier to connect to her. Each of these places has its own subtle energetic differences, and so different types of offerings, spells, divination, or magical workings can be done at each one.

### Caves

Caves are seen as either the bosom or the womb of Mother Earth. As the womb, they are useful for doing reflective internal work, initiations, and transformation. As the bosom, they are seen as a place of refuge and comfort when in peril.

### Canyons

Entering a canyon can become an experience of true union with Mother Earth. Canyons reveal the deeper depths of Earth, and touching the walls can intimately connect you with Maty Zemlya. Use canyons for creating more meaningful connections with Mother Earth.

### Cemeteries

Cemetery dirt can be used for spirit contact, to receive the blessings of the spirits, to honor the ancestors, or to call forth the assistance of death deities.

### Fields

Open fields are used for calling up the power of fertile Mother Earth. The image of the verdant field is called forth in many incantations, such as, "I go out into the open field, into the green grasses. I stand on the damp ground; I look to the east." Crops that feed and nourish us are grown in the fields, so this is the place to encounter the abundant nurturing nature of Maty Zemlya. Backyard gardens, window boxes, and potted herbs can bring Mother Earth's field energy into smaller spaces, but stepping into a field with the wide sky above you is an excellent place to honor her and call forth abundance.

### Forest

The edges of the forest are seen as a liminal place of magic. This is another place where one can encounter spirits, otherworldly beings, and the wildness of nature. Work with Mother Earth at the borders of the forest or in thickets when you wish to encounter her untamed spirit.

### Houses

The earth from one's own home and property strengthens, blesses, and protects the family. This can be the dirt from a beloved home or from the home where you were born and grew up. Dirt from under a threshold is especially powerful when carried as a talisman.

### Meadows

Meadows channel the life-giving healing nature of Mother Earth. Meadows freely provide edible and medicinal herbs and so represent the unconditional love of Maty Zemlya. Herbs collected in the meadow are empowered by Mother Earth, and walking barefoot in a meadow is an exceptional way to connect with her. Morning dew collected from meadows is charged with powerful magic. If you wish to receive the love and blessings of Mother Earth, meet her in a meadow.

### Mounds

*Kurhany* are burial mounds of earth and stones dating back thousands of years. These ancient sites represent the accepting nature of Mother Earth, connect us to our most ancient ancestors, and are mystical places of power. At these burial mounds, we can connect to the receiving nature of Maty Zemlya and our ancestral line.

### Mountains

Mountains invoke the sturdy power and magnificence of Mother Earth. Climbing to the top of a hill or mountain to perform rituals brings strength and a clarifying and energizing power to any magical working. Spiritual people may go to the mountains to connect with Mother Earth as a source of solitude and peace, to find wisdom, or to find self-acceptance. Magical work for achieving seemingly unreachable goals is supported by working in the mountains, and it is said that Maty Zemlya will grant blessings that she has promised when she is petitioned in the mountains.

### Standing Stones

*Kam'yani baby*, or stone women, are very ancient standing stones dating back more than six thousand years. Standing stones or stone circles delineate ancient holy places of power. These earthy portals can be used for time-shifts, traveling to other worlds, or honoring ancestral lines.

### Wilderness

Wilderness or pristine, untrodden areas are often used in cleansing magic. Water from a spiritual cleansing should be left in places where people don't walk so that no one picks up the curse or illness that is being banished by accidentally stepping on it. Objects can be buried in the wilderness to become pure again, as pristine Mother Earth has the power to transform any negative energy. Go into uninhabited wilderness to cleanse or heal or collect dirt from an untrodden area to create a talisman for removing negativity.

## The Deep Connection to Maty Zemlya

Baba Yaga herself has a deep connection to the earth. There are many stories where she rules over an underground realm. This fairy tale idea of a world underground corresponds to ancient notions of the lower world in the World Tree.[160] It can be said that through this life she lives underground, she is intimately entwined with Maty Zemlya, just like the snake and dragon figures she so easily can shape-shift into.[161] To know Baba Yaga, you must know her realm of the underground: the safe womb of Maty Zemlya, she who gives life to all.

---

160. Johns, *Baba Yaga*.
161. Oleszkiewicz-Peralba, *Fierce Feminine Divinities of Eurasia and Latin America*.

# Chapter 18

# Laznya: The Bathhouse

As Vasylyna sang, the underground creatures of the lower world began to emerge to listen to her song. Earthworms and grubs, beetles and centipedes, rats and moles, spiders and salamanders all began to slither and skitter closer and closer to hear her song. As they gathered around her, she stopped singing, afraid that they would attack her, but instead with their tiny voices, they whispered and squeaked. "Please sing to us some more, Vasylyna."

She was afraid that if she stopped, they might harm her, so she continued to sing, and the creatures circled around her. Song after song she sang. Songs with words that were meant to heal a sick person. Songs that were meant to change the weather. She sang songs from the holidays. Songs for weddings and baptisms and funerals. Finally, she finished the very last song that she knew by heart. Her throat was dry, so she thought that she might get them to converse and give her voice a rest.

"Who are you?" she asked them.

"We are the children of Baba Yaga," they all whispered and croaked.

"Oh!" said Vasylyna, surprised, horrified, and glad to have found them all at the same time. "Will you come with me above ground?"

"No!" they all shouted in unison. "We like it down here."

Vasylyna looked at the slimy, dirty creatures and felt repelled by their appearance. Even if she could get over her disgust enough to touch them, there were too many for her to carry all by herself up to the surface. Then Vasylyna had an idea. She started to sing again but stood up and began to walk toward the tunnel, and the animals followed her. She led them up toward the entrance as she sang on the way.

When Vasylyna reached the entrance to the tunnel, Baba Yaga was waiting.

"What took you so long?" she said gruffly. "It's nearly dawn and there is much work to be done today."

Vasylyna began to explain, but Baba Yaga bent over and picked up the ebony-colored snake and held it so that it hung down, and it resumed its form of a broom. Before Vasylyna could finish her sentence, Baba Yaga clambered back into her mortar and gave it a gentle push back toward her khata. All the creatures scampered and capered behind her, and Vasylyna followed as well, keeping her distance from the scariest and slimiest of the animals.

When they got to the khata, Baba Yaga pulled an old sieve off the wall and handed it to Vasylyna.

"Take this. Go down to the stream and collect some water for the laznya, the bathhouse, and take my children down there to clean them up. I have work to do, and I won't be back until sundown, but I expect to see each of my children bathed and immaculately clean by the time I get back. If not? Well, my pich will finally get a morsel to eat." And at that, Baba Yaga picked up her sack and left, leaving the door wide open.

Vasylyna looked at the horrible creatures scampering and crawling over the house and making a ruckus, and then she looked at the sieve with all the holes in it and felt completely disheartened. Just then, her pocket shifted, and she remembered her motanka and pulled her out.

"Dolly of mine, what am I going to do? I hope you have an answer for me, because to me this looks truly impossible!" She whispered under her breath, so as not to offend the creatures: "It's bad enough that I have to touch these slimy creatures, but how am I going to collect water in a sieve?"

The motanka said,

> To get to the laznya, we follow the path,
> and give these earthy children a bath.
> Bring us all down to the river with you,
> and I will show you what to do.

So, Vasylyna tucked the motanka back into her pocket and picked up the sieve. She looked back at the creatures and began to sing so that they would follow her, and down the path they walked to the river and the laznya.

*When they got there, the motanka told Vasylyna to take the clay from the riverbank, line the sieve, and collect some water to take over to the rickety wooden bathhouse nearby. Vasylyna lined the sieve with clay, filled it with water, and carried it over to the vat in the bathhouse. She set the fire, heated the rocks, and invited all the animals in for a steam.*

*She wet a bundle of leafy branches in some warm water and stroked each of them as they enjoyed the steam. At first she hesitated, but then each creature showed such joy in getting cleaned by her, and they were all so well-behaved waiting their turns that she couldn't help but feel a fondness for them as they each passed through her hands and her care.*

## Baba Yaga Shares the Wisdom of the Laznya

Ah! My children! They aren't what you expected, are they? Or maybe they are. As the mother of the forest, all the creatures of the forest are my children, from the birds in the sky to the slimy creatures you find under rotten logs and cracked stones. And why shouldn't they be? You might have a preference, looking with admiration on the beauty of the deer or the majesty of the eagle, but why should they be admired any more than a toad or a rat or a worm? They are all my children, and I see them all as the miracles that they are.

And as much as we love the blessings of our Mother Earth, at some point my children get a little too blessed by her and have got to get clean. That's where the laznya, the bathhouse, comes in. If you're thinking of a bathroom or a bathtub, you couldn't be more wrong. The laznya has none of these things. What is it? It's what you might call a sauna nowadays, but that doesn't begin to describe all its magic and mystery.

The magic of the laznya goes back millennia. Long before written history, people were making dugouts and tents and huts, sacred places where they would create healing rituals combining the supernatural forces of the four elements—water, fire, air, and earth—to cleanse both body and soul. It was believed that these places were where you could get the favor of the divine elements and cleanse yourself of any sickness, spiritual or physical. It was said that if a patient was not helped by the laznya, then nothing would help them. These wooden huts, usually built near a river or stream where it would be easier to fetch the required living water, were seen as another liminal space, a place where the average person could touch the otherworlds and make magic.

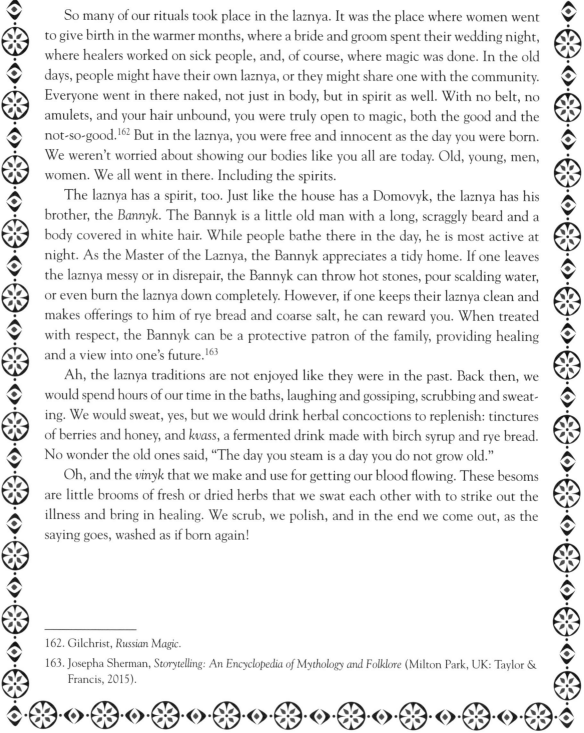

So many of our rituals took place in the laznya. It was the place where women went to give birth in the warmer months, where a bride and groom spent their wedding night, where healers worked on sick people, and, of course, where magic was done. In the old days, people might have their own laznya, or they might share one with the community. Everyone went in there naked, not just in body, but in spirit as well. With no belt, no amulets, and your hair unbound, you were truly open to magic, both the good and the not-so-good.[162] But in the laznya, you were free and innocent as the day you were born. We weren't worried about showing our bodies like you all are today. Old, young, men, women. We all went in there. Including the spirits.

The laznya has a spirit, too. Just like the house has a Domovyk, the laznya has his brother, the *Bannyk*. The Bannyk is a little old man with a long, scraggly beard and a body covered in white hair. While people bathe there in the day, he is most active at night. As the Master of the Laznya, the Bannyk appreciates a tidy home. If one leaves the laznya messy or in disrepair, the Bannyk can throw hot stones, pour scalding water, or even burn the laznya down completely. However, if one keeps their laznya clean and makes offerings to him of rye bread and coarse salt, he can reward you. When treated with respect, the Bannyk can be a protective patron of the family, providing healing and a view into one's future.[163]

Ah, the laznya traditions are not enjoyed like they were in the past. Back then, we would spend hours of our time in the baths, laughing and gossiping, scrubbing and sweating. We would sweat, yes, but we would drink herbal concoctions to replenish: tinctures of berries and honey, and *kvass*, a fermented drink made with birch syrup and rye bread. No wonder the old ones said, "The day you steam is a day you do not grow old."

Oh, and the *vinyk* that we make and use for getting our blood flowing. These besoms are little brooms of fresh or dried herbs that we swat each other with to strike out the illness and bring in healing. We scrub, we polish, and in the end we come out, as the saying goes, washed as if born again!

162. Gilchrist, *Russian Magic*.

163. Josepha Sherman, *Storytelling: An Encyclopedia of Mythology and Folklore* (Milton Park, UK: Taylor & Francis, 2015).

## Madame Pamita Teaches the Magic of the Laznya

I remember the first time I went to a real sauna. For me, it might have been the first time I was completely nude in a public place in front of other people. I remember the feelings of insecurity that it brought up for me and the voices that swirled around in my head: "Are people looking at me? Are they judging my body?" After several minutes, however, I realized that no one was looking and no one really cared, and I was able to settle down and enjoy the experience.

The alien feeling of being completely exposed can initially create a jolt for us that eventually settles into a feeling of acceptance. But when I think about a laznya in the old days, I wonder about the extra feelings of vulnerability that would arise. We all have had the experience of going into an uninhabited building—the eerie feeling of liminality and the heightened senses that prickle our nerves.

Now imagine a windowless wooden hut, a bit distant from the houses in the village. It's dark and musty inside, with just simple sitting shelves on the walls and a stove with rocks in the corner for heat. Now, envision going into this uninhabited hut and removing your clothing, your talismans—everything that would protect you in your day-to-day life. Even just thinking about it conjures up feelings of unease. No wonder the laznya was seen as a mysterious and slightly creepy place.[164]

## The Laznya Today

Today, most bathhouses in big cities are well-lit, clean, and modern—far from being the sketchy, spooky places that country bathhouses were in the past. In fact, for the most part, bathhouses are seen as a special indulgence meant to fortify and heal the body and relax the spirit. Rather than just a place to get cleaned up, the bathhouse is meant to be rejuvenating, where one can cleanse from the inside out, replenish with herbal teas, and be massaged with aromatherapeutic branches. While people today might not have the intense experience of stepping into liminal space when they go into the laznya, they still know the healing power of the bathhouse.

A typical public bathhouse ritual today starts with readying yourself for the laznya by removing your clothes in a locker room and receiving a terrycloth robe, towel, or sheet; shower shoes; and a wool felt beanie to keep your head from overheating. Next,

---

164. Ryan, *The Bathhouse at Midnight.*

you go to the showers, where you take off your robe and cap and take a shower without soap or shampoo. Once you are rinsed off, you are ready for the steam room. Put on your cap and head into the moist steam room to sit or lie down on the sheet or towel for one fifteen-minute session, or several shorter sessions. The steam room can be very hot (160–170 degrees Fahrenheit/70–77 degrees Celsius), so many people take it in a few sessions and step out to drink hot herbal teas, kvass, or fruit-infused water in between.

Once the pores are sufficiently open after a total of fifteen minutes, you can lie down in the steam room, and a friend or a bathhouse employee will take the vinyk and gently stroke and then swat you with the bundle of branches to stimulate circulation and exfoliate the skin. Finally, you will be doused with cold water, take a cold shower, or go for a dip in a cold-water pool to close the pores. If you're in a country laznya in the winter, this last step can be an exhilarating naked roll around outside in the snow.[165]

## Making Magic with the Laznya

In days past, mystery and mysticism were incorporated into bathing rituals. The laznya was considered a liminal place of magic, and so there were strict rules for behavior in the bathhouse. The bath was always done during the day, and the number of participants had to be odd for good luck. Only living water taken from a flowing, clean source was used in the laznya. Special healing and magical effects were attributed to this living water. The bath besoms called vinyky were made of leafy branches of special plants and trees chosen for their healing and magical powers and decorated with ritual ribbons. They were often created with the intention of casting out illness or evil. Fire was used to heat stones, and it was endowed with extraordinary healing and magical properties for burning away negativity.

While you might not have a dedicated bathhouse or sauna of your own, you can still incorporate the healing of the laznya into your magical rituals through the practice of aromatherapeutic steam, massage with the vinyk, communing with the Bannyk, and performing divination. If you are fortunate enough to have access to a sauna, you can do these rituals there. If not, you can transform your bath or shower into a ritual laznya.

---

165. Gilchrist, *Russian Magic*.

### Steaming with Herbs

It is possible to emulate at least some of the healing qualities of the laznya by steaming with herbs. Herbs can be added to a hot bath, a hot shower, or a pot of hot water on the stove to breathe in the benefits of their essential oils as they are released. There are several ways you can do this:

If you are working in a laznya, the easiest way is to simply spread the twigs of dried plants on the shelves of the steam room. In a few minutes, the plants will soften from the heat and moisture and will give off an amazing and slightly intoxicating aroma. Alternatively, you can take the dried branches or stems, dip them in hot water for ten minutes, and then spread them on the top shelf in the sauna. The remaining infusion can be sprinkled on the stones to make a fragrant and healing steam.

You can also create a decoction by adding fresh or dried herbs to an enamel pot of water on the stove. After the water boils, reduce the heat to a low simmer for one hour. Pour this infusion over the stones in the laznya or let it cool and store it in the refrigerator for use in the bath up to one week later.

If you're working in a bathtub, you can add this herbal infusion to your bathwater or simply put the herbs in a muslin bag and put them directly into the bath. If you're doing your laznya ritual in the shower, you can tie up fresh bundles of herbs or put dried herbs in a muslin bag and hang them from your showerhead. There is a helpful list of herbs that can be used for a fragrant steam bath in appendix I.

### Making a Vinyk

There is a saying, "A bath without a vinyk is like a table without salt." The besom is an integral part of the laznya for both healing and magic. These little massage brooms are put together from the branches of magical and medicinal trees and herbs. If you're using fresh branches, these bundles need only be rinsed in warm water before using, but dried branches should be soaked in cold water overnight to soften them before use.

If you are working your magic in a laznya, having someone else slap your skin with the vinyk is the more traditional way to receive the treatment, but you can certainly do this yourself in a steamy shower. Keep the besom moist, dipping it in water from time to time. Stroke and lightly slap your skin with the besom to increase your circulation. The goal is to stimulate the skin and get the blood *flowing*, not to draw blood. It's never a good idea to beat yourself up, figuratively *or* literally. As you do this, you may say the traditional incantation: *"As these vinyk leaves hit the body, may good health enter the body."*

If you are cutting your own fresh branches of deciduous trees such as birch, oak, linden, or rowan, spring and early summer are the best times to harvest them. Pine, juniper, spruce, and other coniferous branches can be cut at any time of year. These tougher branches with needles should be soaked in boiling water to soften them before using them as a vinyk. With either deciduous or evergreen trees, choose young supple branches with soft new leaves. Tie them together with string or twine to make the besom. A complete list of branches traditionally used in making vinyky can be found in appendix I.

When gathering branches for a besom, you should only cut a few branches from each tree until you have built up a nice fluffy handful. As you do, you can speak the following incantation:

> *On the sea, on the ocean, on an island, stands a century-old forest.*
> *It stands still and doesn't move, and every leaf is motionless.*
> *As this forest is strong with trunks and leaves,*
> *so may I borrow your strength.*
> *Mother Earth, help me take these twigs with your blessing.*

When you dip the vinyk in hot water to prepare it for the massage, you can ask the Bannyk to charm the besom for healing by saying the following incantation:

> *Bannyk, you Bannyk, Master of the Laznya,*
> *enchant me against illness and diseases of all*
> *kinds: big and small, dry and wet.*
> *As the leaves fall from this broom, may illness fall from me.*
> *My lips and teeth are a lock; my tongue, the key,*
> *and I will fling the key into the sea, and my mouth shall remain locked.*

Or, if you are using a birch vinyk specifically, you can say this incantation:

> *As this white birch stood in a clear field,*
> *knowing neither curses, nor jealous glances,*
> *so I, [name], will know neither curses, nor jealous glances,*
> *and I will have health and longevity.*

## The Magic of the Bannyk

The Bannyk is the spirit of the laznya. He is naked except for the clothing he fashions from scavenged leaves that have fallen from the vinyky. Like his brother the Domovyk, he lives behind the stove or under one of the resting shelves. He likes his laznya to be clean, so to respect him as the Master of the Laznya, you should always keep the bathhouse tidy and leave him with a bucket of water, some soap, and a broom so that he can maintain his space. Leaving him an additional offering of some rye bread and salt will keep him friendly and protective.[166]

The Bannyk has strict rules for the use of the laznya. First, you should never go in with a bad attitude. It is also offensive to the Bannyk to bring alcohol into the laznya or go in after you have been drinking—a good rule to have, because this can also be physically dangerous and even deadly. People are free to use the laznya during the day, but after dark, it is his domain. He likes to use the laznya as well, so every fourth steam is an offering to him. Fragrant herbs and decoctions are poured onto the stones, and the laznya is closed off to humans so that he and his spirit friends can enjoy a bath.[167]

Should you offend the Bannyk and find yourself in a predicament where he is attacking you, back out of the laznya and call for the help of the Domovyk. A copper or iron rod is also good defense against a troublesome or angry Bannyk.

## Divination with the Bannyk

There is an unusual divination that was done on New Year's Eve by young people. They would leave an offering of rye bread and coarse salt on the stove for the Bannyk and then stand outside the laznya with their naked backsides stuck through the door, asking the Bannyk to reveal their fortune for the coming year. If the year was going to be a good one, they would feel the warm touch of the Bannyk gently stroking their back. If the year was going to be a difficult one, they would feel his cold hand and his nails running down their spine.

The same method was used to get a specific divination from the Bannyk. They would ask a yes/no question of the Bannyk, and if a cold touch or scratch from his claw was felt, it meant *no*. If a warm touch or caress was felt, it meant *yes*.

---

166. Ryan, *The Bathhouse at Midnight*.

167. Kennard, *The Russian Peasant*.

Young single women would also use this technique to ask the Bannyk if they were going to get married in the year. If they felt his touch, they could expect a wedding that year, and the type of touch they felt would predict who the groom would be.

- If the hand was hairy, the groom would be wealthy.
- If the hand was smooth, the groom would be poor.
- If the hand was rough, the groom would be difficult.
- If the hand slapped, the groom would be a bully.
- If the hand pinched gently, the groom would be playful and mischievous.

### Laznya Divination with Mirrors

There are many divination techniques done in the laznya to see who your future love could be. One of the simplest is to fall asleep on one of the resting shelves so that you can see their face in your dream.

A more complicated and riskier version requires you to go to the bathhouse, or some other uninhabited building, at midnight, bringing with you a beeswax candle, a ritual comb, a large mirror, a smaller mirror, and a cloth big enough to cover the small mirror.

Making sure the fires are not lit and the room is completely dark, remove all belts, amulets, and charms, and undo any knots or buttons on your clothes. Set up the large mirror behind you and the smaller mirror in front of you so that you see your repeating reflection. Light the beeswax candle and place it between you and the smaller mirror that you are looking into.

Unbind your hair to open yourself up to the spirit world. Comb it while looking in the mirror, repeating the following incantation: "The one who is destined to be with me, appear before me." Eventually, you should see a shadow behind your left shoulder, a spirit disguised as your future love. As soon as you get a glimpse, throw the cloth over the small mirror and say, *"Chur me." Chur* is thought to be a magic word of protection, calling in the assistance of an ancient god or one's ancestors.[168] It was believed that if you didn't take this last precaution, the spirit could reach out of the mirror and slap you or pull you into the otherworld.[169]

---

168. Dixon-Kennedy, *Encyclopedia of Russian and Slavic Myth and Legend*.
169. Kruchkova, *Slavic Seasonal Rituals and Divinations*.

### Laznya Divination with Water and Ashes

This is another type of bathhouse divination that uses a basin of water. To perform this ritual, you will need a handful of ashes, a basin, a vinyk, and water. First, place the basin of water in front of you. Slowly stir the water with the vinyk in a clockwise direction and ask, *"Will my wish for [name the wish] come true this year?"* Then throw a handful of ashes in the basin and divine the answer to your question.

- If the ashes clump together, the wish will come true this year.
- If the ashes spread evenly over the surface of the water, you may have to wait longer than a year for the wish to come true.
- If the ashes sink to the bottom, immediately dump the water onto the laznya floor to banish any negativity that may be associated with this desire.

### Laznya Scrying Divination

To see a vision of your future, you can use this unusual scrying technique in the laznya or in another uninhabited building at midnight. Bring a clear glass bottle or decanter filled with water, two beeswax candles, and a small mirror. Place the mirror on a table, the glass decanter of water in front of the mirror, and a candle on either side of the decanter. Sit at the table so that you can see the mirror through the decanter. The images you see in the mirror can be interpreted as your predictions for the upcoming year.

### Laznya Binding Love Spell

Love spells can be done in the laznya when the moon is full. If you and your partner are not getting along or your lover has stopped paying attention to you, you can perform the following spell. First, cut seven branches from seven birch trees to make a vinyk, saying this incantation:

*As the birch branches bend to the ground,*
*so let my darling reach out to me.*
*As strong as a birch is how strong their love is for me.*
*Whoever caresses me with this birch besom will be paired with me forever.*

The charmed besom should be used in the laznya for one full moon cycle, from full moon to full moon. Have your lover use the vinyk on you during this month, and their feelings for you will warm up.

### Laznya Spell for Banishing a Third Party

If your lover is being unfaithful, you can ask for the Bannyk's assistance in banishing a rival by doing the following ritual at midnight at the laznya. Bring a candle, a vinyk, a bucket of water, bread, and salt to the laznya. Upon entering the bathhouse, stop and bow to the Master of the Laznya and leave him an offering of bread and salt on the stove. Pour cold water into a bucket, dip the vinyk into it, and say, "Master of the Laznya, help me. Drive my rival out of the house."

Splash the water outside the laznya and place the vinyk inside, near the door, with the handle down. It must stand in this position for a week. After seven days, if the Bannyk will assist you, the vinyk will still be standing handle-down, and the spell will take effect. If the vinyk has fallen over, the Bannyk is telling you that he will not help you with your cause.

### Laznya Spell to Increase a Lover's Interest

Visiting a laznya, especially after a bride had washed herself in there, was considered a magical way to increase one's popularity and become more attractive to a potential lover. However, since most of us don't share a laznya with people in our village, there is another ritual that can be done in your bathroom or in a private sauna.

Bring some honey, an apple, a small piece of paper, some rose petals, a new knife, a pink ribbon, a basin, a piece of black cloth, some water, and a cold piece of burned wood from the laznya fire or any piece of wood that has been previously burned. On Friday, as soon as you wake up, heat up the laznya or start a hot shower or bath. Take off your clothes and whisper the following incantation:

> Water, help.
> Sky, bless.
> Sun and fire, protect.

With the burned stick, write the name of your loved one on the piece of paper. Cut the apple in half with the knife and place the folded paper with your lover's name between the halves of the apple. Tie it together with the ribbon. Place the apple in the empty basin and fill it with water and put the basin on the windowsill. Splash the water on your face and then apply honey to your face. Say the following:

*Look how sweet I am.*
*As bees fly to honey, so you fly to me.*

Use the rest of the water to rinse the honey off. Pour more water into the basin and float the rose petals on the surface. Look at your reflection in the basin with love and admiration and say,

*Look how beautiful I am.*
*As bees love honey, so you love me.*

Pick the apple out of the basin. Hide it in the most inaccessible place in the laznya or bathroom and say,

*As an apple dries up without white light,*
*so you will dry up without me.*
*My word is strong.*

Take the basin to the base of a tree and dump the water and rose petals there. Leave the apple in its hidden place for three days. In a few days' time, you should see your target's affection increase, and after three days, you may bury the apple under a tree.

## The Mystery of the Laznya

The bathhouse was a part of life for Slavs in times past: a dark and mysterious out-of-the-way place that was a portal to the liminal. While we might not have daily access to a laznya where we live, it's essential to understand the essence of the bathhouse and its magic to understand Baba Yaga.

While the bathhouse is part of quite a few of her stories, it's the risky magic of the laznya that is so emblematic of who she is. Do bathing rituals wherever you can, but every once in a while, find an isolated space that puts a tingle in your spine to do your magic, and you will understand the laznya, and the Bannyk. And maybe, just maybe, Baba Yaga herself will ask you to collect water with a sieve, and you'll know exactly what to do.

# CHAPTER 19

# ZHYVA I MERTVA VODA: THE WATERS OF LIFE AND DEATH

*efore she knew it, all the animals were clean, their skins and carapaces and fur glistening brightly. She looked out the door at the sun outside and saw that it was almost all the way down, so she quickly gathered up her things, and the creatures followed her willingly back to the khatynka.*

*When they got back in, the creatures quickly lined up, and Baba Yaga came into the hut only seconds later. She squinted her eyes and looked at Vasylyna and walked up and down the row, inspecting each creature, picking them up, looking under their chins, rubbing their bellies, and patting their heads.*

*When she got to the last one, she turned to Vasylyna.*

*"Hmph. Not bad," she said. "Not bad. Ah well, my pich will have to go hungry yet another day." She put some wood into the stove and began to cook some food. She opened the door and scattered some crumbs in the yard, and all the creatures left the khata and went outside.*

*Baba Yaga bade Vasylyna to sit. The two ate their meal, and, of course, Vasylyna did not forget to give a small bite to the motanka in her pocket. After the long night and day, Vasylyna was quite tired, so as soon as she was finished helping with the dishes, she made up her bed on the bench, tucked her doll beside her, and fell fast asleep.*

*In the middle of the night, Vasylyna could feel herself being shaken awake. Baba Yaga's bony hand was on her shoulder.*

*"Come girl," she said. "We have work to do."*

Vasylyna threw on her skirt and shawls and followed Baba Yaga out into the yard. The sky was dark with no moon to be seen, only the sprinkling of glittering stars.

Baba Yaga stood in her giant iron mortar holding the pestle and a broom. With her bony arms, she lifted Vasylyna into the mortar, and with one powerful shove of the pestle, up they flew into the sky, high up over the pines and spruce trees, flying over the forest. From high above, she could just make out the shadows of Chuhaister and the other Lisovyky frolicking in the forest, the Mavky wandering at the crossroads, and the Rusalky and the Vodyanyky, the dangerous deepwater mermen, splashing playfully in the water.

Baba Yaga steered the mortar over miles of forest, fields, and steppes, and finally they flew over the sea, where all Vasylyna could see were the dark waters below them. They flew for what seemed like hours, until Vasylyna saw a speck of land, an island in the middle of the ocean, with rolling green hills dominated by an enormous oak tree reaching high up into the clouds above them.

Baba Yaga gave a twist to the pestle and down they flew toward the land. She skillfully settled the mortar on a grassy hill near the tree with a gentle thump, jumped out, and grabbed Vasylyna by the hand to pull her out and put her feet on land.

"Come! Come!" Baba Yaga waved her hand impatiently, and together they clambered up toward the massive tree, Baba Yaga leading and Vasylyna close behind. As they got closer, Vasylyna could see that the tree was as big as the tallest mountain she had ever seen, and at its base, two natural springs trickled. Beautiful ebony snakes languidly twined themselves around its massive, tangled roots, while crows cawed in the branches high above. Even though it was nighttime, she could see their shiny jet-black feathers as they flapped their wings, and she could just make out a glimpse of what looked like a human face or two peeping down from high in the branches above.

Baba Yaga stopped at the base of the tree, and from her sack she pulled out two corked bottles, one black and one white. From the spring to the left of the root, she collected water into the black bottle, and from the spring on the right, she filled the white bottle.

Vasylyna wondered to herself, "What is so special about this water that we had to travel all this way to get it?" And as if she could read her thoughts, Baba Yaga turned around to her sharply.

"These are no ordinary waters, girl," snapped Baba Yaga. "Kings have given all their gold for just a drop of these."

*She held the black bottle up to Vasylyna's face.*

*"This is the Water of Death."*

*Then she held the white bottle out for Vasylyna to see. "And this is the Water of Life."*

*Baba Yaga placed the bottles carefully in her bag and stamped her way back down the hill toward where they had left the mortar and pestle. She quickly jumped in, and Vasylyna followed right behind and got in the mortar just as Baba Yaga gave a strong push of her pestle. In moments, they were back in the air and flying over the sea. Vasylyna sat on the floor of the mortar and looked up at the stars in the sky, and she began to hear them sing a lullaby, and soon she was asleep.*

## Baba Yaga Shares the Wisdom of the Zhyva i Mertva Voda

Now, we get to the good stuff. My favorite vacation getaway, *Vyriy*. Oh, you haven't heard of it? Well, I can imagine why. It is terribly exclusive, after all. It's the land of the spirits, both those who have had a good life and are ready for a refreshing break and those who are eagerly waiting to be born. Sometimes those are one and the same.

This fertile island in the west is filled with warm springs of healing water, lush groves, and natural beauty—not so very different from our world, but much more radiant. It is not only the place for the spirits, but also the place where birds and other animals go for the winter. It's always beautiful there, so when the weather gets cold in the land of the living, the birds fly away to Vyriy for the winter and return to their nests in the spring. The cuckoo holds the keys to this otherworld, and so she is the first bird to fly there and the last one to return. Vyriy is also the home of the sun, so in the winter months, the sun spends more time in the warmth of the island than in the cold of the land of the living.[170]

You want to know how to get there? Well, first you have to get a flying mortar and turn left at the Thrice Ten Kingdom and then cross the waters of the Kingdom of the Sun, Moon, and Stars. Some say it's to the west, others say it's to the south; don't ask me. I just follow the Milky Way, and there it is at the end.

---

170. Kukharenko, "Traditional Ukrainian Folk Beliefs about Death and the Afterlife."

Some people call it *Iriy*, *Rai*, or Paradise, but it's so much more. It's the place where we can find the World Tree, that giant oak of all oaks that connects the lower world, the middle world, and the upper world.[171] The spirits and the birds sit up high in its branches, while the snakes are the guardians of the earth below. It's the place where all the weather of the world comes from, and, of course, the Waters of Life and Death. This is the real treasure of Vyriy.[172]

From beneath the roots of the tree flow two natural springs. Of course, any natural spring is considered holy, but these twin springs are the most sacred of all. The Water of Life, well, that is a simple one. If a person has perished, you can pour the Water of Life on them, and they return. But things are not always so simple. Bodies can be destroyed: burned, dismembered, gnawed away by forest creatures. Pour the Water of Life on something like that, and it isn't pretty. You get an upyr, a ghoul, a vampire—the living dead. So, in some cases, we need the Water of Death just to restore the body to being intact.

If someone is cut or their bones are broken, a sprinkle of the Water of Death will draw their body together without a scar. Even if their body is chopped to bits and buried in the east and the west, or burned and destroyed, the Water of Death will pull the smallest crumbs of flesh back and knit them together again to make the body whole. After the body is brought together with the Water of Death, a sprinkle of the Water of Life will call the spirit back to the body, even if the soul has left the land of the living.[173]

## Madame Pamita Teaches the Magic of the Zhyva i Mertva Voda

I have always believed in the magic power of water. From spiritually cleansing baths to waters blessed by the moon, from potions made with herbs steeped in water to holy water from sacred sites, I have always had a love of this live-giving element. It may have

171. Valeriy Voitovych, *Ukrayins'ka Mifolohiya* (Kyiv, Ukraine: Lybid', 2015).

172. W. R. S. Ralston, *The Songs of the Russian People, as Illustrative of Slavonic Mythology and Russian Social Life* (London: Ellis & Green, 1872).

173. Gilchrist, *Russian Magic.*

been my mother who first introduced me to this. In going to Catholic church, we would dip the tips of our fingers in the holy water font at the door and touch our forehead, heart, left shoulder, and right shoulder. There was even an urn in the vestibule of the church where you could fill your bottles of holy water to take home, and my mother would do this regularly.

Several years after my mother had passed away, I was having a hard time and missing her. I looked through a drawer of hers that I had looked through many times before, and I found something that hadn't been there in all the times I had previously looked: three jelly jars, one labeled "Holy Water," another labeled "Lourdes Water," and a third labeled "Jordan Water." Years before, my mother had bottled up these waters, and her spirit brought them to my attention just when I needed to feel her close to me.

I am a collector of waters of all kinds these days. I collect rainwater and water from sacred springs, I make moon water regularly, I bless water with krashanky. Some I put in fancy bottles, but sometimes I put them in jelly jars, label them, and use them for my magic, just like my mother did.

## Zhyva i Mertva Voda Today

Slavic people from the most ancient times have revered water. The old saying "water is life" only scratches the surface of the level of devotion to rivers, lakes, seas, wells, gentle rains, and, of course, springs. Even the introduction of Christianity couldn't wipe out the adoration of these water sources. The only way the early Christian missionaries could get some of the ancient Slavic people on board was to conveniently "find" an icon sitting beside a holy pond or spring, signaling that their saints were sanctioned by the older, and more powerful, holy waters.[174]

Water was also designated as living or dead, healing or depleting. Living water gives strength, and dead water takes strength away. Water is the ultimate purifier. Like fire that burns away unclean forces, water washes away and drowns all evil. In past times, people would take off their hats in respect before drinking water. They never spit in bodies of water or threw trash in water. They wouldn't even speak harsh words near water.

---

174. Dixon-Kennedy, *Encyclopedia of Russian and Slavic Myth and Legend.*

Even today, people make pilgrimages to natural bodies of water that are said to have miraculous healing powers. They feed their sacred lakes and ponds with offerings such as bread. They leave gifts of ribbons and cloth by springs. They decorate wells with verdant greenery and flower wreaths. During the spring when rivers overflow their banks, people make an offering to the Vodyanyk, the spirit of deep waters, to calm the surge.

## The Magic of the Vodyanyk

Deep under the water of the rivers, lakes, swamps, and ocean, next to the snags and beneath the whirlpools and eddies, lives another spirit cousin of Baba Yaga, the Vodyanyk. This old man of the water looks part human but has fishlike scales on his skin, gills on his neck, tangled green hair, and a beard that resembles algae. Just as the Lisovyk rules over the forest, the Vodyanyk is the Lord of the Waters.[175]

More dangerous than most spirits, if a Vodyanyk is upset, he can create all kinds of havoc: tangling nets, flooding riverbanks, breaking dams, destroying water mills, and capsizing boats. When disrespected, he is known to pull people down under the water to drown them. It is believed that drunk people who are swimming in his waters are particularly vulnerable to being caught by him.[176]

Fishermen, whose livelihoods depend on his blessings, throw offerings of bread, boiled fish, salt, vodka, or tobacco into the water to appease the Vodyanyk and even offer him the first of their catch to keep him happy. Fish are the livestock of the Lord of the Waters, and the first caught fish can be returned to the waters as an offering to him with the brief incantation "go and bring your father, mother, aunt, uncle…" and so on to invoke a successful fishing day.[177] If the Vodyanyk was pleased with an offering, he would bestow a good catch for the day and improve the fisherman's livelihood, and so their efforts would not only protect them but reward them.

## The Magic of Zhyva Voda

Water is so important that it is associated not just with the Rusalky and Vodyanyky, but with other spirits as well. Mother Earth is often called Maty Syra Zemlya, Moist Mother

---

175. Gray, *Mythology of All Races Volume 3*.

176. Voitovych, *Ukrayins'ka Mifolohiya*.

177. Voitovych, *Ukrayins'ka Mifolohiya*.

Earth, to emphasize the power of water in the fertile soil. Earth and water go together, hand in hand. "Be rich like the earth, and healthy like water!" is a beautiful blessing that acknowledges this connection.

Living water, *zhyva voda*, is not just the water that Baba Yaga collects to revive the dead—it is also the name given to any water that is especially empowered for magical purposes. There are so many magical versions of living water. Water is never just generic. Each type has a different energy. There are the earthly waters of the wells, springs, rivers, ponds, and lakes that are seen as motherly, and there are the heavenly waters of rain, mist, and snow that are seen as fatherly. Each type of water has its special blessing and magic.

### Spring Water

Spring water is highly revered for magic. Rushnyky and precious hair ribbons are still tied to nearby trees as offerings to the spirits of the springs. Waters collected from different springs have different properties that can be used to one's advantage in healing. For example, the deep springs that consistently and generously bubble up from the ground are known as "healing waters" and are used to cure illness; a spring that emerges from under a rock is seen as water that has traveled from the lower world and is especially blessed and holy. Even the smallest springs are lovingly protected, because each possesses its own power and has a unique spirit guarding it.

### Well Water

In songs and stories, rustic rural wells have so many positive attributes: health, strength, wealth, fertility, purity, beauty, and fidelity. They are also seen as places where we can soothe the pain of separation and sadness. Because well water comes from deep in the ground, it draws on the power of Mother Earth. Even today, some rural people do not have running water and must go to the well in the morning and throughout the day to get their water for cooking, drinking, and washing. People who rely on these wells consecrate them several times a year on special holidays and surround them with plantings of protective willow trees and flowers year-round.

There is magic in the gathering of well water. There is a belief that if you are carrying empty buckets on your way to the well, you should steer clear of crossing paths with someone else to avoid jinxing them with lack and poverty. However, if you are returning with your buckets full, you can feel free to encounter another person on the road, because you will bless them with abundance.

Offerings are made at the well. Coins and jewelry are dropped into the well in exchange for blessings. Well water takes on the characteristics of the people who use the well. The wise ones say that "water hears," that it records the energy around it. Wells where people complain, lie, swear, or speak malicious gossip absorb this negativity, and the water brings trouble, quarreling, and tears. Whereas wells where people speak kindly and joyfully are imprinted with happiness, and the water brings blessings.

## Rainwater

Rainwater has many magical properties. It enlightens and cleanses; gives energy, optimism, and strength; accelerates growth; and washes away bad moods and negative thoughts. In folk medicine, it is used for relieving headaches, healing eye diseases, and removing warts. If you wash yourself with water collected from a spring during the first storm of the year, you will remain healthy for the year. Drops gathered from plants during the first rain of the year offer additional potency to spells in which they are used.

## Thunderstorm Water

Water collected from a thunderstorm is another form of living water used to bring justice, banish evil spirits, remove evil in the heart, and punish the guilty. Rain from a nighttime thunderstorm is considered exceptionally powerful. The stronger the wind during the night rain, the stronger the water is.

## Ancestor Water

Rainwater collected at dawn or dusk can be used to contact the ancestors. It is called the Water of the Ancestors and is used to obtain their advice, to protect their property, and to help the dying so that they can either return to the world of the living or pass easily. Ancestor water can also be used effectively for removing curses or jinxes.

## Sun Water

The water of midday rains is called sun water and is used by healers in their work to remove negative energy from a person and bring back health and strength. Sun water is often called for in the preparation of folk medicine potions.

### Morning Dew

The smallest drops of morning dew are packed with amazing powers of magic and healing. Dew is a precious magical tool because so little can be collected. Traditionally, people would bring clean rushnyky to the fields in the morning and use them to soak up the dew, then squeeze them out and collect the water in clay jugs to use as a remedy for various diseases. Just a few drops of dew added to spring water infuses it with powerful properties.

Walking barefoot on dewy grass cleanses and heals the body and spirit, and washing one's face in dew before sunrise imparts one with youth and beauty. Rubbing dew directly onto your body in the morning improves well-being and gives energy to meet the challenges of the day. Dew also helps the animals of the farm to increase their output. Cows given dew to drink are said to increase their milk. Beehives blessed with dew help the bees produce more honey.

### Charmed Water

Charmed water is water that is blessed by a wise person speaking incantations over it. It is primarily used for spiritual healings and removing possession and curses, for the ritual of pouring beeswax into water for a spiritual cleansing, and for potions and brews.

### Holy Water

Water consecrated by spirits or deities is considered a source of creativity and divine power. In ancient times, priests blessed both statues of gods and believers with such water. Holy water has the ability to spiritually cleanse and heal.

### Waters Collected at Certain Times

It is believed that natural water changes its polarity twice a year. The first switch happens at the winter solstice, and the second during the summer solstice. The polarity of water in the period from *Kolyada* (winter solstice) to Kupala (summer solstice) creates living water that is reviving and invigorating. Water gathered between summer solstice and winter solstice is dead water, which can be used for removing or banishing.

### Kolyada Water

Winter solstice water is blessed by ritually carving a large hole in the ice and dipping a silver talisman into it three times, followed by dipping and dousing a lit candle. This ancient ritual was later folded into the Christian Epiphany (January 6 or 19), where this "Jordan Water" is collected by all in the village. Some of the water may be drunk on the spot for healing, and bottles of it are carried home to be stored in the pokut' and sprinkled on the family, the home, and the livestock for healing throughout year. People will also immerse themselves in this icy water three times for healing serious illnesses or for preventing future illness.

### Stritennya Water

Water collected at Stritennya, the midwinter holiday that corresponds to Candlemas, is also considered healing. It is rubbed on the body to heal skin diseases and given as a drink to cleanse curses or remove vroki. It is sprinkled on soldiers to protect them before going into battle or on travelers before they leave to far-off lands.

### Spring Equinox Water

The healing power of water is especially evident in the spring, when rivers and springs thaw, snow turns into rippling streams, and the sky unlocks its rain. Water gathered at spring equinox is especially powerful for protection from evil forces and for attracting blessings. It can be used for washing away fevers, as well. It is also good for protecting the land. If it is poured onto a field, it protects the farmland from lightning strikes (which can cause fires), hail (which can destroy crops), and excessive flooding. Due to the syncretism of Christianity and Paganism, this water is sometimes collected on the Feast of the Annunciation (March 25) and is called Annunciation Water.

### Yuriy Vesnyanyy Water

Dew can be collected from flowers on the spring holiday of Saint George's Day, *Yuriy Vesnyanyy* (May 6), the holiday midway between spring equinox and summer solstice. According to Christian folk beliefs, spring dew is released by Saint George, who unlocks the moisture from the sky with his keys. If it is collected before sunrise, it is especially healing, as it absorbs the energy of the flowers themselves. This water is believed to be quite healing in folk medicine. People touch it to their eyelids to resolve vision problems or wet their heads with it to stave off headaches. It also has the power of attraction, and some wash their faces with it for beauty, to increase popularity, and to improve their stature in the community. It is also good for livestock, and sprinkling your chickens with it is said to improve their fertility.

### Kupala Water

Water collected on Kupala (summer solstice or syncretized with Saint John the Baptist's Day, June 23–24 or July 6–7) also has exceptional healing properties. River and lake water and dew collected before dawn on this day are infused with this power. People with skin diseases swim in the river on this day before sunrise for healing. Washing the eyelids with water fetched from four different wells on Kupala or with dew collected before sunrise is said to cure eye diseases. And washing yourself with dew on the morning of Kupala was thought to bathe yourself in popularity and good reputation.

Kupala dew was often collected by spreading white cloth in the fields of rye. When the cloth was damp with the dew, the precious water was squeezed out and infused with the special Kupala herbs for healing.

### Star Water

Star water is collected from three different wells at dawn and left out under a clear, starry sky that night. After it is blessed in this way overnight, it can be used for spells to draw abundance.

### Untapped Water

Untapped water, sometimes referred to as "unopened water," is healing water from a well, river, or other body of water collected in silence before sunrise. The method of collection is what empowers this water. The collector should set out with a bucket before dawn and scoop well water in a counterclockwise direction—or, if taken from a running source, scoop against the current. When returning home with the water, the collector should not look back toward the well or river. If they see someone before reaching home, they are not to speak to them, or else the water will lose its healing power.[178]

---

178. Artyukh, "Vohon' i Voda v Systemi Zvychayevykh Zaboron," 31–41.

# Water Spells

Water from different sources has power to be used in different spells. All water has power, and truly any water can be used in these spells, but for their maximum effectiveness, try collecting these special waters, if possible.

### *Divination and Cleansing Spell*

To perform a divination and cleansing when someone has been cursed, two people are needed. One to perform the ritual, and the other to receive the cleansing. Untapped water is the special ingredient in this combination divination and cleansing spell. Collect the water before dawn that morning and perform this spell work at sunset. In addition to the water, you will need three cloves of garlic, a wooden bowl, a knife, and a book of matches.

At sunset, pour the water into the wooden bowl and add the three cloves of garlic. Have the person receiving sit facing the east and place the bowl on a table in front of them. Make a sign of the sun, a cross, over the water with a knife and say the following incantation:

*Fire and water, save [name] from all negativity.*
*Save them from the evil hour.*
*Save them from the evil eye.*
*Save them from all ill-wishing men.*
*Save them from all ill-wishing women.*
*Save them from all ill-wishing children.*
*Save them from all ill-wishing thoughts.*
*Save them from all ill-wishing words.*

Light nine matches one at a time, and as you light them, throw the lit matches one by one into the water while whispering the following charm:

*Not nine, but eight.*
*Not eight, but seven.*
*Not seven, but six.*
*Not six, but five.*
*Not five, but four.*
*Not four, but three.*

*Not three, but two.*
*Not two, but one.*
*Not one, but none.*

When the ninth match is thrown into the water, check to see how many matches float and how many sink. The more matches that sink, the heavier the negativity surrounding the person. If one match sinks, then the negativity is very light. If all nine sink, there is a heavy negativity surrounding the person.

If all the matches float, the person's energy is clear, and you do not have to do the rest of the ritual. If any matches sink, complete the cleansing portion of the ritual below and repeat the divination again the following day and cleanse, if necessary. Repeat each day until all negativity is completely cleansed.

The recipient should then take four sips of this water, one from each of the four sides of the bowl. After that, dip the back of your hand in the water and rub the water from left to right across the forehead, across the upper chest above the heart, down each arm, down each inner wrist, above the navel, and down each leg. Repeat this process of wiping them down two more times.

Pour the remaining water and matches at the base of a tree, at a crossroads, or on the threshold, and say the following incantation:

*"Go back to where you came from."*[179]

### Healing Spells with Dew

Morning dew collected on any day can be used in healing spells. You can also simply wash yourself in the morning by applying dew directly from the flowers, grasses, and flowering trees. It can be wiped over the skin to heal and rejuvenate the body and can be used to speed the healing of wounds. Those who perform negative magic use dew to remove negative energy from themselves after rituals. Dew can be added to healing infusions to enhance the effect of herbs.

In folk medicine practices, dew was rubbed on the scalp to make hair grow faster and thicker. Dew was dropped in the ears for earaches, applied to the nose to speed healing

---

179. Len'o, "Vykorystannya Vohnyu u Narodniy Medytsyni Ukrayintsiv Zakarpattya (Na Osnovi Suchas-nykh Pol'ovykh Materialiv)," 123–126.

from the common cold, and added to infusions for toothaches. Walking barefoot on dewy grass was said to help get rid of fatigue and heal issues with the feet.

### Love Spells with Dew

You can combine the magic powers of bread and dew to make someone fall in love with you. Collect dew from the field with cloths, handkerchiefs, or rushnyky. Create a small round loaf of wheat bread with a hole in the middle and knead it on the dew-covered cloth. Once it's baked, it is said that if you take it outside and look through the hole first at the sun and then at someone you admire, they will fall in love with you.

If you'd like to get a marriage proposal or have a marriage proposal accepted, dip breadcrumbs in dew and feed them to your loved one.

### Healing Spells with Dew from Different Plants

Dew collected from different flowers, herbs, and trees has different healing powers in folk medicine practices. Collect morning dew with rushnyky or clean white cloths of cotton or linen and squeeze the dew into a clean glass container. Dew can be kept and used over the next seven days; however, keep in mind that dew is strongest when freshly gathered and loses its power as time passes.

- Oat, rye, or wheat field dew is used to beautify skin and reduce acne and inflammation, freckles, and pigment spots. It is also used in the treatment of eye diseases.
- Dew from plants growing under oak trees can be used to bring freshness, healthy color, and softness to the skin.
- Apple leaf and blossom dew is used in spells to improve mood and cure sleep and chronic fatigue issues. Washing with this dew from the head to the waist will also give a surge of strength and energy.

### Dew Collected during Different Moon Phases

Dew collected during different phases of the moon also has different powers. Dew collected during the waxing moon phase is used in spells to preserve youth and beauty, to promote health, and to perform rituals of love magic. Dew collected during the waning moon phase is used in spells for removing curses, hexes, and the evil eye, and for weight loss spells. Dew collected on the night of the full moon is used in spells to restore or increase personal or financial success or to improve relationships with others.

### Thunderstorm Water Spell

Thunderstorm water can be used to charge and empower ritual tools, talismans, and amulets. The more powerful the storm, the more power the water will impart. When a thunderstorm is expected, hang tools and amulets on trees where they can be exposed to the lightning and rain and where no one else will touch them. Once the storm passes, bring the items into the house to dry.

### Beauty Bathing on the Full Moon

Magical practitioners who strive for eternal youth perform their beauty rituals during the full moon. The most effective ritual to restore beauty and youth is monthly bathing under the full moon. Go to a pond, a slow river, or any other natural body of water where you can see a reflection of the moon. Undress and dive into the water headfirst, so that the water washes over you from head to toe. After the first dip, say the following incantation:

> *I do not hide my nakedness; I wash during the moon.*
> *As water spills over my body, so youth and beauty return to me.*
> *As the water around my body turns, so health*
> *and strength will return to me.*

Dip under two more times and say the words of the spell after each dip. After the third dip, get out of the water, and do not towel off. Instead, let the water dry on your body, then get dressed and go home without talking to anyone or turning around to look back at the water.

### Creating Spring Water Full Moon Elixir

To make a full moon elixir to maintain beauty and youth, you will need spring water, a crystal bowl, a jar or bottle, a small pink beeswax candle, and rose petals.

When the full moon appears in the sky, light the candle and pour the spring water into the crystal bowl. Drop rose petals into the water and say the following incantation:

*As fresh as this water is, so let me be young.*
*As beautiful as this rose is, so let me be beautiful.*
*The power of the moon helps me.*

Place the glass with the water and rose petals in a place where the moonlight will fall on it. Place the candle next to the bowl, let it burn completely, and then go to bed.

In the morning, take the remains of the beeswax candle and bury them under a young tree. Pour the water into a jar or bottle and use it as a wash by either wiping it over your skin or adding it to your bathwater.

### Full Moon Spring Water Beauty Spell

If you would like to regain the youth and beauty you once had, this ritual will refresh and reinvigorate your looks. On the night of the full moon, pour a glass of spring water or other holy water into a glass. Undress and stand naked with moonlight shining on you, indoors or outdoors, and hold the glass of water while saying the following incantation:

*Mother Moon will help me keep my youth.*
*Make me beautiful like a rose, fresh like the wind, and tender like wool.*
*Let people look at me who do not look, admire who do not admire.*
*As this enchanted water merges with my body,*
*it will become young and healthy again.*
*As I say it, so it will come true.*

After the last words are spoken, go to bed, and leave a glass of enchanted water under the moonlight overnight. First thing the next morning, take a sip of the moonlight-infused water, and take one sip upon rising each day over the next several days. To achieve the best results, repeat the ritual every full moon.

### Rituals for Protection with Kolyada Water

When water collected at Kolyada or Epiphany is brought home, the following ritual can be performed by all members of the household. Take a sip of the sacred water and then dip your fingers in it and wipe your eyes to protect your vision. Dip again and wipe your ears to protect hearing. Dip and wipe your forehead to protect your mental capabilities. Dip a final time and wipe your chest, neck, and arms to be as "healthy as water."

The house and any outlying buildings, such as barns, stables, and sheds, can also be blessed with this water by sprinkling them while saying the following incantation:

> *Wash with water, sprinkle,*
> *be blessed for the health of the people who live here.*

If you own a beehive, it, too, can be blessed with the following incantation:

> *Bees, you are divine insects,*
> *I sprinkle you, I bless you in swarms,*
> *I bless your wax, I bless your honey,*
> *that you may come around,*
> *that you may collect sweet nectar and winter well!*

Walkways, paths, and sidewalks can also be sprinkled with the following incantation:

> *Holy water washes you, sprinkles you with good health.*
> *Everything evil and unclean, begone!*

Any water that is left can be poured into a bottle and stored in the pokut' for any healing needs throughout the year.

### Sun Water Spell for Beautiful Hair

If your hair has become thin, weak, brittle, or dull, you can perform this healing spell with sun water collected during a midday rain, preferably in the countryside near a place where long grasses grow. Once you bring it home, leave it in a bowl or bottle overnight under the light of a waxing moon and say the following incantation:

> *Water-water, dear sister, wake up!*
> *Share your power with me, [name].*
> *Absorb the light of the moon,*
> *transmit the magical power to my hair.*
> *As the grass from this water grows strong and beautiful,*
> *so my hair grows stronger, gaining strength. Let it be so!*

The following day, you can rinse and massage your hair with this water as you imagine new hair growing, damaged hair being restored and strengthened, and all your hair shining with health. After the massage, let your hair air-dry. Repeat once a month during the waxing moon phase.

### Sun Water Spell to Uplift Your Mood

Sun water is an excellent tool for banishing the blues or just for lifting your mood. For this ritual, you do not need to collect the water—just go outside when it's raining in the middle of the day and stand in the rain, in the nude if possible.

Stand with your legs slightly apart, raise your arms, and turn your face up to the sky. Feel the raindrops wash over your body as they cleanse you, washing away all your negative feelings, and say the following incantation out loud, repeating it as many times as there are years in your age:

> I call on the forces of the Sun and the Sky,
> I call on the forces of rainwater!
> The force is strong and settles into my body.
> Pure power of water, enter me, cleanse me, and renew me!
> Quickly fill my body and soul with joy.
> The emptiness is filled.
> All evil is driven away!
> Let it be so!

You should allow a minimum of five to ten minutes of the rain falling on you. Afterward, let your body air-dry, then put on clean clothes or, even better, something brand new.

### Rainwater Spell to Get Rid of Bad Habits

If you have a habit that you are ready to release, rainwater will help you let it go. On a piece of thin paper, write out the words of the habit in watercolor paint. Put the piece of paper out in the rain. As the words wash away in the rain, your bad habit will dissolve.

### Rainwater Spells at Different Times of Day

If you walk outside when it's raining, you can wash your face in the rain to rinse away negativity and help in healing. Moisten your face, neck, and hands as you imagine washing away your problems.

Rains during different daylight hours have different powers. The strongest way to work this magic is to wash directly in the rain, but you also have the option of bottling the waters of rains at these different times to use their powers in other spells:

- 6:00 a.m. to 7:00 a.m.—for new ideas, to attract good luck at work.
- 7:00 a.m. to 8:00 a.m.—for relief from headaches of unknown origin.
- 8:00 a.m. to 9:00 a.m.—to wash away the effects of vroki, the evil eye.
- 9:00 a.m. to 10:00 a.m.—to alleviate sadness and depression, prevent bad actions, and drive out unhelpful thoughts.
- 10:00 a.m. to 11:00 a.m.—to energize the heart, encourage creative action, and start new creative projects.
- 11:00 a.m. to noon—to overcome phobias, fears, and stress and harmonize the body and soul.
- Noon to 1:00 p.m.—to eliminate feelings of aggression and revenge and to remove any harassment, corruption, and curses from others.
- 1:00 p.m. to 2:00 p.m.—to develop intuition and clairvoyance.
- 2:00 p.m. to 3:00 p.m.—to calm cravings, normalize mental states, and relieve nervous excitement.
- 3:00 p.m. to 4:00 p.m.—to open up new ideas and knowledge seemingly from out of nowhere. To increase prophetic powers.
- 4:00 p.m. to 5:00 p.m.—to clarify thinking, quench the aggression of your enemies, and promote reconciliation with enemies.
- 5:00 p.m. to 6:00 p.m.—to find the right solution in a critical situation. To bring harmony to family relationships.

### Sun Water for Healing

To help a sick person and increase their strength, you can use the water of the midday rain, collected from any flowering plants. Ideally, this should be done in the countryside. While collecting the rainwater, say the following incantation:

*This water is given by the forces of nature,*
*for the healing of soul and body.*

Leave the collected water in a jar or bottle in the sun for two days. After that, it can be used to make medicinal drinks, such as herbal tea, or drunk by itself.

When drinking the tea or water, say the following incantation:

*Healing water, settle in my body, share your power,*
*protect me from diseases and improve my health. Let it be so!*

## The Magic of Water

In so many of her stories, Baba Yaga teaches the power of water, both to heal and to harm. She gives her visitors impossible tasks such as collecting water in a sieve, but she also shows them the Waters of Life and Death. While we mere mortals might not have the means to go to Vyriy and collect waters that can revive the dead, we can tap into the deeply meaningful ways to incorporate water into our magical practices—to cleanse, heal, and protect ourselves and our loved ones.

# CHAPTER 20

# KISTKY: THE BONES

When Vasylyna woke up, she was no longer curled up in the mortar, but bundled up on the bench in Baba Yaga's hut. Baba Yaga was cooking kutya in the pich, and the delicious scent of the warm porridge made the girl's stomach rumble.

"Get up, girl. For it's time for you to go home."

Vasylyna rubbed her eyes and sat up at the table.

"How did I get back into bed last night? Weren't we flying in the mortar?"

Baba Yaga looked at her quizzically.

"These girls and their fancies," she muttered to herself as she served up the porridge. "I'm glad I'm an old woman who knows the difference between what's real and what's a dream."

She placed the bowl in front of Vasylyna and went back to the woodstove, placed a piece of bread inside, and gave it a gentle pat.

"Well, pich dear, it looks like you will have to settle for a crust of bread for now and wait another day for a real meal."

Vasylyna gave a pinch of her porridge to the doll in her pocket, ate her fill, and then got up and cleared the table. Baba Yaga packed Vasylyna's basket with bread and salt, apples and walnuts, and gave it to her.

"So that you have something to eat for your journey," she said. Then she pulled a small wooden chest down from a high shelf.

"And take this with you, but do not open it until you get back home."

Vasylyna folded up the blankets on her makeshift bed and put them away. She put on her shawls, put the chest in the basket, and put her arm through the handle. Baba Yaga opened the

263

door, and the hut turned and settled so that they could step outside. The old woman pulled a ball of red wool from her pocket and handed it to Vasylyna.

"Take this ball of yarn, throw it in front of you, and follow it wherever it goes. It will lead you straight back to your stepmother's home."

Then, Baba Yaga reached up to her fence, and with her two hands, she wrested down one of the skull lanterns from its bony fence post.

"And here is the fire that you can give to your stepmother."

Vasylyna took the skull lantern from Baba Yaga and bowed her head.

"Thank you, babusya." Vasylyna felt a pang in leaving Baba Yaga behind. She shyly stepped up to her and gave her a hug.

Baba Yaga held her for a moment and then patted her on the head.

"Go on, little one. The day is short and the journey is long." Vasylyna looked up and thought she saw the corners of Baba Yaga's mouth turn up slightly. But before Vasylyna could say anything, Baba Yaga composed herself, and without another word, she turned and went back into her hut and shut the door behind her. The hut stretched and stood up, scratched at the ground, and turned its back to Vasylyna.

So, Vasylyna did as Baba Yaga had told her to do and threw down the ball of red yarn. Propelled through its own magical force, it rolled ahead of her, and she followed it as it wound through the forest.

Vasylyna held her skull lantern aloft in the dim light and followed the magic ball of yarn as it continued to roll ahead of her. On the way, she left bread and salt for the forest spirits, stopped and ate and fed her doll, drank some cool water from a spring, and by the time the sun was beginning to set, the ball of yarn finally unwound completely, right at the front door of her stepmother's cramped little khata.

When she stepped through the door, the stepmother and the stepsisters looked surprised.

"You're back?" said the stepmother. But then realizing that she was giving away her plan, she composed herself and began accosting Vasylyna in the usual manner.

"Where have you been? We've been trying to start a fire in the pich, but every time we get a spark, it goes out straightaway. We've been freezing here all last night and all day today."

Vasylyna was confused. She was sure she had been gone for longer than a day.

"I brought you the fire from Baba Yaga." And she held the skull out to them. Her stepmother looked in fear at the lantern but took it from her as if it were exactly what she had expected.

"Very good. I'll start the fire, but we will need more wood. Vasylyna, go to the edge of the forest and get us some wood to feed the fire." So, without even having a bite of food, something to drink, or even the chance to take off her shawls or put down her basket, Vasylyna stepped back out the door again. As soon as she started for the wood, her doll tugged at her skirt once more.

> Although your stepmother told you so,
> into the wood you must not go.
> Quickly and quietly as a mouse,
> scamper back to your father's house.

So, instead of going into the wood, she took the road in the other direction and ran as fast as she could back to her father's old house. When she got there, there was her father alone and pacing nervously, waiting for her.

"Vasylyna!" he said as he wrapped his arms around her. "Where have you been?" Vasylyna showed him the little chest that Baba Yaga had given her. She opened it up, and inside were a store of rare and magical objects: a beautiful rushnyk embroidered with magical symbols and made from the cloth that Vasylyna herself had spun and wove, a golden mortar and pestle, a red egg decorated with protective images, a silver comb, a golden spindle, and the white bottle and the black bottle carrying the Waters of Life and Death.

She and her father marveled over the precious items as Vasylyna told him the story of her adventure with Baba Yaga.

When she told her father what her stepmother and stepsisters had done, he said, "They hid their wickedness for so long, but no more! We must go to them so that they can own their deeds and make amends to you." And so Vasylyna packed up the precious items, and she and her father went back to the house in the woods, but when they got there, there was nothing but a pile of burning embers where the house had been. The stepmother, the stepsisters, and the little khata had all burst into flame with the fire from the skull. Thinking quickly, Vasylyna used the Water of Death to bring back their bodies from the ashes, but when she sprinkled the Water of Life on them, their bodies turned back into ash.

The motanka whispered to Vasylyna,

> From the fire they did burn,
> and to ashes they must return.
> Their empty souls cast far away,
> never to harm you another day.

So, as there was nothing more to be done, Vasylyna and her father returned home.

## Baba Yaga Shares the Wisdom of the Kistky

Every story must have an end, but what is an end but the beginning of something new? The end of initiation is the beginning of mastery. Even the end of life is the beginning of new life. One sails across the divine seas to the serene island of Vyriy to rest and revive and wait to be reborn again. An initiation is an initiation. Whether I initiate you into being a vidma or take you to the otherworld, I walk alongside you for that ending of one life and the beginning of the new one.

We old ones really knew how to show a soul into that new beginning. I don't have a bone fence around my yard just to scare away the weak ones, although it does do a good job of that. I don't need a necklace of bones to *look* like a boss lady—I *am* a boss lady. The bones are not there to make a statement. The kistky, the bones, hold the soul. As long as there are bones, the spirit lives on. In the oldest times, we would exhume the bones of our loved ones and decorate them with ash or red ochre to honor them.[180] Or, if the bones were scattered here and there, we would gather them back together to replenish and revive the spirit that resided in them. We still speak of this in our legends, where the heroes are cut up, then put back together and revived as someone new. That's the purpose of the Waters of Life and Death—something is destroyed, it's brought back together, and then we give it a new life. It won't be the same as before. That life before has to be left behind to bring in the evolved version, and isn't leaving the old self behind and emerging as someone new what initiation is all about?[181]

When I gave Vasylyna the skull, I was giving her more than just a fire for her stepmother. Skulls are part of some of our oldest practices. If the bones are the home of the soul, the skull is the seat of the spirit's consciousness. With the skulls of our beloved ancestors, we could call them back and consult with them, ask for their protection, and seek their advice. I not only gave Vasylyna the fire she asked for, I gave her back her connection to her loving ancestors.[182]

---

180. Kristina Killgrove, "Painted Bones Spark 4,500-Year-Old Burial Mystery in Ukraine," *Forbes*, July 27, 2018.

181. Yatchenko, *Ukrayins'kyy Shamanizm*.

182. Clarissa Pinkola Estes, *Women Who Run with the Wolves* (New York: Ballantine Books, 1992).

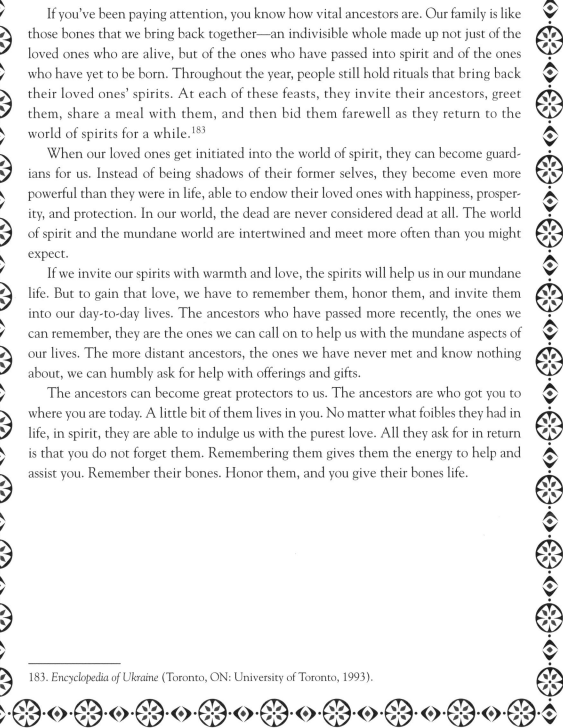

If you've been paying attention, you know how vital ancestors are. Our family is like those bones that we bring back together—an indivisible whole made up not just of the loved ones who are alive, but of the ones who have passed into spirit and of the ones who have yet to be born. Throughout the year, people still hold rituals that bring back their loved ones' spirits. At each of these feasts, they invite their ancestors, greet them, share a meal with them, and then bid them farewell as they return to the world of spirits for a while.[183]

When our loved ones get initiated into the world of spirit, they can become guardians for us. Instead of being shadows of their former selves, they become even more powerful than they were in life, able to endow their loved ones with happiness, prosperity, and protection. In our world, the dead are never considered dead at all. The world of spirit and the mundane world are intertwined and meet more often than you might expect.

If we invite our spirits with warmth and love, the spirits will help us in our mundane life. But to gain that love, we have to remember them, honor them, and invite them into our day-to-day lives. The ancestors who have passed more recently, the ones we can remember, they are the ones we can call on to help us with the mundane aspects of our lives. The more distant ancestors, the ones we have never met and know nothing about, we can humbly ask for help with offerings and gifts.

The ancestors can become great protectors to us. The ancestors are who got you to where you are today. A little bit of them lives in you. No matter what foibles they had in life, in spirit, they are able to indulge us with the purest love. All they ask for in return is that you do not forget them. Remembering them gives them the energy to help and assist you. Remember their bones. Honor them, and you give their bones life.

183. *Encyclopedia of Ukraine* (Toronto, ON: University of Toronto, 1993).

# Madame Pamita Teaches the Magic of the Kistky

Like Baba Yaga's khata that spins in the forest, life comes back around. The journey of writing this book began when the bones of my babusya began to sing, and here we are again, back at the bones.

Bones connect you to the spirit of your loved ones. On each of my ancestor altars, I have some small symbol of the bones—a tiny crystal skull, a deer scapula found in the forest, some chicken bones. They aren't spooky or scary to me. They represent the bones of my ancestors and loved ones who lie in graves well-tended or long-forgotten. The spirits of our ancestors survive just as their bones survive, and these tiny stand-ins bring them symbolically closer to me.

When first my mother and then my father were at the ends of their lives, they had the opportunity to have hospice care where we could be at home with them and spend their last days together. My mother was insistent that she wanted to die at home and not in a hospital. We set up a medical bed for her in the living room, and even though it was the middle of August, she wanted to have the fire in the fireplace going every day. Perhaps it was an intuitive knowing that this would connect her to her loved ones who were ready to welcome her in Paradise. Though she was in great pain at times, we would find moments to laugh and talk and visit and enjoy the crackling of the fire. During the last few days of her life, she slipped into a coma, but I still would talk to her and tell her that I loved her and how much she meant to me.

When the afternoon came that her spirit was ready to leave, I held her hand, and when she passed, I opened the window so her spirit could fly. I find it so magical that while she was passing, one of her favorite old movies was playing quietly in the background on the TV: *Born Yesterday*. I like to think that she was sending me a sly message, telling me that death really isn't the end and that her spirit would be back soon.

## Kistky Today

The kistky, the bones of the ancestors, are remembered. Since ancient times, Ukrainians have always seen the afterlife as an extension of this life. Loved ones who have passed are still considered to be nearby, and people celebrate with the deceased at special ritual feasts offered throughout the year.

In spring, people invite their beloved ancestors back during a celebration called Provody. They welcome them with a warm bowl of kutya and a lit candle in the window and then go to the cemeteries to clean their loved ones' graves and enjoy a picnic with them. They bring them brown bread, white bread, shots of *horilka* or vodka, wine, beer, pies, and cakes. They place a few krashanky on the grave during the picnic, and at the end, they might even break one on the headstone before eating it, saying, "Here is my family, here is my [mother/father/grandmother/grandfather/etc.], and one day I will also rest here!"[184]

Provody can become quite a spirited party. Along with the food and drink for the ancestors, they sing songs to them, catch them up with stories about what has been going on in their lives, and generally offer up their joy to them. The ancestor spirits meet them for these reunions at their graves and enjoy when they are remembered with kind words by living relatives.[185]

At the holidays surrounding winter solstice, people also invite their beloved ancestors to join them in their homes for the celebrations of the new year. There is kutya offered, of course, but also a special ritual sheaf of grain, called a didukh, which is set up at the pokut' for the spirits to reside in during the festive holiday season.

Those who are in the world of the spirits have been initiated and have passed through this world into Vyriy. But like the process of all initiations, it can be challenging, and so there are traditions to help our loved ones as they move to the land of the spirits.

### Funeral Rituals

In the most ancient of times, when the dead were buried, there was a custom called the double sepulcher. After lying in the arms of Mother Earth for several years, the bones of the loved ones were exhumed from the grave, washed, and placed in the pokut', a way to invite our beloved ancestors back into their special sacred place in the home. This practice eventually evolved so that instead of the bones, the ritual cloth used to wash them was placed in the pokut' instead.[186]

---

184. Kukharenko, "Traditional Ukrainian Folk Beliefs about Death and the Afterlife."

185. Gilchrist, *Russian Magic*.

186. Mircea Eliade et al., *A History of Religious Ideas* (Chicago, IL: University of Chicago Press, 1981).

In times past, people were born at home and passed at home. While we have gained so much with medical interventions in the last century, we have lost something as well. At one time, the families would tend to their loved ones, midwifing them into the world of spirit just as they midwifed them into the world of the living when they were born. While today we have the ability to spend our last moments in the hospital where pain can be alleviated, a great relief to some, we also have the option of hospice care where someone can be in their own familiar home and with their loved ones as they make this great transition. In either case, being surrounded with loving care when traversing that liminal state can be a great comfort and can ease this journey.

In old times, and even in some more traditional homes today, when someone was about to die, rituals were performed to assist the dying person's transition. Peace was maintained around the person who was transitioning. Normal life chatter and house-keeping were kept to a minimum, as it was believed that these everyday activities would keep them unnecessarily attached to the land of the living. Any actions in the home were carried out quietly, and conversations, if any, were done in hushed tones.

Generations ago, if the dying person were carrying worry or a heavy emotional burden of any kind that was keeping them tied to the earthly plane, the family might temporarily cut a hole in the roof to allow their spirit to let go. These days, people still open a window in the room where the person is lying to aid their transition. They might also do an obkuryuvannya and cense the person with the smoke of bundles of fragrant herbs—oregano, cedar, pine, juniper, or wormwood—to help them release their unfin-ished business and aid their passage. The dying person might also be given a candle to hold to light their way to the afterlife.[187]

In villages where everyone knew each other, friends and relations would visit the one who was dying in their home so that they had an opportunity for saying their good-byes and making peace. They might apologize to each other if they had done anything wrong and offer graceful forgiveness to bring a sense of peace. If someone missed the chance to apologize while their loved one was still alive, they still had an opportunity after they expired. There was a belief that the spirit lingered near the head of their body

---

187. Artyukh, "Vohon' i Voda v Systemi Zvychayevykh Zaboron," 31–41.

for three days following bodily death, so people could still seek or give forgiveness by addressing the body after death.[188]

After someone died in the home, the family would cover any mirrors so that the spirit wouldn't get confused and take a wrong turn into a portal. They would wash and dress the body and place it on a bench with the head toward the pokut' and the feet toward the door.[189] The water that was used to wash the body was called dead water and would be collected and poured where someone would not walk, usually at the base of a tree that did not produce fruit.[190]

While their loved one's body remained in the house for three days, they would do no work except what was required for the funeral, and the house would not be swept during the funeral proceedings. Over these three days, the body was never left alone or in the dark so that mischievous spirits did not have a chance to distract or influence it. Candles were kept alight throughout the night, and visitors would come by to pay a visit and say their final goodbyes, especially at night. Midnight suppers were held, and little ones were allowed to play funeral games to elevate everyone's mood and remind the spirit and us that there is still pleasure in the world.

In preparing for the funeral, gifts were slipped into the coffin: rushnyky, motanky, bread, vinoky, flowers, prayer books, favorite pieces of jewelry, or other items. Coins wrapped in a handkerchief were slipped into the deceased's hands or placed over the eyes so that they had the fare to pay the psychopomps who would carry their spirit across the underground river or over the sky-sea.

On the day of the funeral, they would leave out a bowl of water and a towel so that the spirit could take one last drink and use the towel to wipe away their tears. Mourners, however, would never drink water while near the deceased. On this day, close family and friends had a chance to give the deceased a final kiss and make a toast to their safe passage before they closed the casket and carried them to the cemetery.[191]

---

188. Svitlana Bohdanivna Pakholok, "Proyavy Narodnoho Etyketu u Pokhoronniy Obryadovosti Ukrayintsiv," *Naukovyy Zhurnal Natsional'nyy Pedahohichnyy Universytet Imeni M. P. Drahomanova*, 2004.

189. Kukharenko, "Traditional Ukrainian Folk Beliefs about Death and the Afterlife."

190. Artyukh, "Vohon' i Voda v Systemi Zvychayevykh Zaboron," 31–41.

191. Kukharenko, "Traditional Ukrainian Folk Beliefs about Death and the Afterlife."

As they carried the casket out of the house, they would tap the coffin against the threshold three times so that the spirit could bid a last farewell to their home.[192] The coffin was carried to the grave feetfirst, and the mourners followed behind to prevent the deceased from "seeing" them and becoming too attached to this world.

### Food for the Dead

Sharing food with the beloved dead is a practice that has been going on for millennia. Even in village funeral processions today, you will see someone carrying a bowl of kutya in front of the coffin as they walk the bones to their final resting place. Kutya is also the first course of a funeral meal and is what is served at the gatherings held throughout the year to honor the ancestors.

Kutya is cooked from wheat berries, poppy seeds, walnuts, and raisins or other dried fruit bits. This labor-intensive dish requires soaking the wheat overnight and then cooking it on the stove for hours, while stirring it so that it doesn't burn. It is truly a labor of love for our ancestors to make kutya in their honor.

For forty days after a soul leaves their body, their belongings remain untouched as their spirit is still believed to be among the living, visiting places they knew and loved. People are careful never to speak ill of the one who has passed, especially during this sensitive time when they are so close and might overhear what is said.

During this forty-day period, the family and the community have memorial feasts on the third, ninth, and fortieth days after the death. They also have feasts on the six-month and one-year anniversaries of their loved one's passing. It is customary to invite their beloved spirits to these feasts with the words,

*You must have grown cold in the moist earth,*
*and perhaps the road here was not warm.*
*Warm yourselves, our own ones, at the stove.*

The family spoons out the first serving of kutya for the spirit-guests with the words,

*You are tired, our own ones,*
*take something to eat.*

---

192. Lecouteux, *The Tradition of Household Spirits*.

When the family has finished eating, they take the long rushnyky that were used to lower their loved ones' casket into the earth and hang them out the window. Then, they escort the spirits from the stove to the linens in the window, saying,

*Now is time for you to go home, and your feet must be tired.*
*The road you will travel is not a short one.*
*This path is softer for you.*
*Bless you and farewell!*

And the spirits descend by means of the linen back to the otherworld until the next spirit gathering.

### Making a Didukh

During the winter solstice celebrations, Ukrainians invite their ancestors to celebrate with them by creating a didukh. This ceremonial sheaf of grains is a symbolic sacrifice of the best of the harvest and symbolizes the circle of life, the cycles of the seasons, and the rebirth of the sun. When we create a didukh, we invite the ancestors and their spirits into our homes for their blessings of health, wealth, fertility, and peace. *Didukh* means "grandfather spirit" and represents the idea that when we create this artifact, we are inviting all our beloved ancestors to join us. The construction of the didukh is reminiscent of the structure of the World Tree with its roots, trunk, and branches and reminds us of our connection to the three worlds.

Traditionally, the didukh was made from the last sheaf of the harvest. This sheaf was ceremoniously reaped and then wrapped with a red ribbon, decorated with guelder rose, and "fed" beer or wine. It was carried in procession from the field by a young single woman from the community who was considered hardworking and of high reputation. She would walk in the front while the rest of the community followed behind and sang harvest songs.

The procession made its way to the home of one of the community leaders, where a festive dinner was prepared for all. The host of the party received the sheaf from the woman, gave her a small amount of money, and all would be invited into the home for a festive meal celebrating the end of the harvest. The sheaf was kept in a storeroom until the night before the winter solstice, when it was retrieved and wrapped and the resulting didukh was ceremoniously placed in the pokut'.

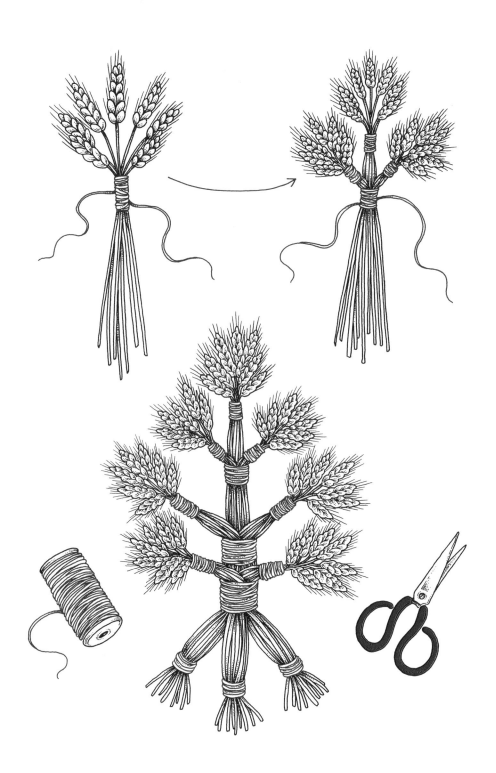

### *How to Create a Didukh*

You can create your own didukh to place on your ancestor altar.

### Ingredients

- Whole stalks of dried wheat, barley, flax, rye, or oats (a minimum of 21 but any multiple of 7)

- Cord or sturdy thread

- Optional: dried flowers, guelder rose branches, poppies, cornflowers, dried herbs, ribbons, paper flowers, or woven straw decorations

### Instructions

1. Soak the stems of the stalks for 10 to 15 minutes in hot water to make them soft and supple.
2. Sort the stalks by size into groups of 7.
3. Wrap the bundles of 7 firmly around the middle several times with the cord.
4. Gather the bundles together, sorting them by levels to get a beautiful graduated treelike top, and wrap with the cord.
5. Divide the lower half of the tree into three (or more) legs to make a tripod and wrap these with the cord.
6. To make the didukh more stable, you can add a few stronger straws to the base.

The didukh can be crafted as a simple sheaf or made to look like a tree. It can be left plain or decorated with flowers, herbs, or woven straw ornaments. When it is brought into the house, the one who brings it in says, "Holidays are coming!" while the family replies, "Holidays have come!" and, "We respectfully invite the ancestors to visit us, too." Then the didukh is placed at the pokut', and the family says, "Didukh in the house, trouble out of the house."

While the didukh is in the home, it is believed that the ancestors are visiting. Some keep the didukh for only one night, others for twelve nights. At the end of the visit, they dismantle the didukh, remove the blessed grains, and add them to those to be planted the following year to bless the whole crop with abundance. They then burn the remaining straw at the crossroads to allow their ancestors to travel back to Vyriy and simultaneously to "let the warm spirit in," an ancient rite of burning winter to invoke an early spring. People jump over this small bonfire to burn away all negativity, and the ashes are collected and distributed around the garden so that the plants will be fertile.[193]

Create a ritual with the didukh to honor your own loving ancestors and invite them into your home in the winter season. Remember the cycle of the seasons and pay your respects to the harvest and to the traditions of long ago.

## Baba Yaga and the Kistky

Baba Yaga is so many things, but one of her attributes is found in the symbol of the bones. Bones surround her home, protecting her space in the woods. These bones remind us that when we step into her yard, we are entering the space of the ancestors.

One of her many names is Baba Yaga Bony-Leg, with one leg that either resembles a bony bird's leg or is simply made up of bones. Either way, her leg tells us that Baba Yaga has one foot in the land of the living and one foot in the land of the dead. She belongs to both worlds and can traverse them easily.

The world of the spirits can be so daunting and mysterious. Baba Yaga is by our side to remind us that, whether we are helping our loved ones on the journey to the other side or the time has come for us to make the journey, we are never alone.

---

193. Artyukh, "Vohon' i Voda v Systemi Zvychayevykh Zaboron," 31–41.

# CHAPTER 21

# KOLO:
# THE CIRCLE

After Vasylyna and her father returned home, life soon settled back into a peaceful rhythm. Vasylyna's father went to get the things for their shop, while Vasylyna traded with the villagers and crafted other items to sell. She used the golden spindle to spin thread that she then wove into cloth so fine and silky that it was admired throughout the land. She used the golden mortar and pestle to make miraculous healing potions that people came from miles around to receive. And when people needed healing or help, she used the other magical items to protect and empower the spells that she cast for them.

She and her father lived in comfort and prosperity. She lived a long life of happiness, health, and plenty. When she herself grew to be an old woman, the children of the village would come to her home. Some would come to pick up something for their parents, others would shyly watch her make her remedies or weave, and still other bolder ones would ask her a million questions about what she was doing. To each one who came to visit, she would ask, "Did you come on an errand or of your own free will?" And to the ones who came to learn, she would sit them down and serve them a bowl of warm kutya. Then, she would sit across from them, light her pipe, and teach them the old ways.

And whenever old Vasylyna had a question herself, she would bring her dear motanka out of her pocket and listen to her wise advice.

## Baba Yaga Shares the Wisdom of the Kolo

The khorovod, the circle dance—have you ever done one, little one? Young and old get together and sing and step and kick and twirl around the circle, holding the hand of the person on the left and the person on the right. They make their way around the kolo, the circle, until they end up back where they started, and then they go around again. Circle dances are rituals that have existed for thousands of years to bring abundance, blessings, and happiness to a community.[194]

All of life is that circle dance. The seasons cycle through spring, summer, fall, winter, and back to spring again. The spirits come down as babies who are born, grow up, perhaps have babies of their own, and then fly back to Vyriy to refresh themselves and come back again. As young ones, we learn from good teachers so that we can grow up and teach the next generation. You come in as initiate, die to your old self, come out as a new person, and then, when you are ready, come back to learn your next lesson and go to the next level. The learning never ends, the journey never ends. Everything comes back around again.

## Madame Pamita Teaches the Magic of the Kolo

The older I get, the more I see the cycles of life. When I was young, I thought of my life's journey as being like a road trip where I was headed for a destination. I believed that life would be perfect when I got to the next town just down the highway, to the love or the money or the career or the thing that was going to fix everything. What I didn't know then was that life is much more like that circle dance: you are always progressing, but you come back to the beginning over and over again, hopefully with a little more wisdom under your belt each time. The circle dance of life is less about looking forward to the destination and more about finding joy in the steps where you are right now.

---

194. Rudnyts'koyi, *Ukrayins'ke mystetstvo u polikul'turnomu prostori* (Min-vo osvity Ukrayiny, Akademiya pedahohichnykh nauk Ukrayiny, Kyyiv: EksOb, 2000).

Meeting with Baba Yaga is like that circle dance. If you spend any time with her, you will realize that she challenges you in the most unforeseen ways. She gives you a task that from your viewpoint may feel impossible. If you back away from it, it may come back to you another time for you to try again. However, if you trust her wisdom and step into it, you will find that you do not have to do it alone. Like Vasylyna, you have the help of your inner guidance, the support of your ancestors, and the assistance of the spirits to help you to get through to the other side.

My hope is that this book and each of the tasks that it lays out for you become that circle dance. An initiatory journey that you return to again and again, each time with more wisdom, always with appreciation, and with a sense of growth and accomplishment as you transform and emerge as someone new.

# Magical Plants
# and Their Meanings

*—Fresh herbs, flowers, branches, and plants used for making a vinok/wreath

†—Flowers and plants included in the twelve traditional flowers of the Kupala vinok

‡—Woods used in making a vereteno/spindle

¶—Branches or flowers used for making a vinyk/bathhouse besom

§—Herbs for a fragrant magical steam bath

(D)—Donor tree

(V)—Vampire tree

(Th)—Herbs used to make Thursday salt

(H)—Herbs for magical hair rinses

Acacia (D)—healing, feminine power

Alder ‡(V)—peace and domestic harmony

Apple blossom *†(D)—maternal love and devotion, love, beauty, fertility, feminine strength, attractiveness, and sexuality

Ash ‡—clairvoyance and blessings

Aspen *‡(V)—banishing negative energy, healing, spiritual cleansing, protection from negativity

Beech ‡—wisdom and divination

Bellflower *—gratitude

Birch *¶§(D)—favorite of the Rusalky, youth, beauty, healing, femininity, strength to the weak and sick, optimism, protection, rebirth, purity, fertility, fragility, modesty, happiness, and well-being

Burdock *(H)—healing

Carlina *—strength, health

Cedar *§—deflects negativity, increases power, replenishes energy, restores strength, enlightens the mind, purifies the soul, awakens spirituality

Chamomile *†§(H)—protection against physical attacks, tenderness, kindness, youth, love, fidelity

Cherry/cherry blossom *†¶—maternal love and devotion

Clover *—fidelity, protection from curses, reuniting couples

Coltsfoot *—love, attraction, spirits, prophecy, wealth, peace

Consolida *—protection of nature, abundance

Cornflower *†—tenderness, cooperative love, compassion, kindness, beauty, simplicity, modesty, humanity, tenderness

Costmary *—truth, honesty

Daisy *—peace, tenderness, loyalty, and love

Dandelion *—dreams, wishes

Dill *—protection, childhood

Elecampane *—strength and health

Fern *—intensifies telepathic and telekinetic powers, calming and connecting to spirits

Forget-me-not *†—stability, fidelity, protection for long journeys

Garlic scapes *—counteracts malefic magic, removes evil eye

Guelder rose (kalyna) *†—health, fertility, beauty, companionship, loyalty, true love, immortality, bravery, fiery heart

Hazel ‡(H)—protection and happiness

Heather *—independence

Hemp *—contact with the otherworld and protection from malevolent spirits

Hops *†—flexibility, wisdom, reason, solutions to complicated issues, fertility

Immortelle *†—controlling the wind, health, healing, and longevity

Juniper ¶§(Th)—cleansing and attracting love

Laurel *§—success and fame

Lemon balm (Th)—healing and attracting love

Lily *†—maiden charm, purity, virtue

Lily-of-the-valley *§—charm, virtue, innocence, element of water

Linden/bass ‡§(D)—success and luck

Lovage *†(H)—invites love, devotion, health, harmony

Mallow *†—attract love, beauty, faith, and hope

Maple (D)—transmutation of energy and emotions, emotional healing, strength, peace, balance, and self-confidence

Marigold *†—invites love

Marjoram *—maternal love

Mint *§(Th)(H)—protection from curses, protecting children, health, protection from mischievous spirits, prosperity, beauty

Mugwort *(Th)—protection against malevolent spirits and curses, astral travel, empowerment, spirit contact

Myrtle *—immortality, soul, love, purity, and beauty

Nettle *¶(Th)(H)—protection against evil forces, banishing

Oak *¶(D)—courage, strength, connection to the World Tree, prevention of nightmares, fertility, wealth, mental clarity

Oregano *§(Th)—motherly love, protection from curses, children's health, peace

Pansy *—protection from jealousy

Pear ‡—spirituality and marriage

Peony *†—longevity, faith, hope, and love

Periwinkle *†—attracts long-term love, fidelity, life, immortality, beauty, tenderness, memory, family well-being

Peppermint *§—protection from curses, protecting children, health, protection from mischievous spirits

Pine ‡§(D)(Th)—calmness, optimism, balancing, spiritual enlightenment, masculine sexuality, protection, blessing

Poplar §(V)—spiritual balancing and equilibrium, spiritual cleansing, mental recalibration

Poppy *†—protection from evil spirits, protection from ill-intentioned people, fertility, youth, beauty, dreams

Raspberry leaf (Th)—healing, banishing

Rose *†—hope, love, fidelity, benevolence, prosperity

Rowan *¶—magic and healing

St. John's wort *§(Th)—protection from evil thoughts, new love, cleansing

Spruce *¶§—banishing curses and spell casting

Sunflower *—devotion and loyalty

Tansy *§—general protection, spiritual protection from illness

Thistle *(Th)—calmness, ability to see spirits, psychic awareness, dream work, courage, healing, protection

Thyme *§(Th)—spiritual protection, beauty, strength

Wild poppy *—invites the protection of Baba Yaga, improves fate, invites peace, hope, flower of dreams, symbol of fertility, beauty, and youth

Wild rose *—faith, hope, and love

Willow *(D)(V)(H)—sacredness, fertility, family, hearth and home, drawing what is desired, releasing what is unwanted

Wood cow-wheat (Kupala and Mavka) *—protection from curses

Wormwood *§(H)—protection from curses, fidelity, added to a bridal wreath for protection of the marriage

Yarrow *†§(Th)—independence, strength, steadfastness, draws good people to you, protects against enemies, courage, healing

# Magical Color
## Correspondences

*—Colors traditionally used for embroidery[195]

†—Colors traditionally used in vinok ribbons/wreath ribbons

‡—Colors traditionally used in nauzy/talismanic knots

¶—Colors traditionally used in pysanky and krashanky/decorated eggs

**Black**\*‡¶—the earth and its fertility, wealth and prosperity, completion, boundaries, binding, confidence, grounding, balance, calm, respect, womb, the otherworld, constancy, spirits, the spirit realm, wisdom, the ancient ones, cronehood, ancestors

**Blue**\*‡¶—power of the sky and water, healing from illness, peace of mind, spirituality, insight, communication, creativity, hidden talents, truth, faithfulness, higher mind, spirit of the air

**Brown**‡¶—perseverance, achieving goals, support for hard work, Mother Earth, life, gifts, rewards, hidden treasure, animals

**Dark blue**†—blessings of the water, cleansing, and protection

**Dark green**†—blessings of the trees, strength, and beauty

**Green**\*‡¶—life, growth, youth, beauty, serenity, spring, wealth, creativity, career, well-being, protection from envy, fertility, healing, hope, freedom, bounty, abundance, spirit of the water, nature

**Light blue**†—blessings of the sky, clarity of thought and word

**Light brown**†—blessings of the earth, source of all life

**Light green**†—blessings of the plants, youth, and vigor

---

195. Dobrovolska, "Filosofiya Ukrayins'koyi Vyshyvky."

**Light pink**†—blessings of the blossom, well-being and prosperity, tender love, romance, protection from relationship jealousies

**Magenta**†—blessings of the fruit, sincerity, and truth

**Orange**†‡¶—blessings of the bread, abundance, needs being met, joy, optimism, new beginnings, attraction, confidence, sociability, success, strength, endurance, worthy ambition, spirit of the fire

**Purple/violet**†‡¶—blessings of the stars, wisdom and insight, confidence, strength, leadership, inspiration, abilities, faith, patience, trust, purity

**Red**\*†‡¶—positive life force, love, life, joy, blessings of the blood, magic and ancestors, strength, passionate love, health, protection from prychyna, action, energy, joy, love, family ties, protection, motherhood

**White**\*†‡¶—innocence, protection from misfortune and jealous glances, restores energy reserves, blessings of the moon, psychic awareness, spirituality, health, protection, wishes, education, protection from conflicts, harmonious relationships, birth, beginnings, light, purity, innocence, maidenhood

**Yellow/gold**\*†‡¶—honey, wheat, prosperity, abundance, wealth, joy, blessings of the sun, mental activity, thoughts, protection from envy, health, family happiness, light, harvest, youth, hospitality, recognition, reward, stars

# Glossary

**baba (s.)/baby (pl.)** баба баби: Old woman/women, grandmother(s).

**baba sheptukha (s.)/baby sheptukhy (pl.)** баба шептуха/баби шептухи: "Grandmother whisperer." Spellcaster who uses whispered incantations.

**babusya (s.)/babusy (pl.)** бабуся/бабусі: Granny/grannies.

**Bannyk** Банник: Spirit of the bathhouse.

**Berehynia** Берегиня: Ancient pre-Christian female guardian spirit and goddess.

**bezkonechnyk** безконечник: Infinite line design.

**Blazhenni** Блаженні: The "blessed ones." Spirits of those who have gone to the afterlife.

**chaklun (s.)/chakluny (pl.)** чаклун/чаклуни: Powerful sorcerer(s).

**chaklunka (s.)/chaklunky (pl.)** чаклунка/чаклунки: Powerful sorceress(es).

**chasnyk** часник: Garlic.

**chetverhova sil'** четвергова сіль: Thursday salt.

**chub** чуб: Long forelock of hair on the top of the head. Worn by the kozaky as a symbol of initiation and warrior status.

**Chuhaister** Чугайстер: Male guardian forest spirit.

**dendroterapiya** дендротерапія: Dendrotherapy (using the energy of trees for therapeutic purposes).

**Derevo Zhyttya** Дерево Життя: The Tree of Life; a decorative design and another name for the World Tree, a concept of the three worlds of spirits, the living, and divine beings.

**did (s.)/didy (pl.)** дід/діди: Grandfather(s).

**didukh** дідух: "Grandfather spirit." The sheaf of wheat displayed in the house that represents the ancestors.

**didus'** дідусь: Grandpa.

**dolya** доля: Fate, good fate, the name of the positive half of the pair of fates.

**Domovyk** Домовик: Ancestral male house spirit.

**drymba** дримба: Jaw harp. A musical instrument that is played by plucking a metal reed over the teeth, creating a droning twang. Used for inducing trances.

**dub** дуб: Oak.

**holosinnya** голосіння: Songs of lamenting with magical incantations for helping the spirits travel to the afterlife.

**holubtsi** голубці: Stuffed cabbage.

**horilka** горілка: Vodka, strong alcohol spirits.

**Hospodynya Lisu** Господиня Лісу: "Mistress of the Forest." The female spirit who watches over the forests, sometimes associated with Baba Yaga.

**hradovyy nizh** градовий ніж: "Hail knife." A knife used by a molfar or molfarka as a tool of magic.

**hrebinets'** гребінець: Comb.

**hromnytsi** громниці: "Thunderbolts." Beeswax candles consecrated at the midwinter holiday, Stritennya. Used for protection and blessing throughout the year.

**Hromnytsya** Громниця: "Thunderstorm." Another name for Stritennya, the midwinter holiday considered to be the day when winter and spring meet.

**hromova palytsya** громова палиця: "Thunder stick." A blessed stick used for controlling the weather.

**hromovytsi** громовиці: "Thunderbolts." Pieces of wood from a tree struck by lightning used in magic.

**hryby** гриби: Mushrooms.

**ikona** ікона: Icon; holy image of a saint or deity imbued with miraculous powers.

**Iriy** Ирій: Paradise.

**kalyna** калина: Guelder rose or *viburnum opulus*, a bush that produces clusters of small white flowers followed by bright red berries.

**kaminchyky** камінчики: Pebbles or small stones.

**kam'yani baby** кам'яні баби: Ancient standing stones carved as female figures.

**kasha** каша: Cooked grain porridge.

**kharaktérnyky** характéрники: Cossack sorcerers.

**khata (s.) khaty (pl.) khatynka (dim.)** хата хати хатинка: Hut or cottage.

**khata stupa** хата ступа: Mill house.

**khlib** хліб: Bread.

**khorovod** хоровод: Circle dance.

**khrest** хрест: Cross.

**khvylyasti liniyi** хвилясті лінії: Wavy lines in traditional embroidery.

**kistka (s.) kistky (pl.)** кістка кістки: Bone/bones or the wax stylus used to write pysanky.

**klyuch (s.) klyuchi (pl.)** клюу клюуі: Key(s).

**kovbasa** ковбаса: Sausage.

**kolo** коло: Circle.

**Kolodiy** Колодій: Old Pagan midwinter holiday corresponding to Shrove Tuesday, Mardi Gras.

**Kolyada** Коляда: The traditional Slavic name for the period from Christmas to Epiphany or a winter festival celebrated at the end of December in honor of the sun.

**kompot** компот: Stewed fruit juice.

**kosa** коса: Braid.

**kozak (s.) kozaky (pl.)** козак козаки: Cossack(s)—member(s) of democratic, self-governing, semi-military communities originating in the steppes of Eastern Europe.

**krashanky** крашанки: Eggs dyed one solid color.

**krayka** крайка: Woven sash or belt.

**kryvi tanets** кривий танець: "Serpentine dance." A meander design used in embroidery and pysanky.

**kum (m.) kuma (f.) kumy (pl.)** кум кума куми: Godfather, godmother, godparents, but can also refer to bosom friends.

**Kupala** Купала: Midsummer "bathing" holiday, originally celebrated at the summer solstice but moved with the Julian calendar to July 6–7.

**kurhany** кургани: Ancient burial mounds.

**kutya** кутя: Wheat berry, poppy seed, and honey porridge.

**kvadrat** квадрат: Square in traditional embroidery.

**kvass** квас: A fermented drink made with birch syrup and rye bread.

**laznya** лазня: Bathhouse.

**Lisova Baba** Лісова Баба: Forest Woman.

**Lisoviy Cholovik** Лісовий Чоловік: Forest Man.

**Lisovyk (s.) Lisovyky (pl.)** Лісовик Лісовики: Literally "the forest man." The spirit of the forest.

**Lysa Hora** Лиса Гора: "Bald Mountain." Legendary mountain near Kyiv where witches are reported to gather.

**mak** мак: Poppy.

**Matusya** Матуся: Mommy.

**Maty Syra Zemlya** Мати Сира Земля: Moist Mother Earth.

**Maty Zemlya** Мати Земля: Mother Earth.

**Mavka (s.) Mavky (pl.)** мавка мавки: Female forest or river spirit. From the Proto-Slavic word *навь*, "the dead."

**med** мед: Honey.

**Mokosh** Мокош: Mother goddess, goddess of weaving.

**molfa** мольфа: Ritual sacred object of the molfar or molfarka.

**molfar (m.) molfarka (f.)** мольфар молфарка: Carpathian shamanlike figure.

**mosyazhni** мосяжні: Protective brass jewelry.

**motanka** (s.) **motanky (pl.)** мотанка мотанки: Sacred ancestral spirit doll.

**mukhomor** Мухомор: Fly agaric mushroom.

**nalysnyky** налисники: Crepes.

**nasinnya maku** насіння маку: Poppy seeds.

**nauzy** наузи: Magical knot charm.

**nedolya** недоля: Misfortune; the name of the negative half of the pair of fates.

**oberih (s.) oberehy (pl.)** оберіг обереги: Charms, talismans, amulet.

**obkuryuvannya** обкурювання: The burning of dried herbs for censing or fumigation.

**Paraskeva P'yatnytsya** Параскева П'ятниця: Saint Paraskeva Friday, a folk saint associated with weaving who sprang from the older goddess Paraskeva.

**pasichnyk** пасічник: Beekeeper; the beehive spirit.

**pasichnyk-charivnyk**: "Beekeeper magician." The name given to experienced male beekeepers, akin to "bee whisperers."

**pavuk** павук: Spider.

**Pekun** Пекун: Dangerous monster chained to a cliff who sends his minions out into the world to count how many pysanky have been created each spring.

**Petrykivka** петриківка : Painting style with flowers and birds.

**pich** піч: Oven; in older times, a woodstove.

**pokut'** покуть: The home altar corner.

**povna rozha** повна рожа: "Full face"; mallow flower in full bloom.

**Provody** Проводи: Ancient holiday commemorating the dead that takes place after Easter where families bring a picnic to the graveyard to share with their beloved dead.

**prychyna** причина: A curse or black magic spell.

**pysanka (s.) pysanky (pl.)** писанка писанки: Intricately decorated talismanic eggs made with the wax resist method.

**pysaty** писати: To write; the root of the word *pysanka/pysanky*.

**Rahkmany** Рахмани: Blessed ones, spirits who inhabit a distant mythic land akin to the lower world.

**Rai** Рай: Paradise.

**rhomb** ромб: A diamond shape; lozenge in traditional embroidery.

**rozdorizhzhya** роздоріжжя: Crossroads.

**Rozhanytsi** Рожаниці: Ancient goddesses who control fate.

**Rusalia** Русалія: Ancient spring festival honoring the water spirits, the Rusalky.

**Rusalka (s.) Rusalky (pl.)** русалка русалки: Female water spirits akin to naiads.

**Rusal'nyy Tyzhden'** Русальний Тиждень: Ancient spring festival honoring the water spirits, the Rusalky.

**rushnyk (s.) rushnyky (pl.)** рушник рушники: Embroidered cloth ritual towel.

**salo** сало: Pork belly.

**sertse** серце: Heart in traditional embroidery.

**shevrony** шеврони: Chevrons in traditional embroidery.

**sil'** сіль: Salt.

**sopilka** Сопілка: Shepherd's flute.

**Stritennya** Стрітення: Literally "meeting"; the holiday when winter meets spring on February 15. Corresponds to Candlemas.

**stupa** ступа: Mortar for grinding herbs or grains.

**svarga** сварга: Sun symbol.

**Sviaty Vechir** Святий Вечір: Holy Night, Christmas Eve.

**tkats'kyy verstat** ткацький верстат: Loom.

**totemy** тотеми: The magical tools of the molfar.

**trembita** трембіта: Long mountain horn.

**trykutnyk** трикутник: Triangle in traditional embroidery.

**Trypillian** Трипільська: From the Neolithic culture of Eastern Europe that flourished between 5500 and 2750 BCE.

**upyr** упир: A ghoul, a vampire, the living dead.

**uzvar** узвар: Drink made from boiled dried fruit.

**varenyky** вареники: Dumplings.

**vazon** вазон: "Flowerpot." A stylized design representing the Tree of Life or the goddess.

**vidma (s.) vidmy (pl.)** відьма відми: Witch/witches.

**vid'myne kil'tse** відьмине кільце: "Witch ring." Circles of mushrooms believed to be enchanted.

**vinok (s.) vinoky (pl.)** вінок вінки: Wreath or flower crown.

**vinyk (s.) vinyky (pl.)** віник віники: Besom; small broom of fresh or dried herbs used in the bathhouse.

**vodyanyk (s.) vodyanyky (pl.)** водяник водяники: Deepwater mermen spirit(s).

**volossya** волосся: Hair.

**vorozhka (s.) vorozhky (pl.)** ворожка ворожки: Fortune-teller(s).

**vroki** вроки: Jealous, harmful glances; the evil eye.

**vylyvaty visk** виливати віск: Pouring wax; a healing ritual done by pouring beeswax into a bowl of water held over the head.

**vynohrad** виноград: Vineyard, grape design.

**Vyriy** Вирій: Paradise; a temperate place where souls reside and birds fly to in the winter.

**vyshyvanka (s). vyshyvanky (pl.)** вишиванка вишиванки: Embroidery; traditional Ukrainian embroidered clothing.

**vytynanky** витинанки: Cut paper art.

**yaytse (s.) yaytsya (pl.)** яйце яйця: Egg/eggs.

**yizha** їжа: Food.

**Yuriy Vesnyanyy** Юрий Весняний: Saint George's Day, celebrated on May 6; the holiday between spring equinox and summer solstice (Julian calendar).

**zaklynannya** заклинання: Incantations, spell words.

**Zeleni Svyata** Зелені Свята: "Green Feast" or "Green Week." Traditional Ukrainian holiday associated with summer.

**zerno** зерно: Grain.

**zgarda** зґарда: Hutzul sun medallion worn as a talisman.

**zhaba** жаба: Frog; design element on embroidery.

**zhayvoronky** жайворонки: Larks, lark-shaped buns.

**Zhyva i Mertva Voda** жива і мертва вода: Waters of Life and Death.

**znakharka** знахарка: Wise woman, healer, rootworker.

**zori** зорі: Morning star. Dawn.

# Bibliography

Adams, Bruce Friend, Edward James Lazzerini, and George N. Rhyne. *The Supplement to the Modern Encyclopedia of Russian, Soviet, and Eurasian History*. Gulf Breeze, FL: Academic International Press, 1995.

Artyukh, L. F. "Vohon' i Voda v Systemi Zvychayevykh Zaboron." *Narodna Tvorchist' Ta Etnolohiya* 3 (2012): 31–41.

Aveela, Ronesa. *A Study of Household Spirits of Eastern Europe*. North Billerica, MA: Bendideia Publishing, 2019.

Barford, P. M. *The Early Slavs: Culture and Society in Early Medieval Eastern Europe*. Ithaca, NY: Cornell University Press, 2001.

Berdnyk, Hromovytsia. *Znaky Karpat·S'koyi Mahiyi*. L'viv, Ukraine: Terra Incognita, 2019.

Bezuhla, S. V. "Narodni Uyavlennya pro Rusalok u Konteksti Svyatkuvannya Triytsi u Skhidnykh Slov'yan." *Isnyk Student·S'koho Naukovoho Tovarystva Donnu Imeni Vasylya Stusa* 1, no. 7 (2015): 43–48.

Bezuhla, S. V. "Narodni Uyavlennya pro Rusalok u Konteksti Svyatkuvannya Triytsi u Skhidnykh Slov'yan." *Visnyk student·s'koho naukovoho tovarystva DonNU imeni Vasylya* 1, no. 7 (2015): 43–48.

Bloshchyns'ka, V. "Kul't Karpat·S'koyi Mahiyi Yak Fenomen Hutsul's'koyi Kul'tury." *Karpaty: lyudyna, etnos, tsyvilizatsiya* 5 (2014): 277–293.

Bosyy, Oleksandr. "Svyashchenne Remeslo Mokoshi." In *Tradytsiyni Symvoly Ta Mahichni Rytualy Ukrayintsiv (Typolohiya. Semantyka. Mifostruktury)*, 39–40. Vinnytsya, Ukraine: Vydavnytstvo-drukarnya «Dilo» FOP Rohal's'ka IO, 2011.

Boyan, S. P., and N. Bayurchak. "Mol'fary Ukrayins'kykh Karpat: Typolohichnyy Analiz." *Halychyna* 27 (2015): 45–51.

Bozóky, Edina. "Mythic Mediation in Healing Incantations." *Health, Disease and Healing in Medieval Culture* (1992): 84–92. https://doi.org/10.1007/978-1-349-21882-0_5.

Bulhakova-Sytnyk, Ludmyla, Lubow Wolynetz, and Natalie O. Kononenko. *The Tree of Life, the Sun, the Goddess: Symbolic Motifs in Ukrainian Folk Art*. New York: Ukrainian Museum, 2005.

Buyskykh, Yulia. "Domovyk u Tradytsiynykh Viruvannyakh Ukrayintsiv: Pokhodzhennya Obrazu." *Etnichna istoriya narodiv Yevropy* 26 (2008): 120–127.

Chumarna, Mariya. *Tainopys Vyshyvky*. L'viv, Ukraine: Apriori, 2018.

Cohen, Deatra, and Adam Siegel. *Ashkenazi Herbalism: Rediscovering the Herbal Traditions of Eastern European Jews*. Berkeley, CA: North Atlantic Books, 2021.

"Cold at Home." EnAct. Accessed May 14, 2021. http://www.coldathome.today/cold-at-home.

Danchenko, A. *Folk Art from the Ukraine*. Leningrad, Russia: Aurora, 1982.

Dixon-Kennedy, Mike. *Encyclopedia of Russian and Slavic Myth and Legend*. Oxford: ABC-Clio, 1999.

Dmytrenko, Alla. "Zbyrannya Trav i Arkhayichni Elementy Svitohlyadu Polishchukiv." *Etnichna istoriya narodiv Yevropy* 11 (2001): 14–18.

Dmytriw, Olya, and Anne Mitz. *Ukrainian Arts*. New York: Ukrainian Youth's League of North America, 1955.

Dobrovolska, O. V. "Filosofiya Ukrayins'koyi Vyshyvky." *Visnyk Kharkivs'koho Universytetu*, no. 57 (2017): 140–144. https://openarchive.nure.ua/handle/document/7029.

Dorosh, Andriy. "The Phenomenon of a Ukrainian Pich (Stove)." Dorosh Heritage Tours, February 11, 2019. https://doroshheritagetours.com/the-phenomenon-of-a-ukrainian-pich-stove/.

Eliade, Mircea, Diane Apostolos-Cappadona, Willard R. Trask, and Willard R. Trask. *A History of Religious Ideas*. Chicago, IL: University of Chicago Press, 1981.

*Encyclopedia of Ukraine*. Toronto, ON: University of Toronto, 1993.

Estes, Clarissa Pinkola. *Women Who Run with the Wolves*. New York: Ballantine Books, 1992.

*Ethnologia Slavica*. 1. Vol. 1. Bratislava, Slovakia: Slovenske pedagogicke nakl., 1969.

*Etnografichnĭĭ Zbirnik: Vidae Naukove Tovaristvo Imeni Shevchenka.* L'viv, Ukraine: Nakladom Naukovoho tovarystva Imeny Shevchenka, 1895.

Frazer, James George, and Robert Fraser. *The Golden Bough: A Study in Magic and Religion.* London, England: The Folio Society, 2018.

Gilchrist, Cherry. *Russian Magic: Living Folk Traditions of an Enchanted Landscape.* Wheaton, IL: Quest Books, 2009.

Gimbutas, Marija Alseikaité. *The Slavs.* London, England: Thames and Hudson, 1971.

Glants, Musya, and Juri Toomre. *Food in Russian History and Culture.* Bloomington, IN: Indiana University Press, 2014.

Grabowicz, Oksana I., and Lubow Wolynetz. *Rushnyky: Ukrainian Ritual Cloths.* New York: Ukrainian Museum, 1981.

Gray, Louis Herbert. *Mythology of All Races Volume 3.* London, England: M. Jones, 1918.

Grimassi, Raven. *Old World Witchcraft: Ancient Ways for Modern Days.* San Francisco, CA: Weiser Books, 2011.

Halaychuk, Volodymyr. "Narodnyy Kalendar Zarichnenshchyny v Obryadakh, Zvychayakh Ta Fol'klori." *Naukovi zoshyty istorychnoho fakul'tetu L'vivs'koho universytetu* 13–14 (2013): 43–83.

Hanchuk, Rena Jeanne. *The Word and Wax: A Medical Folk Ritual among Ukrainians in Alberta.* Edmonton, AB: Huculak Chair of Ukrainian Culture and Ethnography, 1999.

Hrusevs'kyj, Mychajlo S. *History of Ukraine—Rus'.* Edmonton, AB: Canadian Institute of Ukrainian Studies Press, 1997.

Hrushevs'kyy, Mykhaylo, Fedor Pavlovych Shevchenko, Valeriy Andriyovych Smoliy, A. I. Smoliy, and Volodymyr Mykhailovych Rychka. *Ukrayintsi: Narodni Viruvannya, Povir'ya, Demonolohiya.* Kyiv, Ukraine: Libid', 1991.

Hrymashevych, H. I., and Yuliya Vasyl'chuk. "Povir'ya, Zvychayi Ta Obryady, Pov'yazani z Tkatstvom." *Student·s'ki linhvistychni studiyi* 2 (2011): 39–46.

Hubbs, Joanna. *Mother Russia: The Feminine Myth in Russian Culture.* Boulder, CO: NetLibrary, 1999.

Hunter, Clare. *Threads of Life: A History of the World through the Eye of a Needle.* New York: Abrams Press, 2020.

Illes, Judika. *Encyclopedia of Spirits: The Ultimate Guide to the Magic of Fairies, Genies, Demons, Ghosts, Gods & Goddesses.* New York: HarperCollins, 2010.

Ivanits, Linda J. *Russian Folk Belief.* Armonk, NY: M. E. Sharpe, 1992.

Johns, Andreas. *Baba Yaga: The Ambiguous Mother and Witch of the Russian Folktale.* New York: Peter Lang, 2010.

Johnson, Kenneth. *Slavic Sorcery: Shamanic Journey of Initiation.* Woodbury, MN: Llewellyn Publications, 1998.

Kapaló James Alexander. *The Power of Words: Studies on Charms and Charming in Europe.* Budapest, Hungary: Central European University Press, 2013.

Kelly, Mary B. *Goddess Embroideries of Eastern Europe.* McLean, NY: StudioBooks, 1996.

Kennard, Howard Percy. *The Russian Peasant.* New York: AMS pr, 1980.

Killgrove, Kristina. "Painted Bones Spark 4,500-Year-Old Burial Mystery in Ukraine." *Forbes,* July 27, 2018.

Kivelson, Valerie A., and Christine D. Worobec. *Witchcraft in Russia and Ukraine, 1000–1900: A Sourcebook.* Ithaca, NY: Northern Illinois University Press, an imprint of Cornell University Press, 2020.

Kmit, Ann, Johanna Luciow, and Loretta Luciow. *Ukrainian Embroidery.* New York: Van Nostrand Reinhold Co., 1978.

Kolodyuk, I. "Suchasnyy Stan Polis'koho Znakharstva (Za Espedytsiynymy Materi-alamy Na Polissi)." *Volyn'-Zhytomyrshchyna* 13 (2005): 134–42.

Kononenko, Natalie O. *Slavic Folklore: A Handbook.* Westport, CT: Greenwood Press, 2007.

Korniy, Dara. *Charivni Istoty Ukrayins'koho Mifu.* Kharkiv, Ukraine: Vivat Vydav-nytstvo, 2018.

Kotova, Nadiia, Dmytro Kiosak, Simon Radchenko, and Larisa Spitsyna. "Microscopic Examination of Mesolithic Serpent-like Sculptured Stones from Southern Ukraine." *Antiquity* 92, no. 366 (2018). https://doi.org/10.15184/aqy.2018.249.

Kotsur, V. P. *Slovnyk Symvoliv Kul'tury Ukraïny*. Kyiv, Ukraine: Milenium, 2005.

Kruchkova, Olga. *Slavic Seasonal Rituals and Divinations*. Teaneck, NJ: Babelcube, 2019.

Kukharenko, Svitlana P. "Animal Magic: Contemporary Beliefs and Practices in Ukrainian Villages." *Folklorica* 12 (2010). https://doi.org/10.17161/folklorica .v12i0.3784.

Kukharenko, Svitlana. "Traditional Ukrainian Folk Beliefs about Death and the Afterlife." *Folklorica* 16, no. 1 (2011). https://doi.org/10.17161/folklorica .v16i1.4209.

Lajoye, Patrice. *New Researches on the Religion and Mythology of the Pagan Slavs*. Lisieux, France: Lingva, 2019.

Lecouteux, Claude. *The Tradition of Household Spirits: Ancestral Lore and Practices*. Rochester, VT: Inner traditions, 2013.

Len'o, P. Y. "Vykorystannya Vohnyu u Narodniy Medytsyni Ukrayintsiv Zakarpattya (Na Osnovi Suchasnykh Pol'ovykh Materialiv)." *Naukovyy visnyk Uzhhorods'koho Universytetu: Seriya: Istoriya*, no. 2 (2014): 123–126.

Leshko, Jaroslaw, and Lubow Wolynetz. *In Bloom: Nature and Art*. New York: Ukrainian Museum, 2020.

Levkievskaia, E. E. *V. Krayu Domovykh I Leshykha*. Moscow, Russia: OGI, 2009.

Manko, Vira, Lada Bidiak, Andriy Maslukh, Stepan Onyskiv, Oleh Kutianskyj, and Sophia Burak. *The Ukrainian Folk Pysanka*. Lviv, Ukraine: Svichado Publishing, 2017.

Marley, Greg A. *Chanterelle Dreams, Amanita Nightmares: The Love, Lore and Mystique of Mushrooms*. White River Junction, VT: Chelsea Green, 2011.

Matossian, M. K. "In the Beginning, God Was a Woman." *Journal of Social History* 6, no. 3 (January 1973): 325–343. https://doi.org/10.1353/jsh/6.3.325.

Mercatante, Anthony S., and James R. Dow. *The Facts on File Encyclopedia of World Mythology and Legend*. New York: Facts On File, 2009.

Mineyev, I. M. *Entsiklopediya Traditsionnoy Narodnoy Meditsiny: Napravleniya*. Moscow, Russia: Metody. Praktiki. AST, 2002.

Monaghan, Patricia. *Encyclopedia of Goddesses and Heroines*. United States: New World Library, 2014.

Movna, Ulyana. "The Ritual Complex of Traditional Beekeeping of Ukrainians of Nadsiannia." *The Ethnology Notebooks* 147, no. 3 (2019): 608–621. https://doi.org/10.15407/nz2019.03.608.

Mucz, Michael. *Baba's Kitchen Medicines: Folk Remedies of Ukrainian Settlers in Western Canada.* Edmonton, AB: The University of Alberta Press, 2013.

Oleszkiewicz-Peralba, Małgorzata. *Fierce Feminine Divinities of Eurasia and Latin America: Baba Yaga, Kālī, Pombagira, and Santa Muerte.* New York: Palgrave Macmillan, 2015.

Pakholok, Svitlana Bohdanivna. "Proyavy Narodnoho Etyketu u Pokhoronniy Obryadovosti Ukrayintsiv." *Naukovyy Zhurnal Natsional'nyy Pedahohichnyy Universytet Imeni M. P. Drahomanova* 6 (2004).

Parkhomenko, T. "Vykorystannya Vosku v Narodnomu Znakharstvi." *Etnokul'turna spadshchyna Rivnens'koho Polissya* 1 (2001): 27–38.

Pasternak, Anatoli. *Kozats'ka Medytsyna.* Ukraine: Optyma, 2001.

Pen'kova, O., and S. Boyko. "Tradytsiya Kupal's'koho Vinkopletennya v Ukrayini: Istoriya Ta Transformatsiya v Druhiy Polovyni KHKH St." *Novi storinky istoriyi Donbasu* 22 (2013): 255–268.

Petrusha, Luba. "Pysanky Ukrainian Easter Egg." Pysanky.info, 2021. http://www.pysanky.info/.

Phillips, Sarah D. "Waxing Like the Moon: Women Folk Healers in Rural Western Ukraine." *Folklorica* 9, no. 1 (2004). https://doi.org/10.17161/folklorica.v9i1.3744.

Pistun, Tamara Vasylivna. *Ukrayins'ki Pradavni Oberehy.* Ternopil', Ukraine: Navchal'na Knyha-Bohdan, 2005.

Plachynda, Serhiy. *Slovnyk Davn'oukrayins'koyi Mifolohiyi.* Kyiv, Ukraine: Veles, 2007.

Propp, V. A., Svatava Pirkova-Jakobsonova, and Laurence Scott. *Morphology of the Folktale.* Mansfield Centre, CT: Martino Publishing, 2015.

Propp, Vladimir Jakovlevic, and S. E. Chazanova. *Istoricheskiye Korni Skazki.* Saint Petersburg, Russia: Izd-vo S.-Peterburgskogo Universiteta, 1996.

Pysarenko, P. V., and O. I. Harmash. "Etnohrafichni Osoblyvosti Ukrayins'koho Narodu Ta Yikh Rol' u Stvorenni Ekoposelen' Na Terytoriyi Ukrayiny." *Isnyk Poltavs'koyi Derzhavnoyi Ahrarnoyi Akademiyi* 4 (2016): 83–88.

Ralston, W. R. S. *The Songs of the Russian People, as Illustrative of Slavonic Mythology and Russian Social Life.* London: Ellis & Green, 1872.

Roper, Jonathan. *Charms, Charmers and Charming: International Research on Verbal Magic.* Basingstoke, England: Palgrave Macmillan, 2008.

Rosik, Stanisław, and Anna Tyszkiewicz. *The Slavic Religion in the Light of 11th- and 12th-Century German Chronicles (Thietmar of Merseburg, Adam of Bremen, Helmold of Bosau): Studies on the Christian Interpretation of Pre-Christian Cults and Beliefs in the Middle Ages.* Leiden, Netherlands: Brill, 2020.

Rudenko, Y. M. "Oberehove Pryznachennya Stritens'koyi Svichky Yak Osnovnoyi Rytual'noyi Zakhysnytsi." *Termyny rynochnoy ékonomyky: Sovremennyy slovar'-spravochnyk delovohocheloveka* (2020): 180–183.

Rudnyts'koyi, O. P. *Ukrayins'ke mystetstvo u polikul'turnomu prostori.* Min-vo osvity Ukrayiny, Akademiya pedahohichnykh nauk Ukrayiny. Kyyiv: EksOb, 2000.

Ryan, W. F. *The Bathhouse at Midnight: An Historical Survey of Magic and Divination in Russia.* Stroud, PA: Sutton, 1999.

S., Forrester Sibelan E., Helena Goscilo, Martin Skoro, and Jack Zipes. *Baba Yaga: the Wild Witch of the East in Russian Fairy Tales.* Jackson, MS: University Press of Mississippi, 2013.

Sadovnycha, Viktoriya. *Starovynna Mahiya Ukrayintsiv.* Kyiv, Ukraine: Knyzhkovyy Klub, 2018.

Sapura, O. V., and H. B. Munin. *Ukrainian Folk Arts and Crafts.* Kyiv, Ukraine: Ahent·stvo po rozpovsyudzhennyu druku, 2015.

Sciacca, Frank. "Ukrainian Rushnyky: Binding Amulets and Magical Talismans in the Modern Period." *Folklorica* 17 (2014). https://doi.org/10.17161/folklorica .v17i0.4677.

Shcherbyna, E. B. "Ukrayins'ka Narodna Vyshyvka i Yiyi Terminosystemy." *Visnyk Kharkivs'koyi derzhavnoyi akademiyi dyzaynu i mystetstv* 1 (2010): 79–80. http://nbuv.gov.ua/UJRN/had_2010_1_21.

Sherman, Josepha. *Storytelling: An Encyclopedia of Mythology and Folklore*. Milton Park, UK: Taylor & Francis, 2015.

Simonov, Pyotr. *Essential Russian Mythology: Stories That Change the World*. San Francisco, CA: Thorsons, 1997.

Skliar, S. S. *Starovynni Ukrayins'ki Uzory Dlya Vyshyvannya Khrestom. Mahiya Vizerunka*. Kharkiv, Ukraine: Klub Simeinoho Dozvillia, 2016.

Smolyns'ka, Y. E. "Perezhytky Prymityvnoyi Obryadovosty v Ukrayins'komu Pobuti.(Peredmova d-r. Ist. Nauk. Prof. Valentyny Borysenko)." *Etnichna istoriya narodiv Yevropy* 15 (2003): 77–93.

Stakhurskaya, A. V. "Traditsionnaya Kukla-Motanka V Kul'turakh Vostochno-slavyanskikh Narodov." *Gumanitarnyye nauki v XXI veke: nauchnyy Internet-zhurnal* 6 (2016): 78–90. https://humanist21.kgasu.ru/files/N6-N7_Stahurs kaja_AV.PDF.

Stankevych, Mykhaylo. Thesis. *Vytynanky i Shtuchni Kvity: Porivnyal'nyy Aspekt*, 2008. http://dspace.nbuv.gov.ua/handle/123456789/16748.

Stel'mascuk, Halyna Hryhorivna. *Ukrainian Folk Headwear*. L'viv, Ukraine: Apriori, 2013.

*The Story of Pysanka: A Collection of Articles on Ukrainian Easter Eggs*. Lidcombe, NSW: Sova Books, 2019.

Sumtsov, Nikolay Fedorovich. *Lichnyye Oberegi Ot Sglaza*. Saint Petersburg, Russia: Tipografija Gubernskago Pravlenija, 1896.

Surmach, Yaroslava. *Ukrainian Easter Eggs*. New York: Surma, 1957.

Suwyn, Barbara J., and Natalie O. Kononenko. *The Magic Egg and Other Tales from Ukraine*. Englewood, CO: Libraries Unlimited, 1997.

Tarasova, Ol'ha Oleksandrivna. *Lyal'ky-Motanky*. Kharkiv, Ukraine: Glagoslav Distribution, 2014.

Tarasova, Ol'ha Oleksandrivna. *Taiemnychyi Svit Lialky-Motanky*. Kyiv, Ukraine: Lybid', 2015.

Tkachuk, Mary, Marie Kishchuk, and Alice Nicholaichuk. *Pysanka: Icon of the Universe*. Saskatoon, SK: Ukrainian Museum, 1977.

Toporkov, Andrey. "'Perepekaniye' Detey v Ritualakh i Skazkakh Vostochnykh Slavyan." *Fol'klor i Etnograficheskaya Deystvitel'nost'*, 1992, 114–118.

*Traditional Designs in Ukrainian Textiles: An Exhibition.* New York: The Ukrainian Museum, 1977.

"Ukraine Adopts Land Reform." Official Website of the International Trade Administration, September 30, 2020. https://www.trade.gov/market -intelligence/ukraine-adopts-land-reform.

*Ukraine: A Concise Encyclopedia.* Toronto, ON: University of Toronto, 1963.

Voitovych, Valeriy. *Ukrayins'ka Mifolohiya.* Kyiv, Ukraine: Lybid', 2015.

Voropaj, Oleksa I. *Zvychayi Nashoho Narodu: Etnohrafichnyy Narys.* Kyiv, Ukraine: Vydavnycho-Polihrafichne Tovarystvo Oberih, 1993.

Warner, Elizabeth. *Russian Myths.* London: British Museum, 2002.

Williams, Victoria. *Celebrating Life Customs around the World: from Baby Showers to Funerals.* Santa Barbara, CA: ABC-CLIO, 2017.

Yatchenko, V. F. *Ukrayins'kyy Shamanizm.* Kyiv, Ukraine: Milenium, 2011.

Yefymenko, P. *A Collection of Ukrainian Spells.* Lidcombe, NSW: Sova Books Pty Ltd, 2020.

Yudina, P. N. "Derev'ya–Tseliteli." *Dialog kul'tur* (2016): 169–171.

Zajvoronok, V. V. *Oznaky Ukrayins'koyi Etnokul'tury: Slovnykovyy Dovidnyk.* Kyiv, Ukraine: Dovira, 2006.

# INDEX

# R